Practical Salesforce.com Development Without Code

Customizing Salesforce On the Force.com Platform

Philip Weinmeister

Practical Salesforce.com Development Without Code: Customizing Salesforce on the Force.com Platform

ISBN-13 (pbk): 978-1-4842-0098-8

ISBN-13 (electronic): 978-1-4842-0097-1

Managing Director: Welmoed Spahr
Acquisitions Editor: Jeff Olson
Technical Reviewer: Jonathan Keel
Editorial Board: Steve Anglin, Mark Beckner, Gary Cornell, Louise Corrigan, James DeWolf, Jonathan Gennick, Robert Hutchinson, Michelle Lowman, James Markham, Matthew Moodie, Jeff Olson, Jeffrey Pepper, Douglas Pundick, Ben Renow-Clarke, Gwenan Spearing, Matt Wade, Steve Weiss
Coordinating Editor: Rita Fernando
Copy Editor: Jana Weinstein
Compositor: SPi Global
Indexer: SPi Global

Distributed to the book trade worldwide by Springer Science+Business Media New York, 233 Spring Street, 6th Floor, New York, NY 10013. Phone 1-800-SPRINGER, fax (201) 348-4505, e-mail orders-ny@springer-sbm.com, or visit www.springeronline.com. Apress Media, LLC is a California LLC and the sole member (owner) is Springer Science + Business Media Finance Inc (SSBM Finance Inc). SSBM Finance Inc is a Delaware corporation.

For information on translations, please e-mail rights@apress.com, or visit www.apress.com.

Apress and friends of ED books may be purchased in bulk for academic, corporate, or promotional use. eBook versions and licenses are also available for most titles. For more information, reference our Special Bulk Sales–eBook Licensing web page at www.apress.com/bulk-sales.

Any source code or other supplementary materials referenced by the author in this text is available to readers at www.apress.com. For detailed information about how to locate your book's source code, go to www.apress.com/source-code/.

To my amazing wife, Amy, who gave heartfelt encouragement and selfless support over countless hours to make this book a reality. To Harper—we love you and miss you.

Contents at a Glance

Contents

About the Author

Phil Weinmeister is a principal business analyst at EDL Consulting where he is focused on Salesforce.com implementations and custom solutions tailored to client needs. Phil is a Salesforce.com Certified Force.com Developer, as well as a Salesforce.com Certified Administrator, Advanced Administrator, Service Cloud Consultant, and Sales Cloud Consultant. He has delivered numerous solutions to a variety of organizations on the Force.com platform since 2010. Most recently, he has held key roles in designing and implementing custom Community Cloud solutions that combine social collaboration (Chatter) and e-commerce functionality (CloudCraze).

A graduate of Carnegie Mellon University with a double major in Business Administration (with a focus on information technology) and Spanish, Phil now resides in Powder Springs, Georgia. He spends most of his free time with his lovely wife, Amy, and his children, Tariku, Sophie, Max, and Lyla (due March 2015). When he's not finding ways to make his kids laugh or cheering on the Arizona Cardinals, Phil involves himself in various church-related activities with friends and families in the Cobb County area.

Stay updated on Phil's most recent insights and blog posts by following him on Twitter (@PhilWeinmeister).

About the Technical Reviewer

Jonathan Keel runs 6 Street Technologies, a consulting company specializing in Salesforce.com development and integration. Since founding the company, he has helped many clients realize the full potential of Salesforce.com and the Force.com platform, including AppExchange and mobile application development.

Jonathan is a Salesforce.com Certified Force.com Developer and has more than 14 years of experience delivering web applications using many technologies including Visualforce/Apex, Java, C#, PHP, HTML, JavaScript, and CSS. He has worked in many industries such as retail, education, and finance.

Jonathan lives in San Antonio, Texas, and can be reached at jonathan.keel@6st.co.

Acknowledgments

A number of people contributed to this book directly or indirectly and I would like to recognize and thank them here. Writing this book was quite a voyage and I'm very thankful for all of the input and support I have received.

- Jeff Olson (Apress): Jeff believed that I had what it would take to write an effective 300-page technical book on top of my full-time responsibilities at EDL Consulting. Jeff, thank you for extending me this wonderful opportunity.

- Jonathan Keel (6 Street Technologies): Jonathan provided essential validation and feedback by performing the technical review for this book, which was no small task. He went above and beyond by recreating the different solutions used as examples and asking critical questions to help drive clarity. Jonathan, thank you so much for your time and dedication.

- Adam Torman (Salesforce.com): Adam provided a detailed, extremely valuable review of Chapter 14. His expertise and insights on Salesforce.com security-related topics are second to none. Adam, thank you for your help.

- Sue Fuller (EDL Consulting): Sue was extremely supportive of the opportunity to author a book from the moment it came to light and encouraged me all the way along. Thanks for backing me, Sue.

- Bill Loumpouridis (EDL Consulting): Bill had the trust in me to be able to handle multiple client projects at a top-quality level while writing this book. Thank you for the support, Bill.

- Rita Fernando (Apress): Rita coordinated all the activity that transpired to get to the finish line and she did an excellent job. Thanks for putting up with all of my questions and emails along the way!

- Robert Hutchinson and Jana Weinstein (Apress): Robert and Jana both provided valuable feedback for each of my chapters. Their dedication to quality was apparent and made a material impact on the outcome of the book. Thanks to both of you for all of your input.

- Amy, Tariku, Sophie, and Max (my family): My family allowed me to escape to write for hours on end throughout the year. Thanks for being so loving and encouraging the whole time!

Introduction

If you are scratching your head in response to the book's title, Development without Code, you will be happily surprised to discover that this is not at all a paradox. While typical development requires the knowledge of a particular programming language, the creation of business applications within Salesforce.com does not. Some very intelligent employees at Salesforce.com have spent thousands of hours working away to build a highly configurable interface that is both user friendly and intuitive. I am neither a part of that group, nor an employee of Salesforce.com, but I can say without equivocation that building solutions within this CRM application for the last few years has been extremely enjoyable and quite fruitful, both for clients and my own organizations. In this book, I will share tips, tricks, lessons learned, and the application of Salesforce.com features and functionality that do not require the utilization of code.

If you are a traditional developer, keep reading! The content of this book will serve as the foundation to essentially unlimited customization of the platform. I will not cover Apex, Visualforce, or any other languages; however, it's important to understand that a more traditional approach to development in Salesforce.com is almost always accompanied by "declarative" elements that are implemented via configuration, or "clicks," instead of code. There are numerous occasions in which a particular configuration setting will be preferable over a solution built from scratch. Why reinvent the wheel when you can simply input your specifications and order one up? While the content directly applies to administrators, consultants, and analysts, there is also significant value for any Salesforce.com developer looking to better understand the platform and produce reliable, extensible applications.

Why Develop Without Code?

Regardless of your role, you'll need to be able to make wise decisions when it comes to delivering functionality for your organization or client. Inevitably, you will encounter scenarios in which a solution can be delivered either with or without the use of code. There are unique pros and cons in every situation, but do consider a few key points that may support the decision to avoid using code:

- The need to consider Salesforce.com limits and parameters is significantly reduced or, at times, eliminated completely when building solutions using declarative means.

- Modifications are often more straightforward, as they may only require a change to a configuration setting, not to a line of code.

- No unit testing is required (Apex test classes, in contrast, must be written for custom Apex code).

- Knowledge transfer burdens are reduced, since an understanding of the particular feature or function is typically sufficient to quickly determine what a specific application is intended to do.

- Future maintenance is simplified. If, for example, an individual who built custom applications for you leaves abruptly, picking up the pieces is much simpler if the work was done declaratively.

Don't get me wrong—there are numerous scenarios that do warrant development *with* code. However, developing with code in Salesforce.com is often done based on need; many organizations want to extend the platform to support functionality that simply does not exist "out of the box." Make sure you have a solid justification for developing with code if your business need can be met through configuration.

Code Sightings

I would like to comment on the "no code" aspect of this book. First, you *will* find a few snippets of code sprinkled throughout the book. For example, with formula functions, a few occasions arise that require manual input. Here are two examples from Chapter 2:

```
BEGINS(City, "Ph")
```

```
AND(
    Escalated,
    Subject = "AS400 is no longer functioning"
)
```

In both examples, you can see text strings that have been manually typed (e.g., "Ph" and "AS400 . . ."). While the values were not set via configuration or "clicks," I do not consider this code in the traditional sense. It is expected that some scenarios will emerge that require you to manually input a value.

Second, you will encounter traditional code in Chapter 11. In that chapter, I cover development with the Web-to-Lead tool, for which some HTML-editing capability will come in handy. However, HTML-editing skills are not required to understand the chapter and apply the principles being taught.

In both cases, "code" takes a back seat to declarative development.

Glossary

Let's clarify a few terms that will assist you as you walk through the book. You will also likely encounter these terms often when living in the world of Salesforce.com.

- **Org**: An "org" represents a particular instance of Salesforce.com, whether in production or in a test environment. An org has a unique set of configuration settings and data that formulates the overall user experience.

- **Sandbox**: A *sandbox* is a Salesforce.com-specific test org. There are different kinds of sandboxes, but one thing is common to all of them: they never exist in a production environment. Salesforce.com allows deployments both from and to sandboxes from other sandboxes or even a production environment.

- **Declarative**: This term describes a method for configuration or development that does not require coding or programming but, rather, the utilization of UI-based components to set up an org.

- **Customization**: In this book, *customization* is used to describe the utilization of the Force.com platform to deliver solutions or functionality that are not available to users upon initial org activation. Note that, in the world of Salesforce.com development, some individuals refer to traditional, code-based development as "customization."

- **Out of the box**: This term means different things to different people, so I want to be as clear as possible. For purposes of this book, *out of the box* signifies a feature, tool, or function that is ready for use without significant declarative development and definitely without any custom code. For example, workflow rules are supported out of the box, but a complex, custom-built solution that employs workflow rules would not be considered out of the box. Additionally, anything that requires customization via Apex or Visualforce is not considered out of the box.

Salesforce.com Editions

It is important to understand that a number of different editions of Salesforce.com exist. The edition that you are on depends on the licensing agreement that your organization shares with Salesforce.com. Certain features and tools are only available for particular editions, so make sure you are familiar with your edition and the corresponding functionality. You can find an overview of the different editions of Salesforce.com at `http://www.salesforce.com/crm/editions-pricing.jsp`.

Developer Org/Environment

If you don't already have a Salesforce.com org in which you can follow my examples and build similar solutions, you'll want to obtain one. The good news is that Salesforce.com development environments are free and are provisioned very quickly. Navigate to `https://developer.salesforce.com/signup` and sign up for your own org today. I highly recommend that you follow along and try to create solutions based on what you are learning. Reading is a great thing, but obtaining hands-on experience is what will bring you the most long-term benefit.

If at first you don't succeed, try, try again. There was a starting point for all of us in the development ecosystem, so stay encouraged and motivated. If you are struggling to put a particular takeaway into practice, continue to study and apply what you have learned and you'll find that things will eventually "click." Pun intended . . . now go have some fun!

CHAPTER 1

■ ■ ■

The Salesforce.com Data Model: Objects, Fields, and Relationships

If you have any familiarity with Salesforce.com, you know that it has never had a shortage of rich features and functionality. One facet of its broad development platform clearly stands out as a prime starting point for developing without code in Salesforce.com and will serve as the foundation for the rest of this book. That element is the *Salesforce.com data model*, which consists of *objects*, *fields*, and *relationships*. The data model serves as a framework for almost everything else you can do within the application. Once you understand objects, fields, and relationships within Salesforce.com, the other areas I will cover in this book will start to come into focus.

Because Salesforce.com has a wide variety of features and functionality, readers will vary greatly in terms of knowledge, development experience, business analysis/comprehension, and technical aptitude related to the program. While some of you may see this chapter as a refresher before digging deeper, others will see it as more of a critical starting point.

Throughout this book, you will find step-by-step instructions to guide you through building out the platform yourself. I highly recommend taking a hands-on approach as you make your way through each chapter since it will allow you to recall the details more vividly and possibly answer some of your own questions along the way.

By the end of this chapter, you will:

- understand standard and custom fields, including the corresponding differences

- be familiar with field types and when to use each of them

- know how to effectively create custom fields step by step

- understand standard objects and their purpose

- have learned about custom objects, including how to create your own custom object

- understand how to effectively build relationships between different objects

Salesforce.com Fields

When you want to get familiar with a new system or application, it can help to have a frame of reference. To give you one, I might suggest that the fields in Salesforce.com are similar to the columns that you would find in a relational database table. Like database columns, Salesforce.com fields contain data of a specific type. But whereas in a database table, a column and row intersect to give you a field that contains the actual data, in Salesforce.com, a field is present on a record and can be populated with data.

However, it is important to point out where the comparison between database columns and Salesforce.com fields falls short. To be truly nontechnical, I might refer to a Salesforce.com field as a database column on steroids. A field in Salesforce.com has a number of related attributes and properties that make it much more robust than a simple database column.

■ **Note** A **database column** may also be referred to as a field. Regardless of how it is labeled, a column/field in a database has some significant differences from a Salesforce.com field.

To effectively meet your company's needs within Salesforce.com, having the right fields is an absolute must. As you will see in subsequent chapters, fields will be your most basic building block throughout the development process. You will not only need to identify what fields will be meaningful and valuable within your org, but also to build them with the appropriate attributes. In this chapter, I will review Salesforce.com fields in detail and provide you with a foundation for success when developing without code on the Force.com platform.

Standard vs. Custom Fields

Once you begin developing solutions within Salesforce.com, you'll quickly become familiar with the terms *standard* and *custom*. Standard items, whether fields or objects, are elements that Salesforce.com produces for you. While you can control some of the attributes of standard items, you cannot directly control the creation of those elements. In a sense, standard elements are existing Force.com platform features. I say "in a sense" because some standard elements can be created as part of a separate process after your Salesforce.com instance is initially established. For example, when you create a custom object, standard fields are created automatically. The standard fields come along for the ride; you have no direct control over their presence.

The set of standard fields that is available to you depends on the object containing them. Standard objects each contain a unique, predefined set of fields. I will cover those later in this chapter when we dive into objects. For now, let's look at the minimal set of standard fields–those that are automatically created when an object is created:

- **Record Name:** This can be a manually entered alphanumeric value (Text field) or an "autonumber" automatically generated by Salesforce.com.

- **Owner:** With some exceptions (see the "Master-Detail Relationship" section later in this chapter), the Owner field will be automatically created. Your Owner field will be populated with a User from your system.

- **Created By:** This is a special system-populated field that captures the User that created the record along with the date and time of the creation.

- **Last Modified By:** Although this field is similar to Created By, it captures the User and Date/Time associated with the last record update instead of record creation.

■ **Note** Last Modified By is actually a concatenation of two system fields: LastModifiedById and LastModifiedDate. However, users just see the concatenated Last Modified By field.

Attributes

Every field that you create in Salesforce.com has certain attributes that need to be defined. There are obvious examples, such as Name and, in some cases, Length. Other attributes provide depth for fields and allow them to be used properly in a variety of scenarios. You will want to get familiar with these attributes before creating your own fields; they include:

- **Field Label**: The name of your field that is displayed to users.

- **Field Name**: The unique name of your field. Field Name is typically not shown to users, although it is possible to do so. Field Names can only contain alphanumeric characters and (nonconsecutive) underscores, must begin with a letter, and must end with a letter or number.

- **Description**: The Description field is purely for reference, used to explain the purpose and/or context of the field you are creating. It is highly recommended that you always populate Description even if the reason you are adding a field seems obvious.

- **Help Text**: The bubble text displayed to users upon hovering over a small question mark next to the field. Populating the Help Text field is not required and is most valuable when a user might have trouble understanding how to interact with or interpret a field.

- **Required**: This Checkbox must have a legitimately formatted value present before a record can be created or saved.

- **Unique**: By selecting the Unique Checkbox, you ensure that the field on a new or existing record cannot contain a value that matches that of the same field on another record. Unique can be configured to be case sensitive or case insensitive.

- **External ID**: This Checkbox serves as a record identifier for a field in a system or application outside of Salesforce.com. External IDs have special behavior when corresponding records are imported, either via the standard import wizards or the Apex Data Loader. Note that the External ID by itself does not guarantee that the field values are unique in Salesforce.com—the unique attribute is a separate function.

- **Default Value**: By setting the Default Value on a field, you can set an initial value on every record that is created. This value can be as straightforward as a string ("New") or a number ("5"). However, it can also be a formula that uses Salesforce.com's built-in formula functions and can even derive values from other fields/objects.

■ **Note**　The Field Name and Field API Name attributes are directly related. The API Name is referenced in code and formulas. You might have a custom field with a Field Name of "Book." In the API Name, "__c" (for custom) is automatically appended, making the API Name "Book__c" Standard fields do not have anything appended, so the Field Name is the same as the API Name.

All fields require a Field Label and Field Name. Description and Help Text are not required but are available on every field. The remaining attributes (Required, Unique, External ID, Default Value) are available for selection on a limited number of field types. See Table 1-1.

Table 1-1. *A Matrix of Field Attributes Available by Field Type*

Field type	Required	Unique	External ID	Default value
Auto Number			✓	
Formula				
Roll-Up Summary				
Lookup	✓			
Master-Detail				
Checkbox				
Currency	✓			✓
Date	✓			✓
Date/Time	✓			✓
Email	✓	✓	✓	✓
Geolocation	✓			
Number	✓	✓	✓	✓
Percent	✓			✓
Phone	✓			✓
Picklist				
Picklist (Multi-Select)				
Text	✓	✓	✓	✓
Text Area	✓			✓
Text Area (Long)				✓
Text Area (Rich)				
Text (Encrypted)	✓			
URL	✓			✓

Custom Field Types

Every field within Salesforce.com has an associated type. When you create your own custom field in Salesforce.com, you will need to define a field type. A field's type (e.g., Number, Text, etc.) ensures that certain parameters and governing rules are enforced. It drives how users see and interact with the corresponding field. Salesforce.com provides a number of field types to choose from. The types available to you when you create a custom field are a subset of the full set of field types that exist in Salesforce.com; some types are only available via standard objects. Let's take a look at the custom field types and how they are used within the platform.

■ **Note** The Lookup relationship, Master-Detail relationship, and Roll Up Summary field types will be covered in the "Salesforce.com Relationships" section later in this chapter.

Auto Number

Auto Number fields automatically generate a value for each new record based on a simple algorithm that incrementally inserts the numeric portion of the field's value for each new record. At the most basic level, you can create an Auto Number field ("My Custom Auto Number Field") that starts with a value of 1 and increases by 1 for each subsequent record (see Table 1-2).

Table 1-2. *Auto-Numbering Sequencing*

	Record 1 value	Record 2 value	Record 3 value
My Custom Auto Number Field	1	2	3

While you cannot control the size of the increment—Auto Number fields always increase the numeric portion of the value by 1—you can control the display format and the starting number of the field. The display format consists of two parts: (1) a numeric portion that is automatically increased and (2) optional static text that supplements the number. The numeric part is identified in the field setting with curly brackets ("{}"). The starting number setting identifies the first integer to be used.

■ **Note** When you create an Auto Number field, give careful consideration to how you format the static text component to provide as much meaning as possible. For example, "ANN-{0000}" would be a sensible format for an Announcement custom object and "SCH-{0}" would work for a Schedule custom object. If possible, format the Auto Number field so that a user might understand what it represents without needing to do additional research.

Table 1-3 shows some examples of Auto Number display formats along with the corresponding field values that would actually display on a page, based on display format and starting number.

Table 1-3. *Example Values Based on Different Auto Number Formats*

Display format	Starting #	Record #	Field value
{0}	1	1	**1**
{0000}	1	1	**0001**
ABC-{0}	1	1	**ABC-1**
ABC-{0}	1	155	**ABC-155**
ABC-{0}	1000	1	**ABC-1000**
ABC-{0}	1000	155	**ABC-1154**
ABC-{0000}	1	1	**ABC-0001**
ABC-{0000}	1	11315	**ABC-11315**
ABC-{0000}	1000	1	**ABC-1000**
ABC-{0000}	1000	11315	**ABC-12314**

(*continued*)

Table 1-3. (*continued*)

Display format	Starting #	Record #	Field value
Record_{0}	1	1	**Record_1**
Record_{0}	1	87	**Record_87**
Record_{0}	100	1	**Record_100**
Record_{0}	100	87	**Record_186**
{0000}-abc	1	1	**0001-abc**
{0000}-abc	1	52	**0052-abc**

■ **Note** If you notice unexpected gaps in your Auto Number sequences (e.g., "ABC-1" to "ABC-2" to "ABC-7"), you need to know two things: First, know that you have not lost your mind. It's unlikely that a rogue user is off deleting records; this is probably a result of records being created in Apex Test Classes. Second, you can adjust this. Go to **Setup ➤ Develop ➤ Apex Test Execution ➤ Options**, select "Independent Auto Number Sequence," and click "OK."

Formula

The Formula field type allows you to construct a formula based on functions, statements, calculations, operations, user-defined values, and/or other field values that will be evaluated and return a corresponding value. Most commonly, Formula fields will involve derived values that are pulled in from other fields on the same object or from fields on related objects. For example, you may create a formula that evaluates one of the following values:

- a multiple of a currency value (e.g., amount)
- a date based on an existing date field plus a set number of days
- a true/false value derived from an IF statement that evaluates another field on the object
- text inherited from a Parent object (as is)

Formulas will be valuable to you as you build solutions within Salesforce.com. I will dedicate multiple chapters in this book to understanding how formula fields work and how to effectively create them to address your business needs.

■ **Note** Formulas will serve as one of the cornerstones for development without code in Salesforce.com and will be covered in detail in chapters 2 and 3.

Checkbox

A Checkbox field is a Boolean expression, potentially containing one of two values: True or False. Within the standard Salesforce.com User interface, a Checkbox appears with a check for True and without a check for False. You have the option of setting the default value to either checked or unchecked when defining a Checkbox field.

Numeric Fields

Number, Currency, and Percent are three fields that are very similar in behavior, so I am grouping them together here. These field types store numeric values up to a total length of 18 digits. The digits include the total number of digits to the left of the decimal point (referred to as length) and to the right of it (referred to as decimal places). For example, you can create fields from these field types with a length of 16 + 2 decimal places, a length of 10 + 8 decimal places, and so forth. A field with a length of 18 would not be allowed to have any decimal places due to the total digit limit.

It is worth noting that each of these fields stores the corresponding number without any transformation of the value itself. For example, entering 50 in a Number field, a Currency field, and a Percent field would result in a value of 50 being stored in each field in the database (i.e., not "0.5" in the Percent field). Additionally, it's critical to understand that values with precision beyond the configured number of decimal places are rounded accordingly. For example, in a Number field with a length of 2 + 3 decimal places, a submitted value of "14.1448" would be modified to "14.145." The new value is the one actually stored in the field at that point; it is not simply a shortened representation of a longer field.

■ **Note**   The currency type (e.g., USD, GBP, EUR, etc.) associated with a particular Currency field is not set at the field level; it is determined by a variety of contextual factors at the record, user, and org levels.

Date Fields

Date and Date/Time fields contain date and date and time values, respectively. There are a couple key points to understand about Date and Date/Time fields: First, the format of the value will differ based on your context. In scenarios where a date or Date/Time field will be populated or edited by your users (e.g., within record detail pages, list views, reports, etc.), the format will be: MM/DD/YYYY (e.g., "9/30/2015"). You may enter the year as "YY" and it will be converted to the full four-digit date, YYYY. In other scenarios (e.g., advanced developers using Apex or system administrators using the Data Loader), the format will be: YYYY-MM-DD. See Table 1-4 and Figure 1-1 for how Date fields appear in different contexts.[1]

Table 1-4. *Display/Presentation of Date Values in Different Contexts*

Date	Salesforce.com context	Displayed value
September 30, 2015	Record detail page	**9/30/2015**
September 30, 2015	List view	**9/30/2015**
September 30, 2015	Report	**9/30/2015**
September 30, 2015	Apex trigger/class	**2015-09-30**
September 30, 2015	Data Loader	**2015-09-30**

---

[1]All Salesforce.com screenshots in this chapter © copyright Salesforce.com, Inc. Used with permission.

Figure 1-1. A Date field with the automatic date picker that appears in the UI

Date and Date/Time fields behave similarly. In the standard user scenarios previously described, Date/Time fields will need to be formatted in the UI as: MM/DD/YYYY HH:MM AM/PM. For a.m./p.m., you would enter either "AM" or "PM." Hours should be entered in the 12-hour format. Like with the Date field, users may enter YY for a Date/Time field and allow Salesforce.com to automatically convert the value into a four-digit year. In the more datacentric scenarios previously described, the format will be: YYYY-MM-DDTHH:MM:SSZ." The T and Z should be entered as is and do not need to be modified; the T stands for time and the Z stands for zone, as in time zone. By default, the value is entered in the user's local time zone. You can offset the time to a specific time zone, as shown in Table 1-5 and Figure 1-2. In that case, the Z is replaced with the time offset (e.g., "-05:00).

Table 1-5. Date/Time Values (with Local Time and Time Zone Offset)

Date/Time (UTC)	Time zone	Data Loader/Apex input value	As displayed in UI in the referenced time zone
September 30, 2014 10:30 AM	UTC	**2015-09-30T10:30:00Z**	**9/30/2014 10:30 AM**
September 30, 2014 10:30 AM	EST (UTC-5)	**2015-09-30T10:30:00-05:00**	**9/30/2014 5:30 AM**
September 30, 2014 10:30 AM	PST (UTC-8)	**2015-09-30T10:30:00-08:00**	**9/30/2014 2:30 AM**

Figure 1-2. A Date/Time field with the automatic date picker that appears in the UI

■ **Note** The time displayed to a user depends on the time zone set on his record. So, if a Date/Time field contains a time of 1:00 PM PST, it will display as 4:00 PM for users who have the time zone set to EST.

Email

Email fields are essentially Text fields with specific, built-in formatting validations. Email fields must include:

- an @ symbol
- text before the @
- a period somewhere after the @
- text immediately before and after the period
- no symbols other than underscores, hyphens, periods, characters, and @ symbols

Of course, Salesforce.com cannot fully validate an e-mail based on these conditions. Try it yourself. You can enter "1-_@1.1" in the Email field and the value will be accepted. If you do want to expand the validations on this field, you can use the REGEX function within a validation rule. Both the REGEX function and validation rules will be covered in subsequent chapters.

Email fields have a built-in mailto: link that allows you to send an e-mail to the specified address using your default e-mail application upon clicking on the address.

Geolocation

The Geolocation field type is relatively new to Salesforce.com. Geolocation actually contains two subfields: Longitude and Latitude. You can control how the value is displayed: in degrees, minutes, or seconds (DMS) or as a number with decimal places. Figure 1-3 contains four subfields related to the two Geolocation subfields. The first two fields represent the Longitude and Latitude for a DMS-formatted field; the second two fields represent a Decimal-formatted Geolocation field.

Geolocation Field - DMS (Latitude)	32.7346
Geolocation Field - DMS (Longitude)	35.1913
Geolocation Field - Decimal (Latitude)	33.5111
Geolocation Field - Decimal (Longitude)	36.3064

Figure 1-3. *How the two geodecimal fields (DMS and Decimal) appear when edited*

After saving your edit, Figure 1-4 shows what you will see in each field on the record detail page.

| Geolocation Field - DMS | 32°44'5"N 35°11'29"E |
| Geolocation Field - Decimal | 33.5111 36.3064 |

Figure 1-4. *The two Geodecimal fields after saving*

You can set the number of decimals that are allowed in a Geolocation field. Like with other numeric fields, Salesforce.com will round a value that has more decimal places than it allows. For example, in a field with two allowed decimals places, a latitude of 35.505 would save as 35.51 and a latitude of 35.504 would save as 35.5 (note that the lagging zero is removed).

Phone

The Phone field is similar to the Email field in that it has a very specific context and use: storage of a phone number. In terms of what data is allowed in the field, it is really a simple Text field. However, Phone fields can be used for manual or automatic dialing of phone numbers within certain applications.

■ **Note**　The text allowed in a Phone field goes well beyond the scope of characters/digits that would appear in real-world scenarios. I would recommend building out some validation rules to prohibit invalid entry of phone number values to maintain data integrity. Validation rules are covered in detail in Chapter 5.

Picklist

The Picklist fields, **Picklist** and **Picklist (Multi-Select)**, are used frequently within Salesforce.com and can be extremely valuable when building business processes into your application. Picklists behave most similarly to drop-down fields, although that term is completely abandoned on the Force.com platform. With single Picklists, you can define a list of one or more values that can be selected, or picked, by users through the standard UI. Figure 1-5 shows a Picklist field called Stock Exchange. This field represents the exchange on which an Account's stock trades.

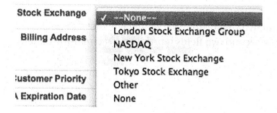

Figure 1-5.　Values from a Picklist field

　　In addition to identifying the values that will be available, you will also define the sequence in which the values will appear and, optionally, the default (prepopulated) value for users.

■ **Note**　Including values such as "None" and "Other" has implications in your business process that need to be considered. Including "Other" may be necessary to prevent user frustration with a finite set of values, but it could have an adverse effect on reporting granularity. "None" is most useful when you want to ensure that users consider and select a value for a Picklist field even if no value applies. Alternatively, you can simply let them avoid making a selection, but there's the risk that the user may skip the field out of hastiness.

　　Multi-Select Picklists allow for the selection of multiple values within a particular field. You can select zero, one, or multiple values from the defined list. Again, you can configure the order of the list. Also, you can define how tall the window is in rows. Figure 1-6 is an example of a Picklist (Multi-Select) on an Account record.

Figure 1-6. *A Multi-Select Picklist field during an edit*

■ **Note** Perhaps the primary factor you will need to consider when creating a Multi-Select Picklist field is the implication for reporting. With a standard (single) Picklist field, you can easily obtain the count of records by Picklist value. That is not the case with a Multi-Select Picklist field.

Text Fields

You can create a variety of text fields in your data model. Table 1-6 is a summary of each.

Table 1-6. *A Matrix of Text Field Types and Their Related Attributes*

Text field type	Max length	# display lines	Formatted text	Images	Links
Text	255	1	No	No	No
Text (Encrypted)	175	1	No	No	No
Text Area	N/A	1–3*	No	No	No
Text Area (Long)	32,768	2–50	No	No	No
Text Area (Rich)	32,768	2–50	Yes	Yes	Yes

You do not have control over the number of lines displayed for a Text Area field; this is driven by the context (page) and the length of the value in the field.

Encrypted fields allow characters to be masked and replaced with "x" or "*." The format of the masking can be configured as well. Standard users will not be able to see encrypted fields without the "View encrypted data" permission.

URL

URL fields are text based and have a specific use and context. These fields store properly formatted hyperlinks and link to the specified URL upon the user clicking the hyperlink. Like Phone fields, URL fields have no restrictions on the amount of actual characters that can be entered. Salesforce.com will take the text input and identify whether a prefix (http://) is required. If the submitted value does *not* start with http:// or https://, Salesforce.com will add the prefix "http://" to the text value in the field. I would recommend some basic validations of this field to ensure that no invalid characters are accidentally included in the URL value.

Additional Field Types

Address and Name field types are not currently available when creating custom field types but are present on some standard objects. Each field type is actually a set of related fields and is referred to as a compound field. The Address and Name fields cannot be directly updated, but the individual field components within them can. For example, you cannot update Billing Address on the Account object, but you can update Billing Street, Billing City, Billing State, and so on. The Address field type is comprised of the following fields: **Street**, **City**, **State/Province**, **Zip/Postal Code**, and **Country**. The Name field type contains the following fields: **Salutation**, **First Name**, and **Last Name**.

Creating a Custom Field Step by Step

Each field type has a unique creation process. I previously described some of the elements that need to be considered when creating a corresponding field according to the field type. What follows is an overview of the creation process along with the key considerations. Keep in mind that the best way to get familiar with the process is to actually create a variety of fields with different field types.

■ **Note**   Relationship fields (Lookup, Master-Detail) have a more detailed creation process than the four-step process described in this section.

---

1. *Select a field type.* Carefully choose your field type from the provided list. Make sure to think about the exact use case and select the field type that makes sense for your business needs.

2. *Configure the field attributes.* Once you select your field type, you will have to set the attributes for the field. Each of these is covered in detail earlier in this chapter.

3. *Set up field-level security.* Establish the permissions to your new field that should be granted to existing profiles. Once you have set the field type and configured the related attributes for your field, you will need to set the visibility of and access to the field across the existing profiles. You have three options that can be applied. Table 1-7 is a matrix showing the Visible and Read-Only columns that you edit along with the CRUD (create, read, update, delete) equivalent of the corresponding combination.

Table 1-7. *Potential Field-Level Security Settings*

Field-level security			
Summary of visibility and access	Visible	Read-only	CRUD equivalent
No visibility / No ability to edit the field			-
Visibility / No ability to edit the field	✓	✓	R
Visibility / Ability to edit the field	✓		RU*

* Create and Delete are managed at the record and Object levels

Keep in mind that field-level security (FLS) may or may not have a direct impact on a user's experience. If a User does not have access to a particular record at all, full access via FLS does nothing to change that—the user still will not be able to see any of the fields on the record. Or she may be granted Read/Write access via FLS but a validation rule (these will be covered later in this book) may override that access and prevent her from editing the record. FLS, whether associated with a profile or a permission set, conveys the maximum access to a field that a user might have; the user might ultimately have less access based on other settings, but she will not have more access to the field than configured via FLS. Figure 1-7 is a look at the FLS settings page during custom field creation.

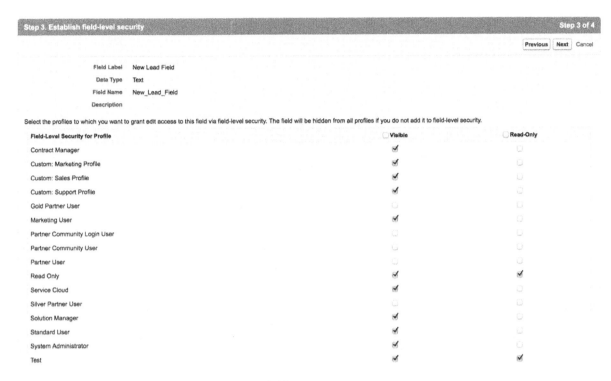

Figure 1-7. *Setting the field-level security for your field*

▪ **Note**   Security considerations, including object and field permissions, are discussed in detail in Chapter 14.

---

    4.   *Add to page layouts.* The last step in the field creation process is only marginally helpful, and I'll explain why. You are given the option to automatically add the field you are creating to any of the page layouts for the corresponding object. If you are creating a Lead field and four page layouts exist for Leads, you can add the Lead field to any of those four layouts at your discretion, as shown in Figure 1-8.

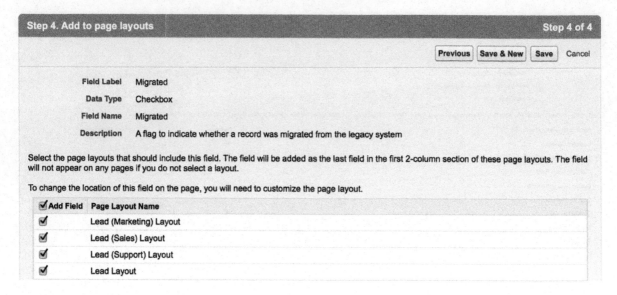

Figure 1-8. *Setting your page layout options*

This sounds like a nice time-saver, doesn't it? The problem is that you have no control over the field's location within the page layout, just whether it is present or not. Fields added to page layouts through this means are always added as the bottom, left-most field in the first section on the page layout, as shown in Figure 1-9.

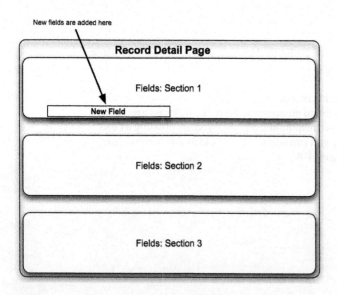

Figure 1-9. *Appearance of a new field when added during the creation process*

Except in the rare situation where you specifically want your field to appear in the bottom-left corner of the top-most field section on your page layout, you will need to go into your layout and edit it to move the field to the desired location. You may want to hold off on automatically adding a field to a page layout and just do it manually for two reasons:

- If you forget to update the corresponding page layout after creating it, your field will be in the wrong location.

- You have to update the page layout anyway and you will have additional control if you handle adding the field and moving it all at once.

That's it! You do want to spend some time thinking about your options before just breezing through the creation. You can always change your field settings later, but it's definitely easier to set up your field properly up front. Now, you're ready to move on to the world of objects.

Salesforce.com Objects

As you have seen in this chapter thus far, it is impossible to cover the breadth of Salesforce.com fields without at least touching on the objects in which those fields are contained. In this section, I will dive into the basics of objects and further prepare you to develop real-world business solutions on the Force.com platform.

Previously, I stated that fields in Salesforce.com are comparable to database columns. Along those same lines, we can compare Salesforce.com objects to database tables (again on steroids). Each object contains a set number of standard fields along with any custom fields you create. At the intersection of those fields and the records will be your field values, similar to database fields. Table 1-8 includes a couple of basic charts that have a similar structure to each other.

Table 1-8. *Comparison Between a Salesforce.com Object and a Relational Database Table*

Salesforce.com object			Relational database table		
	Field 1 (text)	Field 2 (number)		Column 1 (text)	Column 2 (number)
Record 1	My first record	100	Row 1	My first record	100
Record 2	My second record	200	Row 2	My second record	200
Record 3	My third record	300	Row 3	My third record	300

However, there is another layer entirely to objects. Like fields, objects have associated attributes and metadata that build their context and drive their use. I will now walk you through the object creation process, during which you will see the additional information that can be associated with a Salesforce.com object. Figure 1-10 is the initial screen you see when creating a custom object.

Custom Object Information

The singular and plural labels are used in tabs, page layouts, and reports.

Label		Example: **Account**
Plural Label		Example: **Accounts**
Starts with vowel sound	☐	

The Object Name is used when referencing the object via the API.

Object Name		Example: **Account**

Description

Context-Sensitive Help Setting ◉ Open the standard Salesforce.com Help & Training window
◯ Open a window using a Visualforce page

Content Name --None--

Figure 1-10. Typical custom field attributes that can be set during field creation

The first step in creating a custom object is to define its basic, key information. You'll set your label and plural label first. Salesforce.com doesn't want to assume what your grammatical application will be. What if you wanted to make an object called "Fish"? In that case, you might want the plural label to match label. The "Starts with vowel sound" is present for a similar reason: Salesforce.com does not inherently know that the starting letter in hour and hot sound different, but it does want to apply correct grammar rules. Setting that yourself helps to achieve that goal.

Like with Salesforce.com fields, you will need to provide an object name and, optionally, a description. I would again recommend using the object name that is automatically populated, unless it is critical to your business process that you set a specific name for a business purpose. And as tempting as it is to skip entering a description, the ten seconds needed to enter one could pay off in spades. I can say from personal experience that a populated description has helped save a significant chunk of time more than once.

The next step is configuring the Record Name label and format for your object. Figure 1-11 shows the Record Name field, which will be the primary name field for your new records.

Record Name		Example: **Account Name**
Data Type	Text	

Figure 1-11. Record Name as a text field

As shown in Figure 1-12, you can either allow open text entry or you can automate it (without code) by using the Auto Number option. I recommend using the Auto Number option when possible, as it provides you with a built-in ID that is automatically increased, in increments, with the creation of new records. It also serves as a nice reference when looking at a list of records.

Record Name		Example: **Account Name**
Data Type	Auto Number ⇕	
Display Format		Example: **A-{0000}** <u>What Is This?</u>
Starting Number		

Figure 1-12. *Record Name as an Auto Number field*

The last setting in this section determines the source for your content. You can either use the generic custom object page that Salesforce provides or your own custom page. If you don't have a specific help page ready for use, proceed with the Salesforce.com help page.

There are some additional attributes that you'll need to consider when creating your custom fields. Here's a summary of the remaining items:

- **Allow Reports**: Creates a custom report type for the object with which reports can be created for the new object.

- **Allow Activities**: Enables activities (tasks, events) to be associated with the record. Recommended only if activities make sense for the object. If the object does not require activities to be tracked against it, leave it unchecked. You can also enable it later.

- **Track Field History**: Allows changes made to the fields on the object to be tracked.

- **Allow Sharing**, **Allow Bulk API Access**, and **Allow Streaming API Access**: These three settings must either all be enabled or all be disabled. By default, they are enabled, making a custom object an "Enterprise Application" object. Disabling these features will convert the object to a "Light Application" object. The settings themselves allow for more advanced, robust interaction with the object.

- **Deployment Status**: Allows you to select "Deployed" if the object is ready for release to all users.

- **Add Notes and Attachments (related list to default page layout)**: Like with activities, you'll need to assess whether the notes and attachments are relevant. If so, select this option. Otherwise, leave off the clutter.

- **Launch New Custom Tab Wizard (after saving the custom object)**: Will users need to navigate to the records? Then definitely select this option. There's no need to select this option if it has more of a back-end or reporting function.

▨ **Note** The Object attributes that are configured at the time of object creation can easily be modified later by navigating back to the object in the Setup menu. For example, if your reporting needs change after object deployment, you can check the Allow Reports Checkbox when needed.

Salesforce.com Relationships

While relationships in Salesforce.com technically fall under the umbrella of field types, they warrant a closer look outside the scope of other more straightforward field types. Relationship fields are the last piece of the puzzle and allow you to connect everything in your data model together.

Relationship Field Types

To fully understand how relationships within Salesforce.com work, you must first have a firm grasp on the types of relationship fields that can be created.

Lookup Relationship

Along with the Master-Detail relationship field type, which will be discussed in the next section, the Lookup relationship is vastly different from all other field types and has significant implications for your Salesforce.com org. A Lookup relationship field actually modifies the interobject schema by creating Parent/Child links between objects. To clearly see the picture, first take a look at a two disparate, unrelated objects. As illustrated in Figure 1-13, the Contact and Idea objects have no native relationship with each other.

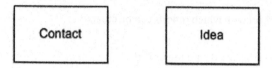

Figure 1-13. *Two disparate objects*

Unlike the Contact and Idea objects, the Contact and Account objects are in fact related. The Contact object has an "Account Name" Lookup relationship that creates a link between the two objects. In Figure 1-14, the Account object is shown above the Contact object since it is the Parent object and the Contact object is the Child.

Figure 1-14. *Related Account and Contact objects, connected via a Lookup field*

Figure 1-14 shows the Crow's Foot entity-relationship notation for the relationship between the Account and Contact. A Contact can look up zero or one Account. An Account can go from zero-to-many Contacts and is not required to have any related Contacts, but can be associated with however many you can add to it within the applicable limits of your org. An important consideration when creating a Lookup relationship field is that it is a loose relationship; deletion of the Parent record that is referenced in the Lookup field does not result in the Child record's deletion. For example, take a look at Figure 1-15. In this image, you can see that the Contact record for George

Jetson has a Lookup relationship to the Spacely Sprockets Account. If you delete the record of the Parent, Spacely Sprockets, George Jetson's Contact record will not be deleted automatically; the Account field will simply no longer be populated.

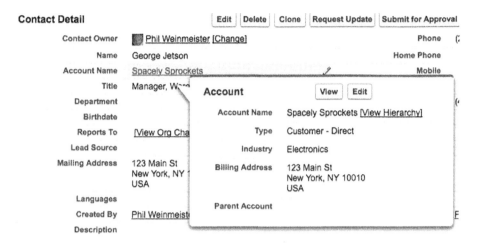

Figure 1-15. *A relationship field on the record detail page*

Salesforce.com does allow you to restrict deletion of a Parent record that is part of a Lookup relationship. By enabling that restriction setting, you require users to first remove or change the value in the Child record's Lookup field before deleting the Parent. In this case, you would edit George Jetson's Contact record, modify the Account Name Lookup, save the record, and then delete the Spacely Sprockets record.

Additionally, you can add a Lookup Filter to a Lookup relationship. A Lookup Filter will restrict the available records in a Lookup field based on defined criteria.

Master-Detail Relationship

The Master-Detail relationship field type is very similar to a Lookup relationship. By creating a Master-Detail field, you build a relationship between a Child record and a Parent record. However, there are some critical differences between these two relationship field types:

- A Master-Detail relationship field must be populated. In other words, you cannot have an "orphaned" Child record that has a blank Master-Detail field. This is not the case with a Lookup field unless you specify that a Parent is required in the Lookup.

- A Child in a Master-Detail relationship does not have a standard Owner field; the owner of the Parent record, via inheritance, determines the owner for this relationship.

- Cascading deletion occurs when Parent/Master records are removed. In other words, all Child/Detail records will be deleted if the Parent record linked via a Master-Detail field is deleted.

- Master-Detail fields allow you to create Roll-Up Summary fields. They will be discussed in the next section.

Although a Master-Detail field must be populated, it can be "reparented" if configured accordingly. That means that you can change the associated Parent record after the Child record is created.

Roll Up Summary

The Roll Up Summary field type does not affect object relationships, but it builds directly upon the Master-Detail relationship. A Roll Up Summary field is a great feature, which Salesforce.com makes available for creation any time you establish a Master-Detail field. The presence of an associated Master-Detail field is a requirement, since the Summary part of the field is directly related to the associated Child records. In Figure 1-16, you can see two different perspectives of how this works. On the left, you see that the Master-Detail field is created on the Detail, or Child, object. However, the Roll Up Summary is set up on the Master, or Parent, object. On the right, you can see examples of actual records that might be present in this Master-Detail relationship. The presence of the Roll Up Summary on the Master record makes sense since the summary will include a downward look across all of the children.

Figure 1-16. *A view of a Master-Detail relationship*

When you create a Roll Up Summary, you are given the following options:

- **Object to summarize**: Note that the objects listed will be limited to those with Master-Detail relationships with the object you're working with.

- **Roll Up type**: (COUNT, SUM, MIN, MAX) COUNT returns the number of all Child records on the selected object. SUM returns the sum of a specified Number or Currency field across Child records. MIN and MAX return the least/first or greatest/last value, respectively, from a specific Number, Currency, or Date field among Child records.

- **Filter criteria**: Allows you to specify criteria based on object fields to limit which Child records are included in the Roll Up.

It might help to look at a few specific examples. Figure 1-17 represents the Master-Detail relationship between the Opportunity and Account objects, and Table 1-9 shows sample records at the detail level.

Figure 1-17. *Three Opportunities and their related Account*

Table 1-9. *Examples of Roll-Up Summary Fields and Their Values Based on the Records in Figure 1-17 Salesforce.com data model:roll up summary*

Roll-Up type	Field	Criteria	Field value
COUNT	N/A	None (All Records)	3
COUNT	N/A	Closed = False	2
COUNT	N/A	Type = Existing	1
SUM	Amount	None (All Records)	$24,500
SUM	Amount	Closed = False	$10,500
SUM	Amount	Type = Existing	$10,000
MIN	CloseDate	None (All Records)	04/01/15
MIN	CloseDate	Closed = False	04/01/15
MIN	CloseDate	Type = Existing	04/29/15
MAX	Amount	None (All Records)	$14,000
MAX	Amount	Closed = False	$10,000
MAX	Amount	Type = Existing	$10,000

Junction Objects

You just read about Lookup and Master-Detail relationships. These field types build the respective foundation for zero-to-many and one-to-many associations between Parent and Child records. What about many-to-many relationships? Can you create those in Salesforce.com, and if so, how? The answer is yes; you *can* create many-to-many relationships in Salesforce.com. I will walk you through a real-world example that requires a many-to-many relationship and explain how to appropriately configure your data model.

Let's say your firm regularly holds sweepstakes contests for marketing and branding purposes and you want to capture the specific individuals who have entered each contest. Those individuals come from your pool of existing Contact records. In this case, the standard Campaign and Campaign Member objects would likely meet your needs, but we will use custom objects for the purposes of this discussion.

You could create a Contest object and relate Contacts to it via a Lookup relationship, as shown in Figure 1-18.

Figure 1-18. *Contact record related to a custom object "Contest"*

However, via a direct relationship to Contest, *a Contact can only be associated with one Contest*. That quickly becomes a problem as your Contacts start to attend multiple Contests. This is where a "Junction object" comes into play. Instead of directly linking your Contact to a Contest, you can create a new custom object called a Contest Registrant and add two relationship fields to it, as shown in Figure 1-19.

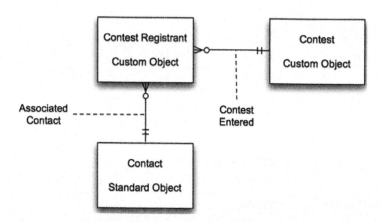

Figure 1-19. *Contest Registrant custom object serving as a Junction object*

Here is a breakdown of the various elements shown in Figure 1-19:

- **Contest Entered:** This Master-Detail field identifies a contest that the registrant is registered for. It is a Master-Detail field because a Contest Registrant cannot exist apart from a Contest.

- **Associated Contact:** This field identifies the person that registered for a particular Contest. Because you don't need a duplicate record of a person, you link to the "source" record, which is the Contact, and add any custom fields to the Contest Registrant record to provide additional context about his role as a registrant. This is a Master-Detail field because a Contest Registrant cannot exist apart from a Contact, at least in this case.

As a result, both Contacts and Contests can be associated with many Contest Registrants. That means that:

- One Contact can be associated with many Contests.

- One Contest can be associated with many Contacts.

If one Contact is registered for five Contests, you would have one Contact, five Contest Registrants, and five Contest records. If one Contest has five registrants, you would have one Contest, five Contest Registrants, and five Contacts.

Some Perspective on the Data Model

The Salesforce.com data model consists of three key parts: objects, fields, and relationships. Since Master-Detail and Lookup relationships are fields, you could make the argument that it is really just two parts, since relationships are field types. However, since the relationship field type is so fundamentally different than other field types, I find it more useful to look at it as a completely separate element.

Figure 1-20 is intended to help you see the Salesforce.com data model from a few steps back. This visual gives a basic perspective of the objects, fields, and relationships that exist within your instance of Salesforce.com. You can use Salesforce.com's "Schema Builder" tool for a detailed view of the same content.

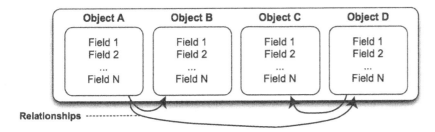

Figure 1-20. *A view of the data model*

More realistically, the creation of your data model will look like Figure 1-21.

Figure 1-21. *A high-level suggested sequence for building out your data model*

This list provides additional clarification for the corresponding numbered items in Figure 1-21:

1. Configure the standard fields on the standard objects relevant to your organization.

2. Create/configure the custom fields on the same standard objects.

3. Create/configure any relationships between standard objects.

4. Create/configure custom object A (Parent, if applicable).

5. Create/configure the custom fields on custom object A.

6. Create/configure custom object B (Child, if applicable).

7. Create/configure the custom fields on custom object B.

8. Create/configure relationships looking up to the custom objects.

■ **Note**   Create Parent objects before Child objects to minimize the number of total steps required to build out your data model. This will allow you to add the relationship from the Child object to the Master object while you are building out the Child object.

Recap

A solid understanding of the Salesforce.com data model is critical for success as a developer on the Force.com platform whether or not you are using code. In this chapter, I examined objects, fields, and relationships in detail and I walked you through the process for setting up a data model in your org. You will build on this foundation as you make your way through the rest of this book.

CHAPTER 2

Formula Functions: Your Building Block in Salesforce.com Formulas

Without hesitation, I would identify this chapter as one of the most important in this book. Along with the first chapter on the Salesforce.com data model, it will serve as the foundation for many of the upcoming chapters, as formula functions are used in a number of development areas within the Force.com platform. If you understand how to properly build and apply functions within Salesforce.com, you will be able to develop successful custom solutions for yourself, your employer, and your clients.

Functions can be used in a number of different areas:

- formula fields

- workflow rules

- field updates

- validation rules

- approval rules

- approval rule steps

- auto-response rules

- escalation rules

- assignment rules

- custom buttons and links

The areas previously listed comprise much of the focus of this book and a significant portion of your arsenal in developing custom solutions within Salesforce.com using clicks, not code. There are over 60 total functions available for use within Salesforce.com and that number continues to grow. In this chapter, I will dissect the most useful and applicable of them. Those functions that are not specifically covered in this chapter can be reviewed in more depth using Salesforce.com's online help documentation.

In this chapter, I will walk you through each function and review the following areas in relation to it:

- **Format**: The format and syntax of the function

- **Summary**: A summary of the function, including a concise description of how the function works

- **Application scenarios**: Examples of how you might apply the function in real-world situations

- **Usability**: The areas in Salesforce.com in which the function can be used

- **Other considerations**: Any additional tips or "gotchas" that might assist you when using the function

Although some of the scenarios described may not closely pertain to you or your business, they can offer a starting point for you to generate ideas. Once you grasp the basics of functions, you can start applying them in complex and powerful ways. In upcoming chapters, I will examine how to pull significant value out of formulas using an array of functions and related fields.

By the end of this chapter, you should:

- be familiar with the most useful Salesforce.com functions

- understand Salesforce.com function syntax

- understand how to apply functions at a basic level

Anatomy of a Salesforce.com Function

Understanding the anatomy of a function in Salesforce.com is the first step in properly utilizing it. Salesforce.com functions can be generally represented as follows:

```
FUNCTION_NAME(argument_1,...argument_n [, optional_argument])
```

Name

The name of the function being used is the `FUNCTION_NAME`. The name will always be followed by the opening parenthesis.

Arguments

The number of arguments in a function can vary. An argument is not required, as demonstrated through such functions as `TODAY` and `NOW`, which return the current date and the current date/time, respectively, without an argument being provided. The type of arguments that can be used in functions can vary. For example, the argument required may be a:

- Number (e.g., `Amount`)

- True or false value (e.g., `Child_Account_Count__c > 0`, `IsClosed`, etc.)

- Text string (e.g., `"On Hold"`)

- Field of a specific type (e.g., a Multiselect Picklist field)

There are many more types of arguments that can found within the array of Salesforce.com functions; these are just a few common examples.

■ **Note**   In functions, fields are represented by their full (API) name. For example, a field labeled "My New Field" might have an API name of `My_New_Email__c`. The label "My New Field" will not be referenced in the function examples; instead, you will see `My_New_Field__c` within the function.

Optional Arguments

An argument that can be provided but is not required is an optional_argument. Brackets, [ ], represent these optional arguments. For example: FUNCTION(text [, optional]) may be used as:

```
FUNCTION(text) or
FUNCTION(text, optional)
```

■ **Note** All functions with optional arguments have specified default behavior for when the optional arguments are omitted. Always know the default behavior before you decide that the optional arguments are unnecessary.

Salesforce.com Development Using Functions

As previously mentioned, functions can be invoked in various areas within Salesforce.com. While it is important to understand function format and syntax, the actual use of functions requires no coding on behalf of the developing user. Salesforce.com provides a declarative method not only for producing a validly formatted function but also for inserting related fields.

The framework does, of course, allow for hard-coded input that falls outside of what Salesforce.com can deliver declaratively. For example, the SUBSTITUTE function calls for text strings as two of the arguments; unless you established each of those values in a custom setting (refer to Chapter 9 for more detail on how to build and use custom settings), you would need to manually type in your text values.

To develop using Salesforce.com formula functions, you can use the provided formula editors that exist in the majority of elements where functions can be developed. The formula editors allow you to use clicks to build your solution without memorizing syntax or format of the related functions you'll be using.

Let's take a look at the components of a formula editor.

The Function Selector

The function selector, when available, is located to the right-hand side of the development area as shown in Figure 2-1.

Figure 2-1. *The function selector allows you to declaratively insert functions into your formulas[1]*

To use the function selector:

1. Select a function category from the list of displayed functions (optional).

2. Scroll down to and select the function to be used.

3. Click the "Insert Selected Function" button.

---

[1]All Salesforce.com screenshots in this chapter © copyright Salesforce.com, Inc. Used with permission.

■ **Note**   You may double-click a function name to insert that function into your formula as an alternative to selecting the function name and clicking the "Insert Selected Function" button.

When you select a function, some information about it will be displayed below the function selector. Once you click the "Insert Selected Function" button, the function will be inserted into the development area as shown in Figure 2-2.

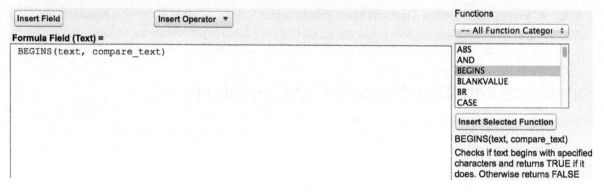

Figure 2-2. *The BEGINS function has been inserted into this formula using the function selector*

In this case, the BEGINS function was selected, and the following text was inserted into the development area:

```
BEGINS(text, compare_text)
```

Inserting a Field

Once you have the function in place, you can replace the default argument text with actual values. For example, you will want to replace text and compare_text in the BEGINS function shown in Figure 2-2. To insert a field:

1. Double-click the text to be replaced.

2. Click the "Insert Field" button.

3. Select the lowest-level object or entity in which your field resides.

4. Select a Lookup field to traverse to a related object; repeat as needed (optional).

5. Select the field you want to insert into your function.

6. Click the "Insert" button.

Figure 2-3 shows the interface for selecting and inserting a field.

Insert Field

Select a field, then click Insert. Labels followed by a ">" indicate that there are more fields available.

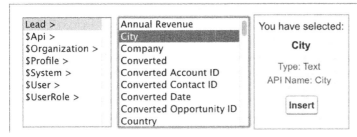

Figure 2-3. *Inserting a field*

Once inserted, the formula function becomes:

```
BEGINS(City, compare_text)
```

Inserting Text

In this example with the BEGINS function, you still have compare_text to replace. It's possible that you may want to replace this with another field, but it's more likely that you will manually replace it with the desired text. To do so, double-click the text and replace it with your desired text within quotes (e.g., "Ph") as follows:

```
BEGINS(City, "Ph")
```

■ **Note** Function operators will frequently be used in your development without code. I will review details of operators in Chapter 3, "Formula Fields."

Checking Your Syntax

Although you are not required to use it, Salesforce.com provides a way to check your syntax before saving your formula and related functions. To use the syntax checker, click the "Check Syntax" button after completing your work in the development area. If the syntax is valid, you will see a message displayed confirming that no errors exist and showing the compiled size of the formula. If it is not, you will see red text communicating that the syntax is invalid along with details of why it will not work properly.

After clicking on the button for the formula function, you get the following message:

```
No syntax errors in merge fields or functions.
```

Done! You've developed your first formula function within Salesforce.com.

■ **Note** Manual validation of syntax is not required because it happens automatically upon saving your formula.

Using the Simple and Advanced Formula Editors

When building formula fields, Salesforce.com provides two types of formula editors to use: simple and advanced. The application of the simple formula editor is extremely limited in comparison to that of the advanced formula editor. Additionally, *you cannot develop with functions declaratively in a simple formula editor*. Figure 2-4 shows the main user interface for the simple formula editor.

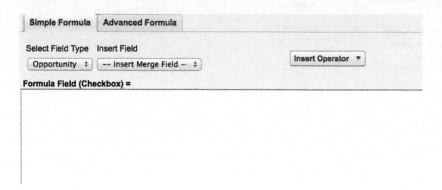

Figure 2-4. *The simple formula editor provides limited functionality when building formulas*

The idea here is that the simple formula editor is easy and quick to use. However, you'll notice a few drawbacks:

- No lookups can be done declaratively to pull in fields for function use.
- Only a limited number of fields are displayed in the field list.
- Operator choices are limited.
- A function "picker" is not available.

Figure 2-5 provides an example of the values displayed within the merge field dropdown when using the simple formula editor.

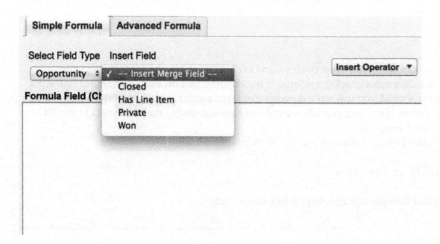

Figure 2-5. *Examples of available fields that can be used with functions in the simple formula editor*

The advanced formula editor provides access to more fields, operators, and most importantly, the function selector. The advanced formula editor is shown in Figure 2-6.

Figure 2-6. *Advanced formula editor*

■ **Note**   Due to the limited scope and declarative capabilities of the simple formula editor, it is recommended that you use the advanced formula editor when building formula fields.

Salesforce.com Formula Functions: A Deep Dive

Understanding basic function syntax and how to create functions using the provided editors lays the groundwork for the development of meaningful functions for real-life business situations. In this section, I will cover specific functions in detail and walk through hypothetical scenarios that show how these functions can be applied within your org. Clearly, there are many more possible scenarios for function usage than described in this chapter; you could write a separate book on example scenarios alone!

■ **Note**   This section will cover key functions to know. Some lesser-used or niche functions are not included here, but you can refer to Salesforce.com help documentation for a list of all Salesforce.com functions and their use.

ABS

The ABS function returns the absolute value of a number. The number can be specified, referenced via a field, or calculated.

Format

```
ABS(number)
```

Application Scenarios

Scenario 1: You want to calculate the difference between two numbers without the concept of sequence or rank among the data points.

Your organization uses Case management within the Salesforce.com Service Cloud. Internal business processes drive all new Cases to queues, from which customer service representatives within the corresponding queue pick them up. Internal service level agreements (SLAs) require that a representative post a Case comment within five minutes of ticket acceptance. The sequence is irrelevant; all that matters that a customer service representative communicates with the customer right around the time that the Case is "picked up" by the representative (i.e., the representative assigns the Case to himself). You would use the following (custom) fields:

Time_to_Initial_Response__c (custom field on Case object);
Time_to_Initial_Acceptance__c (custom field on Case object)
The updated function:

```
ABS(Time_to_Initial_Response__c - Time to Initial Acceptance__c)
```

■ **Note**   Sequence is irrelevant when using the ABS function based on subtraction. ABS (field 1 – field 2) and ABS (field 2 – field 1) will have the same result.

Scenario 2: You want to know the difference between the actual amount and the initial expected revenue on a "Closed/Won" Opportunity. You only care how far off the initial expectation was (in dollars); you do not have interest in which of the two was actually larger. You would use the following fields:

Amount (standard field on Opportunity object)
Initial_Expected_Revenue__c (custom field on Opportunity object)
The updated function:

```
ABS(Amount - Initial_Expected_Revenue__c)
```

Usability

Table 2-1 shows the areas in which the ABS function can be utilized.

Table 2-1. *Allowed ABS Function Usage*

ABS			
Validation Rules	✓	Escalation Rules	✓
Workflow Rules	✓	Approval Rules	✓
Formula Fields	✓	Assignment Rules	✓
Auto-Response Rules	✓	Approval Step Rules	✓
Field Updates	✓	Custom Buttons and Links	✓

Other Considerations

Although ABS will return a Number value, you can apply the ABS function to Percent and Currency fields in addition to Number fields. The ultimate output of your formula will always depend on your formula type, not the value returned by your Formula function. For example:

- **Formula (number)**: ABS (Currency_1 - Currency_2) – Difference between Currency_1 and Currency_2 in number format

- **Formula (currency)**: ABS (Number_2 - Number_1) – Difference between Number_2 and Number_1 in currency format

- **Formula (percent)**: ABS (Percent_2 - Percent_1) – Difference between Percent_2 and Percent_1 in percent format

AND

The AND function checks whether all arguments are true and returns TRUE if all arguments are true or FALSE if one or more arguments are false.

Format

AND(logical1,logical2,...)

Application Scenarios

Scenario 1: You want to flag all opportunities that have an expected revenue greater than $5,000 and a probability greater than 50 percent. You would use the following fields:
Amount (standard field on Opportunity object)
Probability (standard field on Opportunity object)

The updated function:

```
AND(
    Amount > 5000,
    Probability > 0.5
)
```

Scenario 2: You want to identify all cases that are Escalated and have a specific value in the Subject field. Let's assume that Subject line is "AS400 is no longer functioning." You would use the following fields:

Escalated (standard field on Case object)
Subject (standard field on Case object)
The updated function:

```
AND(
    Escalated,
    Subject = "AS400 is no longer functioning"
)
```

Usability

Table 2-2 shows the areas in which the AND function can be utilized.

Table 2-2. *Allowed AND Function Usage*

AND			
Validation Rules	✓	Escalation Rules	✓
Workflow Rules	✓	Approval Rules	✓
Formula Fields	✓	Assignment Rules	✓
Auto-Response Rules	✓	Approval Step Rules	✓
Field Updates	✓	Custom Buttons and Links	✓

Other Considerations

You'll notice the term *Escalated* in the previous function (AND). This can be notated in longer form as *Escalated = true*. Since we're dealing with a Boolean field (Checkbox), the value returned is True or False. So, if you want to evaluate whether a Boolean field is true, the field name itself is sufficient.

■ **Note** When evaluating a Checkbox field within a function, the field name itself is sufficient. There is no need for = *true* or = *false* in the statement.

Another approach for evaluating whether all arguments are AND() is by using the && operator. For example:

```
Amount > 5000 && Probability > 0.5
```

The decision to use the function AND or the operator && is purely based on personal preference. Both can be applied using clicks and there is no advantage to using one vs. the other in terms of how the formula is compiled.

■ **Note** The AND function can be used interchangeably with a pair of ampersands. AND(argument1, argument2) is the equivalent of argument1 && argument2.

BEGINS

The BEGINS function checks if specified text begins with specified characters and returns TRUE if it does. Otherwise, it returns FALSE.

Format

```
BEGINS(text, compare_text)
```

Application Scenarios

Scenario 1: You want to identify all Leads with a particular New York City area code and labeling them as high-priority Leads. In such an example, you would use the following field:
Phone (standard field on Lead object)
The updated function:

```
BEGINS(Phone, "202")
```

Scenario 2: You want to use the standard Product object within Salesforce.com and identify a certain type of product based on the name. You have a simple product-naming standard, with the first three letters conveying the product category. For example, "BRD-02293" is a Blu-ray disc and "DVD-15529" is a DVD. If you want to identify flag Blu-ray discs and emphasize them to users for special attention, you would use the following field:
Name (standard field on Product object)
The updated function:

```
BEGINS(Name, "BRD")
```

Usability

Table 2-3 shows the areas in which the BEGINS function can be utilized.

Table 2-3. *Allowed BEGINS Function Usage*

BEGINS			
Validation Rules	✓	Escalation Rules	✓
Workflow Rules	✓	Approval Rules	✓
Formula Fields	✓	Assignment Rules	✓
Auto-Response Rules	✓	Approval Step Rules	✓
Field Updates	✓	Custom Buttons and Links	✓

BLANKVALUE

The BLANKVALUE function checks whether an expression is blank; if it is, it returns specified substitute text. If the expression is not blank, it returns the original expression value.

Format

BLANKVALUE(expression, substitute_expression)

Application Scenarios

Scenario 1: You want to provide feedback or instruction to a user regarding the value of a particular field that resides on a Parent object. In this case, you would either show the Account Site on the Contact being viewed or, if blank, instruct the User to update the Site field. You would use the following field:

    Account.Site (standard field on Account object, Lookup from Contact)

    The updated function:

```
BLANKVALUE(
Account.Site,
"This Contact's Account does not have a designated Site. Please update the Site field on the Account record.
)
```

Usability

Table 2-4 shows the areas in which the BLANKVALUE function can be utilized.

Table 2-4. *Allowed BLANKVALUE Function Usage*

BLANKVALUE			
Validation Rules	✓	Escalation Rules	✓
Workflow Rules	✓	Approval Rules	✓
Formula Fields	✓	Assignment Rules	✓
Auto-Response Rules	✓	Approval Step Rules	✓
Field Updates	✓	Custom Buttons and Links	✓

Other Considerations

This function's use is not terribly extensive. If you want to identify whether a field is blank, you would use ISBLANK, which is also covered in this chapter.

CASE

The CASE function checks an expression against a series of values. If the expression's value matches any of the provided values (e.g., value1), the corresponding result is returned (e.g., result1). If it is not equal to any of the values, the else_result is returned.

Format

```
CASE(expression, value1, result1, value2, result2,...,else_result)
```

Application Scenarios

Scenario 1: You have a custom `Customer Survey` object within which you want to capture customer feedback related to the handling of a Case. The main field on the `Customer Survey` object is a score that can range from 1-10 or be left blank if not applicable. You want the customer to feel that she can provide granularity in the response, but the ten different values make it difficult to quickly assess and act on the feedback internally. A formula field is built to group some of the values. You will use the following field:

> `Feedback_Score__c` (Custom field on `Case` object)
> The updated function:

```
CASE(
Feedback_Score__c,
1, "Poor",
2, "Poor",
3, "Average",
4, "Good",
5, "Good",
"N/A"
)
```

Scenario 2: You want to show a next step or action item to users based on Opportunity Stage. Here, you'll take each Stage and apply corresponding text to display to users. You would use the following field:

> StageName (standard field on Opportunity)
> The updated function:

```
CASE(
StageName,
"Prospecting", "Gather Opportunity details.",
"Needs Analysis", "Work with Account Mgmt to solidify approach.",
"Value Proposition", "Communicate value to decision makers.",
"Decision Makers", "Review related case studies.",
"Perception Analysis", "Submit proposal to customer.",
"Proposal/Price Quote", "Ensure that customer understands quote.",
"Negotiation/Review", "Work with VP to ensure proper approach.",
"Closed Won", "Opportunity won; file proper paperwork.",
"Closed Lost", "Opportunity lost; no further action needed."
"N/A"
)
```

Usability

Table 2-5 shows the areas in which the CASE function can be utilized.

Table 2-5. *Allowed CASE Function Usage*

CASE			
Validation Rules	✓	Escalation Rules	✓
Workflow Rules	✓	Approval Rules	✓
Formula Fields	✓	Assignment Rules	✓
Auto-Response Rules	✓	Approval Step Rules	✓
Field Updates	✓	Custom Buttons and Links	✓

Other Considerations

Values and results in the Case statement must be of the same return type. For example, value1 and value2 must be of the same return type; however, value1 and result need not be. See the previous example that refers to the Feedback_Score__c field. Also, if you are only dealing with two or three different Case values, you may also want to consider the IF function, which provides additional flexibility.

CONTAINS

The CONTAINS function checks if identified text contains specified characters, and returns TRUE if it does. Otherwise, it returns FALSE.

Format

CONTAINS(text, compare_text)

Application Scenarios

Scenario 1: You want to capture Leads via Web-to-Lead and you want to identify particular text within the Lead Description field; specifically, if you want to highlight the Lead if the word *compliant* is present. You will use the following field:

  Description (standard field on Lead object)
  The updated function:

CONTAINS(Description, "compliant")

  Scenario 1: You have Email-to-Case configured and want to flag any Cases that have the word "Cancel" in the subject line so that they can be handled with special attention. You would use the following field:

  Subject (standard field on Case object)
  The updated function:

CONTAINS(Subject, "Cancel")

■ **Note** Functions are case sensitive. We will look at how to efficiently handle both cases in some formula field examples in Chapter 3.

Usability

Table 2-6 shows the areas in which the CONTAINS function can be utilized.

Table 2-6. *Allowed CONTAINS Function Usage*

CONTAINS			
Validation Rules	✓	Escalation Rules	✓
Workflow Rules	✓	Approval Rules	✓
Formula Fields	✓	Assignment Rules	✓
Auto-Response Rules	✓	Approval Step Rules	✓
Field Updates	✓	Custom Buttons and Links	✓

DATE

The DATE function takes the input of day, month, and year separately and returns a Salesforce,com-formatted date value.

Format

DATE(Year, Month, Day)

Application Scenarios

Scenario 1: The year, month, and day captured from a related record are coming over from a legacy system as separate fields and you want to convert these to a Salesforce.com-formatted date field. You would use the following fields, all of which are custom number fields on a generic custom object:

Year_Captured__c (custom field on generic custom object)
Month_Captured__c (custom field on generic custom object)
Day_Captured__c (custom field on generic custom object)
The updated function:

DATE(Year_Captured__c,Month_Captured__c,Day_Captured__c)

Usability

Table 2-7 shows the areas in which the DATE function can be utilized.

Table 2-7. *Allowed DATE Function Usage*

DATE			
Validation Rules	✓	Escalation Rules	✓
Workflow Rules	✓	Approval Rules	✓
Formula Fields	✓	Assignment Rules	✓
Auto-Response Rules	✓	Approval Step Rules	✓
Field Updates	✓	Custom Buttons and Links	✓

DATEVALUE

The DATEVALUE function creates a date from its date/time or text representation.

Format

```
DATEVALUE(expression)
```

Application Scenarios

Scenario 1: You want to programmatically determine whether a Case was closed on the same date as it was opened. You would use the following fields:

    CreatedDate (standard field on Case object)

    ClosedDate (standard field on Case object)

    The updated function:

```
DATEVALUE( CreatedDate ) = DATEVALUE( ClosedDate )
```

Usability

Table 2-8 shows the areas in which the DATEVALUE function can be utilized.

Table 2-8. *Allowed DATEVALUE Function Usage*

DATEVALUE			
Validation Rules	✓	Escalation Rules	✓
Workflow Rules	✓	Approval Rules	✓
Formula Fields	✓	Assignment Rules	✓
Auto-Response Rules	✓	Approval Step Rules	✓
Field Updates	✓	Custom Buttons and Links	✓

DAY, MONTH, and YEAR

The DAY function returns the day of the month, a number between 1 and 31. MONTH returns the month, in number format. The values will be between 1 (January) and 12 (December). YEAR returns the year of a date, a number between 1900 and 9999.

Format

```
DAY(Date)
MONTH(Date)
YEAR(Date)
```

Note The DAY, MONTH, and YEAR functions do not accept Date/Time fields; only Date fields can be used.

Application Scenarios

Scenario 1: You have Date Opened on the Case object and you also want to know the month, day, and year in separate fields. You would use the following fields:

    CreatedDate (standard field on Case object)

    The updated functions:

```
MONTH(CreatedDate)
DAY(CreatedDate)
YEAR(CreatedDate)
```

Usability

Table 2-9 shows the areas in which the DAY, MONTH, and YEAR functions can be utilized.

Table 2-9. Allowed DAY, MONTH, and YEAR Function Usage

DAY, MONTH, and YEAR			
Validation Rules	✓	Escalation Rules	✓
Workflow Rules	✓	Approval Rules	✓
Formula Fields	✓	Assignment Rules	✓
Auto-Response Rules	✓	Approval Step Rules	✓
Field Updates	✓	Custom Buttons and Links	✓

FIND

The FIND function returns the position of the search_text string in text.

Format

```
FIND(search_text, text [, start_num])
```

Application Scenarios

Scenario 1: You are using Email-to-Case (or Web-to-Lead) to capture incoming information and you want to glean a phone number, if present, in the description field coming over. You would use the following fields:
    `Description` (standard field on Case or Lead object)
    The updated function:

```
FIND("Phone: ", Description)
```

    Once you have the starting position, you may be able to extract the phone number using a different function.

Usability

Table 2-10 shows the areas in which the `FIND` function can be utilized.

Table 2-10. *Allowed FIND Function Usage*

FIND			
Validation Rules	✓	Escalation Rules	✓
Workflow Rules	✓	Approval Rules	✓
Formula Fields	✓	Assignment Rules	✓
Auto-Response Rules	✓	Approval Step Rules	✓
Field Updates	✓	Custom Buttons and Links	✓

HYPERLINK

The `HYPERLINK` function produces a hyperlink for the user to use to navigate to a desired page, either within the Salesforce.com org or outside of it.

Format

```
HYPERLINK(url, friendly_name [, target])
```

    Here, `url` is the URL of the page to which the user will be redirected/linked, `friendly_name` is the display name of the link, and `target` specifies where to open the hyperlinked URL.

Application Scenarios

Scenario 1: You want to provide a quick and easy way to access a key Leads report directly from a Lead record. Instead of requiring that users navigate to the Reports tabs and then find the desired report, the hyperlink function can be used to link directly to the report. You would not use any derived fields here but instead add your own values manually.

The updated function:

```
HYPERLINK("/000x0000000hrah", "Today's New Leads", "_self")
```

Scenario 2: You want to provide a hyperlink to a specific reference document to your whole org, but you do not want to replace the "Help with this page" content itself. You can link to a specific page or document with the following function. You would not use any derived fields here; again, you would add your own text.

The updated function:

```
HYPERLINK("https://org62.my.salesforce.com/help/doc/en/sf.pdf", "How to be Successful with
Salesforce: PDF from Salesforce.com")
```

Usability

Table 2-11 shows the areas in which the HYPERLINK function can be utilized.

Table 2-11. *Allowed HYPERLINK Function Usage*

HYPERLINK		
Validation Rules		Escalation Rules
Workflow Rules		Approval Rules
Formula Fields	✓	Assignment Rules
Auto-Response Rules		Approval Step Rules
Field Updates		Custom Buttons and Links

Other Considerations

The following values can be used in the [, target] attribute:

_blank: Opens page in new window or tab
_self: Opens page in same frame in which the link was clicked
_parent: Opens page in parent frame
_top: Opens page in full body of same window
<framename>: Opens page in custom, named frame
If you are referencing a page outside Salesforce.com, you will need to include http:// or https:// in your URL.

■ **Note** The HYPERLINK function is covered in more detail in Chapter 12 within the topic of user interface development.

IF

IF is a function that will return one of two values conditionally, based on whether the provided logical test is true or false.

Format

```
IF(logical_test, value_if_true, value_if_false)
```

Application Scenarios

Scenario 1: You want to provide a simple message to customers regarding the current status and expected next steps of a Case and, based on customer feedback, the Status field itself will not suffice. You would use the following field:

IsClosed (standard field on Case object)

The updated function:

```
IF(
IsClosed,
"This Case has been closed; please call Support or open a new Case for further assistance.", "This
Case is currently being worked. Please click on "Add Comment" to post updates."
)
```

Since IsClosed is a Boolean field, you are representing it with its name only in order to derived its stored value; you could also use IsClosed = true.

Scenario 2: You have a custom object capturing student course performance (grade). The field is numeric, containing the raw percentage score and is populated via integration from another system. You want to display the overall pass/fail result, instead of the raw score, on the record detail page. You would use the following field:

Grade__c (custom number field on custom object)

The updated function:

```
IF(Grade__c >= 60, "Pass", "Fail") OR
IF(Grade__c >= 60, true, false)
```

You'll notice the two different approaches just looked at. The appropriate approach depends on the formula field return type you want to use. I will cover return types in depth in Chapter 3, "Formula Fields."

Usability

Table 2-12 shows the areas in which the IF function can be utilized.

Table 2-12. *Allowed IF Function Usage*

IF			
Validation Rules	✓	Escalation Rules	✓
Workflow Rules	✓	Approval Rules	✓
Formula Fields	✓	Assignment Rules	✓
Auto-Response Rules	✓	Approval Step Rules	✓
Field Updates	✓	Custom Buttons and Links	✓

IMAGE

The IMAGE function will result in a specific image being returned/displayed, with the ability to specific alternate text and the height and width of the image.

Format

```
IMAGE(image_url, alternate_text [, height, width])
```

Application Scenarios

Scenario 1: You want to display the logo of each of your accounts. You can assume that you are able to capture a web URL of the image showing the corresponding Account's logo and you store it in a custom field Account_Image_URL__c. Additionally, you want the alternate text to contain the Account's name (e.g., "EDL Consulting, LLC Logo"). You can simply reference the Account Name and display the image at the top of your Account detail page using the following:

```
IMAGE(Account_Image_URL__c, Name & " Logo", 125, 250)
```

Scenario 2: You want to display an image of your Product on each Product detail page. You can assume that the product images are stored in the same Web directory with file names matching the Product SKU. Additionally, you want the alternate text to contain the product name (e.g., "EZ-Twist Wrench"). You would use the following field:

Product_SKU__c (custom field on Product object)

The updated function:

```
IMAGE("http://www.company.com/images/products/ & Product_SKU__c", Name, 125, 250)
```

Scenario 3: You want to display a banner image at the top of all Opportunity pages that shows a flow of the Opportunity creation and management process. You have uploaded this image as a Document into Salesforce.com. You will not use any input fields here; all text will be entered manually.

The updated function:

```
IMAGE("/servlet/servlet.FileDownload?file=<DocumentRecordId>", "Opportunity Banner")
```

> **Note** The IMAGE function is covered in more detail in Chapter 12 within the topic of user interface development.

Usability

Table 2-13 shows the areas in which the IMAGE function can be utilized.

Table 2-13. *Allowed IMAGE Function Usage*

IMAGE		
Validation Rules		Escalation Rules
Workflow Rules		Approval Rules
Formula Fields	✓	Assignment Rules
Auto-Response Rules		Approval Step Rules
Field Updates		Custom Buttons and Links

INCLUDES

The INCLUDES function checks a provided text string to see if it is included in the list of selected values within a multiselect picklist. INCLUDES can be seen as the equivalent of ISPICKVAL, but it is used for Multi-Picklists instead of Picklists.

Format

```
INCLUDES(multiselect_picklist_field, text_literal)
```

Application Scenarios

Scenario 1: You have an Account field called `Present_in_States__c` to convey the states in which the organization operates and you want to verify if the account is in Arizona.

```
INCLUDES(Account.Present_in_States__c, "Arizona")
```

Usability

Table 2-14 shows the areas in which the `INCLUDES` function can be utilized.

Table 2-14. *Allowed INCLUDES Function Usage*

INCLUDES			
Validation Rules	✓	Escalation Rules	✓
Workflow Rules	✓	Approval Rules	✓
Formula Fields	✓	Assignment Rules	✓
Auto-Response Rules	✓	Approval Step Rules	✓
Field Updates	✓	Custom Buttons and Links	✓

ISBLANK

`ISBLANK` is a Boolean function that identifies whether a provided expression is blank or not. Although you can use hard-coded text as part of the expression argument, this function is really only useful when using other fields in the expression. In other words, `ISBLANK("String")` is a valid use of the function, but it is not valuable. Typically, you would want to use `ISBLANK` with other functions to return values conditionally (e.g., `IF(ISBLANK("Field"), "value_if_true", "value_if_false")`).

Format

```
ISBLANK(expression)
```

Application Scenarios

Scenario 1: A sensitive field containing personal information is hidden from most users via Field-Level Security, but that information is needed at some point during the sales process. It is important for users to identify whether that information has been gathered. You could use `ISBLANK` to convey this state to users without providing Read access to the sensitive field. You would use the following field:

    `Personal_Information__c` (custom field on Opportunity object)

    The updated function:

```
ISBLANK(Personal_Information__c)
```

Usability

Table 2-15 shows the areas in which the `ISBLANK` function can be utilized.

Table 2-15. *Allowed ISBLANK Function Usage*

ISBLANK			
Validation Rules	✓	Escalation Rules	✓
Workflow Rules	✓	Approval Rules	✓
Formula Fields	✓	Assignment Rules	✓
Auto-Response Rules	✓	Approval Step Rules	✓
Field Updates	✓	Custom Buttons and Links	✓

Other Considerations

You should use `ISBLANK()` instead of `ISNULL()` where possible. `ISNULL` is still supported, but it is considered a legacy function that is less useful than `ISBLANK`. Avoid using `ISNULL` if possible.

ISCHANGED

The `ISCHANGED` function is extremely useful, as it will help you systematically identify whether a field has been modified. It will return `TRUE` if the field has changed in the current operation; otherwise it returns `FALSE`.

Format

`ISCHANGED(field)`

Application Scenarios

Scenario 1: You need to identify when the Amount of an Opportunity has changed programmatically (tracking via field history is not sufficient for you, in this scenario). The values of fields do not matter. You would use the following field:

    `Amount` (standard field on Opportunity object)

    The updated function:

`ISCHANGED(Amount)`

    A second scenario for using this function could be when you want to know if anything on a record has changed. To do this, you can use the Last Modified Date field as the field argument:

    `LastModifiedDate` (standard field on various objects)

    The updated function:

`ISCHANGED(LastModifiedDate)`

Usability

Table 2-16 shows the areas in which the `ISCHANGED` function can be utilized.

Table 2-16. *Allowed ISCHANGED Function Usage*

ISCHANGED			
Validation Rules	✓	Escalation Rules	✓
Workflow Rules	✓	Approval Rules	✓
Formula Fields	✓	Assignment Rules	✓
Auto-Response Rules	✓	Approval Step Rules	✓
Field Updates	✓	Custom Buttons and Links	✓

■ **Note** ISCHANGED must be manually typed into a formula for a custom button or link.

ISNEW

The ISNEW function checks a record to see if it is new or existing; it will return TRUE if the record is new or FALSE if the record was previously created. No argument is provided.

Format

ISNEW()

Application Scenarios

This function is most effectively used in conditional statements with other functions (e.g., IF) to apply behavior based on whether the record is new or existing. This function will always be formatted as "ISNEW()."

Other Considerations

Some uses of this function will always return FALSE, including:

- A workflow rule with a time-based trigger
- A field update for an approval action

Usability

Table 2-17 shows the areas in which the ISNEW function can be utilized.

Table 2-17. *Allowed ISNEW Function Usage*

ISNEW			
Validation Rules	✓	Escalation Rules	✓
Workflow Rules	✓	Approval Rules	✓
Formula Fields	✓	Assignment Rules	✓
Auto-Response Rules	✓	Approval Step Rules	✓
Field Updates	✓	Custom Buttons and Links	✓

■ **Note** ISNEW must be manually typed into a formula for a custom button or link.

ISNULL

Refer to the ISBLANK function section.

ISPICKVAL

Many Salesforce.com functions have known equivalents in other popular applications (e.g., Microsoft Excel). ISPICKVAL is one function that is specific to Salesforce.com. ISPICKVAL() is a Boolean function that identifies whether a specified field (of type Picklist) on the corresponding record has a certain value. ISPICKVAL can be seen as the equivalent of INCLUDES but for Picklists instead of multi-Picklists.

Format

ISPICKVAL(picklist_field, text_literal)

Application Scenarios

Scenario 1: You need to identify whether a particular Lead record has a status of "Working - Contacted." You would use the following field:

Status (standard field on Lead object)
The updated function:

ISPICKVAL(Status, "Working - Contacted")

Scenario 1: You need to identify whether a particular Opportunity record has a Stage of Qualification. You would use the following field:

StageName (standard field on Lead object)
The updated function:

ISPICKVAL(StageName, "Qualification")

Usability

Table 2-18 shows the areas in which the ISPICKVAL function can be utilized.

Table 2-18. *Allowed* ISPICKVAL *Function Usage*

ISPICKVAL			
Validation Rules	✓	Escalation Rules	✓
Workflow Rules	✓	Approval Rules	✓
Formula Fields	✓	Assignment Rules	✓
Auto-Response Rules	✓	Approval Step Rules	✓
Field Updates	✓	Custom Buttons and Links	✓

LEFT, MID, RIGHT

The LEFT, MID, and RIGHT functions return a string of a specified length from identified text. These functions are useful when you a need a subset of the text from a field that has clearly formatted, organized content. For example, you may feel that the "superset" text has unnecessary or redundant text that you'd like to hide, but not delete.

Format

```
LEFT(text, num_chars)
MID(text, start_num, num_chars)
RIGHT(text, num_chars)
```

LEFT returns X characters from the beginning, or left side, of the text. For example, assuming X = 4, LEFT("ExampleText", 4) would return *"Exam."* MID adds an element of a starting position to allow for the capture of a string that is neither at the beginning nor the end of a larger string of characters. MID("ExampleText", 2, 5), for example, would return *"ample."* RIGHT returns X characters from the end, or right, of the text. For example, RIGHT("ExampleText", 4) would return "Text."

Application Scenarios

Scenario 1: You have captured a phone number but all you need is the area code for another use in your org. You would use the following field:

Phone (standard field on Lead object)

The updated function:

```
LEFT(Phone,3)
```

Scenario 2: You need to perform some analysis on your zip code data. You have captured Zip Code + 4 for all addresses. Addresses with an unknown "+4" are assigned 0000 for the value (e.g., 12345-0000). You need to split the first five and second five digits for reporting and analysis purposes. You would use the following field:

PostalCode (standard field on Contact object)

The updated function:

```
LEFT(PostalCode,5)
```

Scenario 3: You have captured a phone number but you need just the middle three digits out of a full ten-digit number for another use in your org. You would use the following field:

Phone (standard field on Lead object)

The updated function:

```
MID(Phone,3,3)
```

Other Considerations

The initial start_num is 0. For example, `MID("ExampleText", 0, 2)` would return `"Ex."`

Usability

Table 2-19 shows the areas in which the `LEFT`, `MID`, and `RIGHT` functions can be utilized.

Table 2-19. *Allowed LEFT, MID, and RIGHT Function Usage*

LEFT, MID, RIGHT			
Validation Rules	✓	Escalation Rules	✓
Workflow Rules	✓	Approval Rules	✓
Formula Fields	✓	Assignment Rules	✓
Auto-Response Rules	✓	Approval Step Rules	✓
Field Updates	✓	Custom Buttons and Links	✓

LEN

LEN returns the length, in characters, of a provided text string.

Format

```
LEN(text)
```

Application Scenarios

Scenario 1: You require a mailing address for all Contacts that are entered into your system; however, you notice that bogus addresses are being entered with a single character to circumvent the requirement. LEN can identify the length of the field to validate that the entered value is of a reasonable length to be a legitimate address. You would use the following field:

MailingAddress (standard field on Contact object)

The updated function:

```
LEN(MailingAddress)
```

Scenario 1: You ask all users to include an error code for all Cases of Type *Application Error* in the Case Description field, with the code being at least eight characters in length. You can use length to determine whether the Description field could possibly contain an error code (if the length is less than eight characters, you know that no error code is present). You would use the following field:

Description (standard field on Case object)

The updated function:

```
LEN(Description)
```

Usability

Table 2-20 shows the areas in which the LEN function can be utilized.

Table 2-20. Allowed LEN Function Usage

LEN			
Validation Rules	✓	Escalation Rules	✓
Workflow Rules	✓	Approval Rules	✓
Formula Fields	✓	Assignment Rules	✓
Auto-Response Rules	✓	Approval Step Rules	✓
Field Updates	✓	Custom Buttons and Links	✓

MID

Refer to the LEFT, MID, RIGHT function section.

MOD

MOD returns the remainder after the number is divided by the specified divisor. Here are examples of values that would be returned by this function:

MOD(3,2) >> 3 can be divided by 2 once, with 1 left as the remainder >> returns 1.

MOD(5,3) >> 5 can be divided by 3 once, with 2 left as the remainder >> returns 2.

MOD(6,3) >> 6 can be divided by 3 twice, with 0 left as the remainder >> returns 0.

MOD(2,2) >> 2 can be divided by 2 once, with 0 left as the remainder >> returns 0.

MOD(1,2) >> 1 can be divided by 2 zero times, with 1 left as the remainder >> returns 1.

This function can be extremely useful when combined with other functions to determine date-related items like the day of the week. I will cover those in more detail in Chapter 3, "Formula Fields."

Format

```
MOD(number,divisor)
```

Usability

Table 2-21 shows the areas in which the MOD function can be utilized.

Table 2-21. *Allowed MOD Function Usage*

MOD			
Validation Rules	✓	Escalation Rules	✓
Workflow Rules	✓	Approval Rules	✓
Formula Fields	✓	Assignment Rules	✓
Auto-Response Rules	✓	Approval Step Rules	✓
Field Updates	✓	Custom Buttons and Links	✓

NOW, TODAY

NOW and TODAY are very simple functions that return the current date (TODAY) or the current date/time (NOW). For example, on December 25th, 2014, at 8:00 p.m., the following would be returned:

TODAY( ) >> December 25, 2014

NOW( ) >> December 25, 2014 8:00 p.m.

Format

NOW: NOW( )
TODAY: TODAY( )

Application Scenarios

These functions will be covered further in the chapter on formula fields; they are very useful in time-based calculations that drive business rules and/or automated behavior.

Usability

Table 2-22 shows the areas in which the NOW and TODAY functions can be utilized.

Table 2-22. *Allowed NOW and TODAY Function Usage*

NOW, TODAY			
Validation Rules	✓	Escalation Rules	✓
Workflow Rules	✓	Approval Rules	✓
Formula Fields	✓	Assignment Rules	✓
Auto-Response Rules	✓	Approval Step Rules	✓
Field Updates	✓	Custom Buttons and Links	✓

OR

The OR function checks whether at least one of the arguments is true and returns TRUE if at least one argument is true and FALSE if all are false.

Format

```
OR(logical1,logical2,...)
```

Application Scenarios

Scenario 1: You want to flag all Opportunities that have an Expected Revenue greater than $100,000 or have a Probability greater than 90 percent. You would use the following fields:

Amount (standard field on Opportunity object)
Probability (standard field on Opportunity object)
The updated function:

```
OR(
Amount > 100000,
Probability > 0.9
)
```

Scenario 1: You want to identify all Cases that are Escalated or have an Account Name of ImportantCo. You would use the following fields:

Escalated (standard field on Case object)
AccountName (standard field on Case object)
The updated function:

```
OR(
Escalated,
AccountName = "CloudCraze"
)
```

Usability

Table 2-23 shows the areas in which the OR function can be utilized.

Table 2-23. *Allowed OR Function Usage*

OR			
Validation Rules	✓	Escalation Rules	✓
Workflow Rules	✓	Approval Rules	✓
Formula Fields	✓	Assignment Rules	✓
Auto-Response Rules	✓	Approval Step Rules	✓
Field Updates	✓	Custom Buttons and Links	✓

Other Considerations

You will notice `Escalated` in the previous scenario. Since we're dealing with a Boolean field (Checkbox), the value returned is `True` or `False`; we can notate it as `"Escalated,"` as opposed to `"Escalated = true."` So, if you want to evaluate whether a Boolean is true, the field name itself is sufficient. Another approach to evaluate whether one or more arguments are true is by using the `||` operator. For example:

```
Amount > 100000 || Probability > 0.9
```

The decision to use the function `OR` or the operator `||` is purely personal preference. Both can be applied using clicks and there is no advantage to using one vs. the other in terms of how the formula is compiled.

PRIORVALUE

The `PRIORVALUE` function returns the previous value for the field. For example, if you are changing the Amount from 5000 to 10000, `PRIORVALUE` would return 5000.

Format

```
PRIORVALUE(field)
```

Application Scenarios

Scenario 1: You want to validate the previous value of Case Status in your calculation to ensure that users cannot skip certain statuses in the Support process. You would use the following field:

    `Status` (standard field on Case object)

    The updated function:

```
PRIORVALUE(Status)
```

Usability

Table 2-24 shows the areas in which the `PRIORVALUE` function can be utilized.

Table 2-24. *Allowed PRIORVALUE Function Usage*

PRIORVALUE			
Validation Rules	✓	Escalation Rules	
Workflow Rules	✓	Approval Rules	
Formula Fields		Assignment Rules	✓
Auto-Response Rules		Approval Step Rules	
Field Updates	✓	Custom Buttons and Links	

REGEX

The `REGEX` function checks a provided text string against a regular expression and returns `TRUE` if a match is found or `FALSE` if a match is not found.

Format

```
REGEX(Text, RegEx_Text)
```

Application Scenarios

Scenario 1: You want to identify if a value in the Social Security field on a custom object is formatted as expected. You would use the following field:

Social_Security_Number__c (custom field on custom object)

The updated function:

```
REGEX(Social_Security_Number__c, "[0-9]{3}-[0-9]{2}-[0-9]{4}")
```

Usability

Table 2-25 shows the areas in which the REGEX function can be utilized.

Table 2-25. *Allowed REGEX Function Usage*

REGEX		
Validation Rules		Escalation Rules
Workflow Rules		Approval Rules
Formula Fields	✓	Assignment Rules
Auto-Response Rules		Approval Step Rules
Field Updates		Custom Buttons and Links

RIGHT

Refer to the LEFT, MID, RIGHT function section.

SUBSTITUTE

The SUBSTITUTE function will replace identified text within a string with alternate text. For example, SUBSTITUTE ("Please contact Tariku about the contract," "Tariku," "Max") would return "Please contact Max about the contract."

Format

```
SUBSTITUTE(text, old_text, new_text)
```

Application Scenarios

Scenario 1: You want to share Cases but hide any references to the Account Name field in the Case Subject. You would use the following fields:

Subject (standard field on Case object)
AccountName (standard field on Case object)

The updated function:

```
SUBSTITUTE(Subject, AccountName, "<Account>")
```

Assuming "<Account>" equal to "Client," "PayCo having issues with TechE application" would become "Client having issues with TechE application."

Scenario 2: Some of your customers have been entering their last name in the Case Description field, but you do not want the last name to be displayed on the Case detail page. You would use the following fields:

Description (standard field on Case object)

Contact.LastName (standard field on Case object; looks up to Contact object)

The updated function:

```
SUBSTITUTE(Description, Contact.LastName, "<Last Name Removed>")
```

"The XY50 is not operating as expected. Our manager, John Smith, has called Support without success" would become "The XY50 is not operating as expected. Our manager, John <Last Name Removed>, has called Support, without success."

Usability

Table 2-26 shows the areas in which the SUBSTITUTE function can be utilized.

Table 2-26. *Allowed SUBSTITUTE Function Usage*

SUBSTITUTE			
Validation Rules	✓	Escalation Rules	✓
Workflow Rules	✓	Approval Rules	✓
Formula Fields	✓	Assignment Rules	✓
Auto-Response Rules	✓	Approval Step Rules	✓
Field Updates	✓	Custom Buttons and Links	✓

TEXT

Although simple, TEXT is a very frequently used function within Salesforce.com. One of the most common uses of this function is to extract the text value from a picklist field.

Format

```
TEXT(value)
```

Application Scenarios

Scenario 1: You want to return the actual value of a Picklist field without using the ISPICKVAL function. You would use the following field:

StageName (Standard field on Opportunity object)

The updated function:

```
TEXT(StageName)
```

Scenario 2: You want to return Opportunity Amount (a numeric value) as text. You would use the following field:
Amount (standard field on Opportunity object)
The updated function:

```
TEXT(Amount)
```

Usability

Table 2-27 shows the areas in which the TEXT function can be utilized.

Table 2-27. *Allowed TEXT Function Usage*

TEXT			
Validation Rules	✓	Escalation Rules	✓
Workflow Rules	✓	Approval Rules	✓
Formula Fields	✓	Assignment Rules	✓
Auto-Response Rules	✓	Approval Step Rules	✓
Field Updates	✓	Custom Buttons and Links	✓

TODAY

Refer to the NOW, TODAY function section.

TRIM

TRIM is used to remove all spaces from a string except for single spaces in between words.

Format

```
TRIM (text)
```

Application Scenarios

Scenario 1: Your customers include extra spaces when submitting Cases via e-mail. You want to strip out extraneous spaces. You would use the following field:
Subject (standard field on Case object)
The updated function:

```
TRIM(Subject)
```

Usability

Table 2-28 shows the areas in which the TRIM function can be utilized.

Table 2-28. *Allowed TRIM Function Usage*

TRIM			
Validation Rules	✓	Escalation Rules	✓
Workflow Rules	✓	Approval Rules	✓
Formula Fields	✓	Assignment Rules	✓
Auto-Response Rules	✓	Approval Step Rules	✓
Field Updates	✓	Custom Buttons and Links	✓

VALUE

VALUE converts numeric values that are stored as text into a number.

Format

VALUE(text)

Application Scenarios

Scenario 1: You have a legacy field of field-type text in which sales people enter Projected Amount. Additionally, you have cleaned up the records and want to run numeric calculations on the field value. You would use the following field:

Projected_Amount__c (custom field on Opportunity object)
The updated function:

VALUE(Projected_Amount__c)

Usability

Table 2-29 shows the areas in which the VALUE function can be utilized.

Table 2-29. *Allowed VALUE Function Usage*

VALUE			
Validation Rules	✓	Escalation Rules	✓
Workflow Rules	✓	Approval Rules	✓
Formula Fields	✓	Assignment Rules	✓
Auto-Response Rules	✓	Approval Step Rules	✓
Field Updates	✓	Custom Buttons and Links	✓

Recap

In this chapter, you dove into the world of functions and familiarized yourself with some of the most important functions to be considered when developing within Salesforce.com. At this point, you should have a fairly solid understanding of function syntax, how to use common functions, and how to properly apply functions to address a specific need within the system. In the next chapter, you will learn more about the application of these functions, specifically within Salesforce.com formula fields.

CHAPTER 3

■ ■ ■

All About Formula Fields

The last chapter examined Salesforce.com formula functions in detail. You familiarized yourself with the anatomy of a function, an approach to declaratively create a function, and the application of simple functions to useful business scenarios. Think of that chapter as Salesforce.com formulas 101: functions. Congratulations! Now that you've passed your intro course, you're moving on to Salesforce.com Formulas 201: fields.

The majority of fields in Salesforce.com are static, meaning that the values present within those fields do not change unless there is a specific update by a user or the system (via an automated action). With formula fields, it's a different ballgame altogether. With some critical thought and the development of the right formula fields in Salesforce.com, you can add a stroke of intelligence to your records and shift from a list of data points to a rich set of valuable, informational fields.

■ **Note** Salesforce.com defines a *formula field* as a "read-only field that derives its value from a formula expression you define. The formula field is updated when any of the source fields change."

How valuable would the right formula fields be to you or your users? Consider a few situations that you may be able to relate to:

- Your users review multiple fields to ascertain a record's "true" state.

- Data is not in a desired or ideal format.

- You want to hide/mask, emphasize, or transform certain data points.

- You rely on users to perform calculations to come up with desired metrics (i.e., to export to Excel).

- Users need to be directed or instructed to understand how they should interact with records.

Formulas themselves are present in many areas of Salesforce.com (such as validation rules, assignment rules, and workflow rules), but it's safe to say that fields come to mind first when thinking of formulas. They are a relatively quick way to get the right data in the right format to the right audience. Don't get me wrong: Formula fields can get extremely complex. However, if you understand how their functions work in conjunction with one another and know how to use them to solve your business problems, you can add some "shock and awe" to your existing org without writing code.

By the end of this chapter, you will:

- Be aware of the preparation needed to make effective, useful formula fields

- Know the different return types of formula fields and when to select each type

- Understand how to combine multiple functions within one formula

- Be able to apply conditional logic to formulas

- Be able to create a formula field from scratch declaratively (using "clicks, not code")

- Solve basic business needs with formula fields

Preparing to Build Your Formula Fields

Before you start to construct a formula field, you should scrutinize your organization's existing data model. Why? Because the source of what you want to convey, calculate, or communicate has to be *somewhere* in the system before you ever touch a formula. Without relevant source fields, Salesforce.com formula fields have little or no value.

You might ask yourself: Does the current data model account for all of the necessary data sources? If not, you'll need to make sure to create custom fields for any sources that you might use in your formulas. Remember, the eventual output will be derived from these fields, so don't be too concerned if your data sources aren't in a desired format; we're talking about raw data here. For example, let's say that you need a Contact's emergency phone number for use in a formula field. If you're currently capturing the emergency number as a text field instead of a phone field, that's okay. You can use the formula itself to manipulate and reformat the derived value. The key is that the data is being captured somehow, somewhere within your org.

You should build out the non–formula fields in your data model first; this includes both the fields on the object you will be working with and the fields on any related objects. Any fields that your formulas will reference must be in place up-front. With proper planning, you can avoid the frustration that emerges when you realize the need for a nonformula custom field only after you've started building out a formula that depends on that field.

The Structure of Formula Fields

Formula fields have a few key components: values (static and derived), functions, statements, and operators. To ensure that you fully grasp formula fields and how to properly build them, I will walk you through each of these underlying elements.

Static Values

One of the simplest elements that can be inserted within a formula field is a static value. A *static value* could be defined as an unchanging value established by the formula developer. Let's take a look at a few examples.

Any calculation that contains values that are not based on fields would reveal a user-provided static value. For example, assume you want to create a formula that adds ten days to the date on which a Lead was created. You could represent that calculation like this:

```
CreatedDate + 10
```

In this instance, "10" is our static value. It is provided by the developer and will not change within calculation unless it is edited or removed within the formula itself.

A formula that looks for a specific string would commonly contain a static value, as well. Let's say that you want to identify when a key negative word appears in your Case subject. You would do that with the following:

```
CONTAINS(Subject, "lawsuit")
```

In this instance, you want to know if the Subject ever contains the same exact string ("lawsuit"). This could also be handled within a custom setting, but it is not always necessary to do that or even the right solution. I will examine custom settings in detail in Chapter 9.

Derived Values

Within formula fields, you can set values directly, as previously described for static values. You can also establish derived values. A *derived value* is a value that is obtained through an existing field within Salesforce.com. I use "existing" to emphasize that the field from which a value is derived must be created before it is used in a formula. This existing field can be any of the following:

- Any standard or custom field of the same object in which the formula field resides (e.g., any field on the Lead object if you are creating a Lead formula field)

- Any standard or custom field on an object to which the formula field's object relates via a Lookup or Master-Detail relationship (e.g., any field on the Account object if you are creating a Contact formula field)

- A custom field within a hierarchical custom setting

- A custom or standard field on a system object

■ **Note**   Static value and derived value are not official Salesforce.com terms but are used to help in understanding specific elements within formula fields.

I'll start with a formula field on the Contact object and look at examples of each derived field type. All of the examples of fields shown would be valid fields to reference within a custom Contact formula field.

The starting point for derived values is on the object itself (Contact). Within a formula field on the Contact object, you can obtain the value from the Mailing City field with very simple syntax (just the field name): `MailingCity`. Referencing a custom field is similar; the only difference is the way API names are formatted for custom fields. For example, if you want to derive the value from a custom field called "Maiden Name," you would use `Maiden_Name__c`, not `Maiden_Name`.

■ **Note**   The *API Name* is the name of an element that is used by Salesforce.com within formula fields, Data Loader, or Apex within API calls; it is not a user-facing string.

Using Lookup or Related Fields

The preceding section examined how to pull in values from fields on the same object as the formula field. Let's expand that thought and look at pulling in values from *other* objects. As discussed in Chapter 1, Salesforce.com allows "looking up," or traversing, objects. Think of it as inheriting fields from a Parent record. Let's say you want to pull in the Date/Time Opened (`CreatedDate`) field from the Account related to a Case and display it on the Contact record. In this case, you need to explicitly capture the Lookup object's name (`Account`). The format is: `Account.CreatedDate.`

Let's keep moving up the chain. Assume you also want to use the Entitlement record to which the Case's Account is related. In this case, you'll be looking at a Grandparent object that lives two lookup levels above the referencing object. Following the format in the last example, you simply add the additional object and an extra period in our syntax: `Account.Entitlement.Name.`

For custom objects, you need to slightly tweak what was done previously for standard objects by using the API Name of the object and replacing the __c with __r. Of course, if you develop declaratively, you don't need to worry about that; however, I think it is valuable to know. If you were to look up one level to a standard field on a custom object equivalent to the fields in the previous examples (for standard objects), the syntax would look like this: `Custom_Object_1__r.CreatedDate`

For two levels, it would look like this: `Custom_Object_1__r.Custom_Field_2__r.Name`

Following are some additional examples.

For fields on a related object with a single lookup, you would use:

- **Lookup to a standard field**: `Account.BillingState`

- **Lookup to a custom field**: `Account.Sales_Region__c`

For fields on a related object with multiple lookups (via standard object), you would use:

- **Lookup to a standard field**: `Account.Owner.LastName`

- **Lookup to a custom field**: `Account.Owner.Badge_Number__c`

For fields on a related object with multiple lookups (via custom object):

- **Lookup to a standard field**: `Account.Admin__r.LastName`

- **Lookup to a custom field**: `Account.Admin__r.Badge_Number__c`

Custom settings and system objects differ from regular object references. Certain custom settings can be referenced from any formula field, which can be extremely useful. Chapter 9 will take a closer look at custom settings. System "objects" contain certain values related to the Salesforce.com org itself.

For fields on a custom setting:

- **Custom field**: `$Setup.Custom_Setting__c.Config_Value_1__c`

- **Custom field**: `$Setup.Custom_Setting__c.Config_Value_2__c`

For fields on a system object:

- **Standard field (Organization)—Id**: `$Organization.Id`

- **Custom field (User)—Badge Number**: `$User.Badge_Number__c`

Functions

The preceding chapter dissected Salesforce.com formula functions, looking at the name, arguments, and optional arguments that come together within a function. That one function, without any added operators, conditions, and or arguments, can serve as a formula, albeit a simple one.

For example, let's say you are using the Web-to-Lead feature to capture Internet Leads and route them directly to your org. Your entire organization is making a huge push to sell one of your newer software products, "RunIt," this month. You do capture Product of Interest in your Web-to-Lead form, but you've noticed that customers aren't always successful at communicating their wants and needs and often do not select RunIt as a Product of Interest. To that end, you've created a formula field of the Checkbox type to identify whether the Lead description contains "RunIt." This formula would be simple, using just the function itself:

```
CONTAINS(Description, "RunIt")
```

Statements and Operators

In addition to deriving values from existing fields, specifying static values, and applying built-in functions, you can assess statements and perform operations to produce the final value to be returned in a formula field. Salesforce.com provides a number of operators that can be used for these purposes. To comprehend the full scope of what is possible, you'll need to examine the operators that are available, as shown in Table 3-1.

Table 3-1. *Salesforce.com Operators*

Add	+	Opening parenthesis	(	Greater than	>
Subtract	-	Closing parenthesis	)	Less than or equal to	<=
Multiply	*	Equal to	=	Greater than or equal to	>=
Divide	/	Not equal to	<>	And	&&
Exponentiation	^	Less than	<	Or	||

Add, Subtract, Multiply, and Divide

The Add, Subtract, Multiply, and Divide operators perform basic addition, subtraction, multiplication, and division operations on numeric values, including those of the following field types: Number, Percent, Currency, Date and DateTime.

Some examples follow:

```
CreatedDate + 2
Amount + 1000
Expected_Resolution_Date__c + Return_Period_in_Days__c

ClosedDate - 3
BudgetedCost - 1000

Probability * 0.85
Units_Requested__c * Unit_Cost__c
Tax * 1.07

Months_Duration__c / 12
```

■ **Note** Think carefully about the data types of the operands and the formula field type when applying Add, Subtract, Multiply, and Divide operators in formula fields. Here is an example of why this is important: CreatedDate + 3 and Amount + 3 are both valid, but the 3 in each calculation uses a different unit of measure (days and currency units, respectively).

Exponentiation

The Exponentiation operator performs exponentiation on numeric values, including the following field types: Number, Percent, Currency, Date, and DateTime.

Some examples:

```
ExpectedRevenue ^ 2
Case_Worked_Duration__c ^ 2
```

Opening and Closing Parentheses

The Opening and Closing Parentheses operators allow for certain operations to be prioritized higher in the order of operations. In the following examples, the operation within parentheses will be evaluated first, based on the standard order of operations.

Example 1:

Formula:

```
Expected_Resolution_Date__c - (Return_Period_in_Days__c + 10)
```

Assumption:

```
Expected_Resolution_Date__c = 12/31/2014
Return_Period_in_Days__c = 30
```

Result:

Example 1 will return **11/21/2014** (12/31/2014 - 40).

Example 2:

Formula:

```
(Expected_Resolution_Date__c - Return_Period_in_Days__c) + 10
```

Assumption:

```
Expected_Resolution_Date__c = 12/31/2014
Return_Period_in_Days__c = 30
```

Result:

Example 2 will return **12/11/2014** (12/01/2014 + 10).

Here, you see that a small difference in parenthetical location has a direct impact on the evaluation of the formula.

Here are a couple of other examples of where you might want to use parentheses within a formula:

```
(ClosedDate - CreatedDate) * 2
(Units_Requested__c * Unit_Cost__c) - 500
```

Equal To and Not Equal To

The Equal To and Not Equal To operators evaluate a statement expected to have equivalent values (equal) or different values (not equal) to determine whether it is true or false. If true, the statement will return TRUE; if not, it will return FALSE.

Some examples:

```
CloseDate = DATEVALUE("2015-01-01")
NumberofResponses = 0
Probability = 1
Description = "Test"

Days_Remaining__c <> 0
Quantity <> 2
Subject <> "Test"
```

You can approach the previous statements slightly differently, depending on what type of formula you are trying to build. For example, you can represent a Checkbox (a Boolean field) in the following ways:

```
IsClosed
IsClosed = true
```

You can represent a statement evaluation for a Picklist field in the following ways:

```
ISPICKVAL(Status, "Working")
TEXT(Status) = "Working"
```

Also, for Not Equal, you can use NOT on a corresponding Equal statement:

```
NOT(Probability = 1)
```

Less Than, Greater Than, Less Than or Equal To, and Greater Than or Equal To

The Less Than, Greater Than, Less Than or Equal To, and Greater Than or Equal To operators evaluate a comparative statement to determine whether it is true or false. If true, the statement will return TRUE; if not, it will return FALSE.

Examples:

```
CloseDate < TODAY()
Number_of_Complaints__c < 2

Amount > 1000000
NumberofResponses > 1000

Probability <= 0.5
LastModifiedDate <= ClosedDate

NumberOfEmployees >= 100000
Age_in_Days >= 10
```

And

Like the AND function, the And operator (&&) will check whether all included arguments are true. It returns TRUE if all arguments are true or FALSE if one or more arguments are false.

Examples:

```
Probability > 0.8 && Amount > 10000
ISPICKVAL(Status, "Working") && (Case_Age_in_Days__c + Business_Days__c) <= 10
```

The And operator (&&) and AND function can be used interchangeably. For example, these return the same value.

Using the AND function:

```
AND(
 IsClosed,
 (ClosedDate - CreatedDate) < 15
)
```

Using the And operator:

```
IsClosed && (ClosedDate - CreatedDate) < 15
```

Or

Like the OR function, the Or operator (II) will check whether one or more included arguments are true. It returns TRUE if one or more arguments are true or FALSE if all arguments are false.

Examples:

```
Probability > 0.75 || Amount > 50000
ISPICKVAL(Status, "On Hold") || IsClosed
```

The Or operator (II) and OR function can be used interchangeably. For example, these return the same value:
Using the OR function:

```
OR(
 NOT(IsClosed),
 (TODAY - ClosedDate) < 2
)
```

Using the Or operator:

```
NOT(IsClosed) || (Today - ClosedDate) < 2
```

■ **Note**   Since you have different options for evaluating multiple statements (&&, AND), you will want to come up with a thoughtful, systematic approach in your development. Always think about the next person who might come along and maintain what you've built, in case you move on to a different position at your job. When possible, stick with one or the other within a formula.

Creating a Formula Field

It's time to build your first formula field in Salesforce.com. The remainder of this chapter walks you in detail through the 11 steps in the process of creating a formula field in the program, pointing out your options when appropriate.

■ **Step 1.**   Navigate to the corresponding object, as shown in Figure 3-1.

Build

▶ **Customize**

▾ **Create**

      Apps

      Custom Labels

➡   Objects

      Packages

      Report Types

      Tabs

Figure 3-1. *Location of setup menu item to access custom objects*[1]

For standard objects: **Setup ➤ Customize ➤ Object_Name ➤ Fields**
For custom objects: **Setup ➤ Create ➤ Object_Name ➤ Fields**

▨ **Step 2.**   Click on the "New" button in the custom fields section, as shown in Figure 3-2.

Lead Custom Fields & Relationships   New

Figure 3-2. *The "New" button allows you to create a new formula field*

▨ **Step 3.**   Select "Formula" for the field type and click the "Next" button, as shown in Figure 3-3.

---

[1]All Salesforce.com screenshots in this chapter © copyright Salesforce.com, Inc. Used with permission.

Lead

New Custom Field

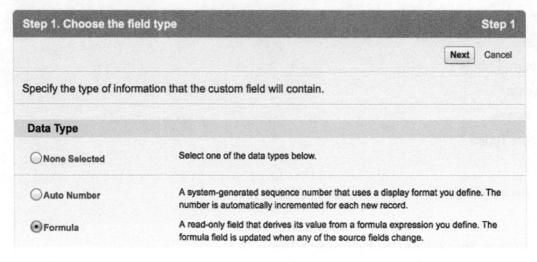

Figure 3-3. Selection of the formula field type

■ **Step 4.** Label and name the field, as shown in Figure 3-4.

| Field Label | My Custom Field | | Field Name | My_Custom_Field | i |

Figure 3-4. The formula's "Field Name" will autopopulate after you populate the "Field Label" and hit the tab key

I recommend that you use the Salesforce.com-suggested name when possible. By default, symbols are removed and spaces are replaced with underscores in the Name field. A custom field labeled "My Custom Field" would become "My_Custom_Field," as in Figure 3-4.

■ **Step 5.** Determine the appropriate formula return type.

This is a critical step in the formula creation process. What you need depends on how your data should be displayed and/or how you intend your users or the system to interact with the field. Much of what you will do with formula fields will center on the Text return type, but I'll cover the others as well.

Let's walk through the options and review when it makes sense to use each of them. The current formula return type options are:

- Checkbox
- Currency
- Number

- Percent
- Date
- Date/Time
- Text

Checkbox

A Checkbox is a relatively new addition to the list of available return types. The clearest way to understand the value of this field and how it can be used is to focus on the fact that it serves as a Boolean operator rather than thinking of it as an actual checkbox. The Checkbox will simply tell us if our formula is true or false, regardless of the complexity of the formula itself. Here are some basic examples of when you might select Checkbox for the return type:

- **Contract object**: You can use this object to determine whether a particular contract is still in effect based on a Start Date and Contract Term by entering the following: `TODAY() > StartDate + (ContractTerm * 12)`

- **Lead object**: This can be used to flag a potentially valuable lead if her organization has a hundred thousand or more employees or brings in a revenue of $100,000,000 or more, as follows: `NumberOfEmployees >= 100000 || AnnualRevenue >= 100000000`

- **Campaign member object**: A checkbox return type on this object could determine if the Campaign to which the Campaign Member is related is inactive or was created over one year ago as such: `NOT(Campaign.Active) || (TODAY() - CreatedDate) > 365`

A Checkbox formula can also be very useful within other formulas (such as formula fields, validation rules, and workflow rules). If you need to determine whether a specific formula is true in multiple areas of your system, consider creating a Checkbox formula field. You'll be able to quickly and easily reference it once the field is set up.

Currency, Number, and Percent

Currency, Number, and Percent are numeric return types that behave similarly when building the corresponding formula field. As long as your formula corresponds to a number, any of these three return types will work; it's simply a matter of how you want the data to be displayed and used throughout the system.

Here are some examples of formulas with a return type of Currency:

- **Opportunity object**: You could use this object to determine what the Expected Revenue would be with an additional upsell of 10 percent of the current Expected Revenue as follows: `ExpectedRevenue * 1.1`

- **Case object**: You could use this object to display the related Account's annual revenue as such: `Account.AnnualRevenue`

Here are some examples of formulas with a return type of Number:

- **Lead object**: This object is used to calculate the age of a Lead: `TODAY() - CreatedDate`

- **Contact object**: This object displays the number of total Contacts associated with the Contact's Account via a custom field on the Account object: `Account.Total_Number_Of_Contacts__c`

Here are some examples of formulas with a return type of Percent:

- **Opportunity object**: This object calculates the ratio of the ClosedAmount to the initial Amount at the time of Opportunity creation: `Amount / Initial_Amount__c`

- **Quote object**: This object displays the ratio of the Quote's Grand Total to the related Opportunity's Amount (assume the Quote is not the primary one): `GrandTotal / Opportunity.Amount`

Date and Date/Time

Date and Date/Time formula fields are used to calculate a date or a date and time and can be extremely valuable for an organization. The decision of selecting Date or Date/Time will probably be more difficult than deciding between these two types and the other return types. The obvious benefit of Date/Time is the additional detail; however, it can be a problem if the time is irrelevant. Showing "12:00:00" or even a seemingly random time can confuse your users. If you need to capture the time an event occurred or convey a strict deadline that needs to be precise down to the minute, Date/Time is the right return type. For anything else that doesn't require a specific time, it is better to just create a Date field.

Date:

- **Opportunity object**: This is used to calculate a date that precedes the CloseDate by 10 days, serving as a "reminder" date to increase efforts to close the open Opportunity as follows: `CloseDate - 10`

- **Case object**: This calculates a "Follow-up Date" one week after Case closure: `ClosedDate + 7`

Date/Time:

- **Case object**: Calculates an expected first contact date/time one hour from the time of Case creation: `CreatedDate + (1 / 24)`

■ **Note** Operations with Date and Date/Time fields are identical within formula fields; integers are interpreted as days. For example, adding 1 would add one day to either a Date or a Date/Time field within formula field calculations.

Text

Formulas with a Text return type are arguably the most flexible and are my personal favorites. With all other return types, the returned value is always in the same format, whereas a formula field with a return type of Text can contain more than just text; you can include text strings, hyperlinks, and even images. Think of it like a rich-text field. Here are some examples:

- **Lead object**: This object identifies Leads with high Annual Revenues and Ratings as high priority as follows: `IF(AnnualRevenue > 1000000 && ISPICKVAL(Rating, "Hot"), "High Priority", "Standard")`

- **Opportunity object**: This displays a link to the chapter in the Salesperson Guidebook that corresponds to the current Stage: `CASE(StageName, "Prospecting", "http://www.company.com/collateral/salesguidebook#2.1", "Qualification", "http://www.company.com/collateral/salesguidebook#2.3", "Needs Analysis", "http://www.company.com/collateral/salesguidebook#3.1", "http://www.company.com/collateral/salesguidebook#4")`

- **Case object**: This displays an informational message if the Subject field contains certain keywords, such as "Cancel" or "Quit": IF(CONTAINS(Subject, "Cancel") || CONTAINS(Subject, "Quit"), "Case may be related to cancellation; please review ASAP" , "")

Some of your formulas may require extra thought when deciding on a return type. For example, assume you want to display the Account's five-digit Billing Zip Code on the Contact object. Although five-digit zip codes are numeric, your formula return type must be Text. This will handle zip codes that start with zero. Additionally, you don't need to use zip codes in any statements or operations.

Step 6.   Select the applicable "Formula Return Type" and click "Next," as in Figure 3-5.

Lead

Help for this Page 🔵

New Custom Field

Step 2. Choose output type	Step 2 of 5

Previous   Next   Cancel

Field Label   My Custom Field   Field Name   My_Custom_Field   ⓘ

Formula Return Type

○ None Selected   Select one of the data types below.

◉ Checkbox   Calculate a boolean value
                       Example: TODAY() > CloseDate

○ Currency   Calculate a dollar or other currency amount and automatically format the field as a currency amount.
                       Example: Gross Margin = Amount - Cost__c

○ Date   Calculate a date, for example, by adding or subtracting days to other dates.
                       Example: Reminder Date = CloseDate - 7

○ Date/Time   Calculate a date/time, for example, by adding a number of hours or days to another date/time.
                       Example: Next = NOW() + 1

○ Number   Calculate a numeric value.
                       Example: Fahrenheit = 1.8 * Celsius__c + 32

○ Percent   Calculate a percent and automatically add the percent sign to the number.
                       Example: Discount = (Amount - Discounted_Amount__c) / Amount

○ Text   Create a text string, for example, by concatenating other text fields.
                       Example: Full Name = LastName & ", " & FirstName

Previous   Next   Cancel

Figure 3-5. *Selecting a return type for your formula*

■ **Step 7.** Select the advanced formula editor if necessary, as shown in Figure 3-6.

Simple Formula	Advanced Formula

Insert Field   **Insert Operator** ▼

My Custom Field (Checkbox) =

Figure 3-6. The advanced formula editor tab

Once you select your formula return type, you'll be presented with the formula editor, as discussed in Chapter 2. If your formula editor does not automatically default to "Advanced Formula," click on that tab to select this editor, which will then serve as the default going forward. You will select the advanced formula editor through the remainder of this book.

■ **Step 8.** Build your formula.

This step is where all the magic (and fun) occurs. You'll take a formula of midlevel complexity and methodically build it out. The scenario is that you're creating a new Case formula field to provide some additional information to agents about the Case. The formula looks at a few Case attributes, including whether the Case is escalated, whether it is closed, and what the Created Date is.

If the Case is escalated, a direct phone call to the customer is required. Closed cases are automatically de-escalated at your business, so you don't need to add a qualification that the Case is open. You will display the following to agents: "Contact customer directly by phone to address customer needs."

If the Case is not escalated, but it is at least seven days old and it is still open, you will display "Handle Case with urgency; Case has been open over one week."

If neither of those conditions matches the record, then no text will be displayed. Continue to build out this formula step-by-step. You will build this formula declaratively, or by using the clickable user interface that Salesforce.com has provided. However, as you feel more comfortable, you can feel free to type out your formulas. It is completely personal preference whether you use clicks or code when building a formula.

■ **Step 8.1.** Select and insert the IF function to start building the formula as in Figure 3-7.

Insert Field   **Insert Operator** ▼   **Functions**

My Custom Field (Text) =   `-- All Function Categoi ⏷`

```
IF(logical_test, value_if_true, value_if_false)
```

FIND
FLOOR
GEOLOCATION
GETSESSIONID
HYPERLINK
IF

Insert Selected Function

Figure 3-7. The IF function after being inserted into the formula

■ **Step 8.2.**   You have the option to reformat your `IF` statement for a cleaner view, as done in Figure 3-8.

Figure 3-8. *Reformatting the default placement of formula elements*

■ **Step 8.3.**   Select and double-click "`logical_test`" in preparation for replacing the text with the actual test statement, as shown in Figure 3-9.

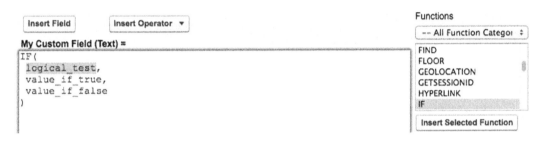

Figure 3-9. *Selecting the text to be replaced*

■ **Step 8.4.**   Insert the Escalated field to determine whether a particular record has been escalated or not, as in Figure 3-10. To do this, click the "Insert" button, select the Case object and the Escalated field, and then click on the "Insert" button to inject the field into your formula, replacing the "`logical_test`" text, as shown in Figure 3-11.

Insert Field

Select a field, then click Insert. Labels followed by a ">" indicate that there are more fields available.

Figure 3-10. *The "Insert Field" menu*

Figure 3-11. *The IF function after being inserted into the formula*

■ **Step 8.5.** Input the display text that you want to appear if a Case is escalated. To do this, select and double-click "value_if_true," in preparation for replacing the text with the text to be displayed, as in Figure 3-12.

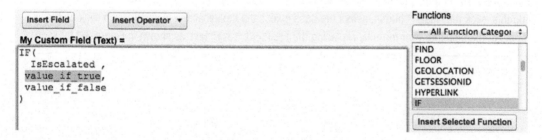

Figure 3-12. *Selecting the text to replace with the second IF function*

■ **Step 8.6.** Paste in the text you would like to display for escalated Cases, as shown in Figure 3-13.

Figure 3-13. *Field that appears after inserting the text to be displayed*

■ **Step 8.7.** Build a detailed IF statement to answer the question, What if my logical test is false? First, highlight the "value_if_false" text, as shown in Figure 3-14, and replace it with the IF statement, as done in Figure 3-15.

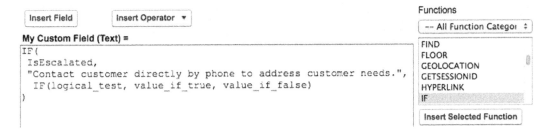

Figure 3-14. *Highlighting the text to be replaced*

Figure 3-15. *Field that appears after inserting the second IF function*

Figure 3-16. *Build your formula and continue to reformat, as needed*

■ **Step 8.8.** To establish the logical test for the second IF statement, highlight "logical_test," as in Figure 3-17, and insert the NOT function, as done in Figures 3-18 and 3-19.

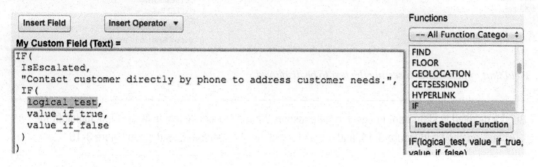

Figure 3-17. *Selecting "logical_test," indicating text to be replaced*

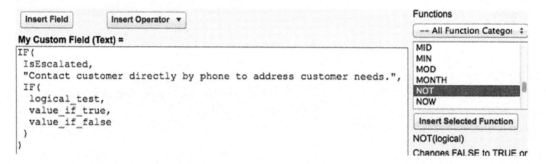

Figure 3-18. *Selecting the NOT function (on the right)*

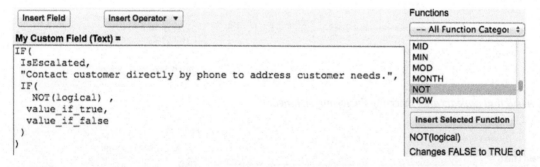

Figure 3-19. *Screen that appears after the NOT function has been inserted*

■ **Step 8.9.** Select the text within parentheses in the NOT function, as in Figure 3-20, and replace it with the Closed field, as is done in Figures 3-21 and 3-22.

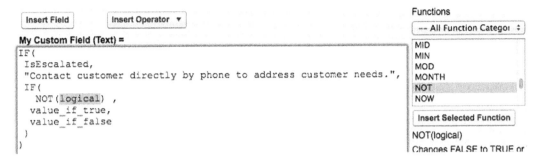

Figure 3-20. *Selecting the text to be replaced within the NOT function*

Insert Field

Select a field, then click Insert. Labels followed by a ">" indicate that there are more fields available.

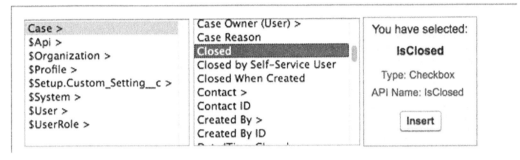

Figure 3-21. *Selecting the Closed field within the "Insert Field" menu*

Figure 3-22. *The IsClosed field once it is placed within the NOT function*

■ **Step 8.10.** You have added the condition that the Case is not closed in our second IF statement. Now, continue and add the age aspect of the condition. First, you need to establish that this needs to be an AND statement by inserting the && operator, as shown in Figure 3-23.

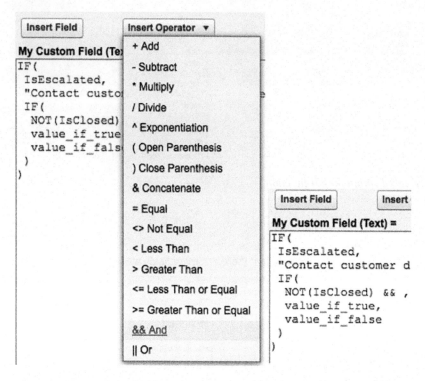

Figure 3-23. *Selecting "&&" and inserting the operator into the formula*

In this case, you could use the AND function instead of the double ampersands. However, with just two statements in the logical test, it's simpler and cleaner to use "&&."

■ **Step 8.11.**   To determine whether the Case is over seven days old, you'll need to build a calculation that takes the difference between the current date and the Case Created Date and assesses whether that value is greater than seven. First, add some parentheses for clarity, per Figures 3-24 and 3-25.

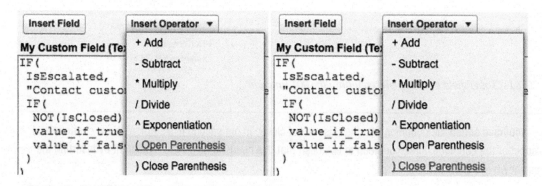

Figure 3-24. *Adding Opening and Closing Parentheses*

Figure 3-25. *The parentheses, after insertion*

Step 8.12. Insert the current date/time by selecting the NOW function and clicking "Insert Selected Function," as in Figure 3-26.

Figure 3-26. *Inserting the NOW function*

Step 8.13. Select and insert a minus sign, as done in Figure 3-27.

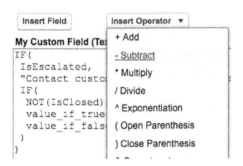

Figure 3-27. *Inserting the Subtract operator*

■ **Step 8.14.** Select and insert the Date/Time Opened field to fill out the calculation of the Case's age, as in Figures 3-28 and 3-29.

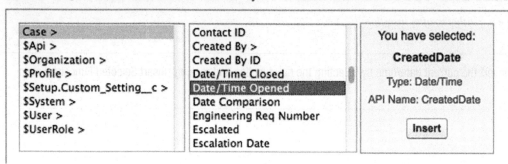

Figure 3-28. *Selection of the Date/Time Opened field*

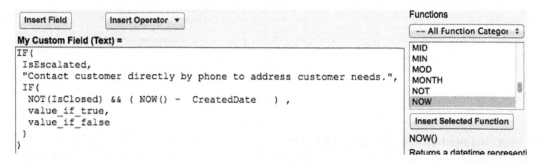

Figure 3-29. *Custom field once* CreatedDate *has been inserted into the formula*

■ **Step 8.15.** Optionally, clean up the formula and place the cursor after "CreatedDate)." You are now going to set up the check of whether the Case Age is greater than seven. You'll first need a greater than symbol, as in Figures 3-30 and 3-31).

Figure 3-30. *Selecting the Greater Than operator*

Figure 3-31. *Field after inserting the Greater Than operator*

■ **Step 8.16.** Type in "7" manually at the end of the IF statement to complete the "logical_test," as done in Figure 3-32.

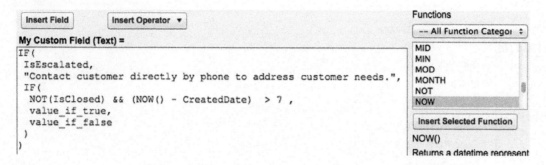

Figure 3-32. *Typing in "7" at the end of your IF statement*

■ **Step 8.17.**   You're almost there! Select and replace "`value_if_true`" with the replacement text, as in Figure 3-33.

Figure 3-33. *Field once "value_if_true," text has been replaced with the text to display*

■ **Step 8.18.**   Replace "`value_if_false`" with double quotations since you do not want any text to display in this scenario, as shown in Figure 3-34.

Figure 3-34. *Field after replacing the "value_if_false" text with double quotations*

▓ **Step 8.19.**   The formula has been built. Now comes the moment of truth. Click the "Check Syntax" button at the bottom of the page to find out if it was built properly, as in Figure 3-35.

Insert Field		Insert Operator ▾

My Custom Field (Text) =

```
IF(
 IsEscalated,
 "Contact customer directly by phone to address customer needs.",
 IF(
  NOT(IsClosed) && (NOW() - CreatedDate)  > 7 ,
  "Handle Case with urgency; Case has been open over one week." ,
  ""
 )
)
```

Check Syntax No syntax errors in merge fields or functions. (Compiled size: 299 characters)

Figure 3-35. *Clicking "Check Syntax" to find out if our formula was built properly*

Congratulations, you have successfully built a meaningful formula field! Give yourself a pat on the back. Make it quick, though, because you have a few more steps left to complete and save the field.

▓ **Step 9.**   Finalize field attributes.

You have completed the formula, but you will still want to populate the Description field; optionally, you can populate the Help Text field. There is one additional choice as well: blank field handling. Within a formula, you can set any derived fields that are blank with a value of zero or leave them blank. In this formula, it does not matter, so you'll leave the default of zeros. However, in some formulas with numeric return types, this can be a critical decision. Populate these fields and click "Next," as in Figure 3-36.

Description

Guidance field for customer support agents

Help Text

[i]

Blank Field Handling

If your formula references any number, currency, or percent fields, specify what happens to the formula output when their values are blank.

(•) Treat blank fields as zeroes
( ) Treat blank fields as blanks

[Previous] [Next] Cancel

Figure 3-36. When building a formula field, you'll need to set "Description," "Help Text," and "Blank Field Handling."

■ **Step 10.** Establish field-level security.

Set the field-level security for each profile. With non-formula fields, you have the choice of making the field hidden (inaccessible), read-only, or editable. However, all formula fields will always be read only since they are based on formulas and cannot be manually edited. This means that your selection for each profile will be hidden or read-only. See Chapter 14 for additional details on considerations when making this decision. Click the "Next" button to proceed to the final step.

■ **Step 11.** Add to page layouts.

Select the page layouts to which your new formula field should be added. Click the "Save" button. Your formula field is now complete!

Recap

There's a lot to Salesforce.com formula fields when you take a close look. Fortunately, you have just taken a very detailed look at the elements of formula fields, when they can be used in a real-world, business context, and how to properly build them from start to finish. Formulas are used extensively within Salesforce.com, and what you have just learned will come in extremely handy as you learn about other areas of the platform in subsequent chapters.

CHAPTER 4

Automating Your Business with Salesforce.com Workflow Rules

At this point, you have added a nice variety of tools to your Salesforce.com development tool belt. You have learned how to establish a meaningful and effective data model using objects, fields, and relationships; how to utilize functions; and how to build formula fields based on calculations, statements, and derived values from other fields. Next, you will take your org to a new place altogether by automating your business processes. Let's start with an understanding of what business process automation means in the context of Salesforce.com.

The one thing you're guaranteed to find in every active instance of Salesforce.com is interaction. It is a given that your users will add, edit, and/or remove data from your org on a regular basis. Consider these updates to Salesforce.com as the first step in your automation efforts. The second step is making Salesforce.com do what you want *based on that initial user interaction* with no further manual activity from users.

What Salesforce.com refers to as a "workflow rule" is an extremely powerful way to take one of these regular, everyday interactions and allow it to drive your business forward without spending the time or money to have additional people or systems make the change happen. At the simplest level, I can describe workflow rules as operating as explained below:

1. Workflow rules look for a particular state of specific data (your criteria).

2. The workflow rules "fire" (i.e., become active) if the state of the data satisfies the configured criteria.

3. The workflow rules trigger designated, automated actions to occur.

Through this process, your organization has taken an additional step forward using process automation. Whether you use workflow rules to notify a colleague that further action is needed or you update a field to reflect the current state of data, you have ensured that some desired action will happen and you did it all with a small, one-time investment of your cerebral efforts as opposed to an ongoing, manual activity.

With the potential value that lies in workflow rules comes a critical need for a solid understanding of these rules and a strategic approach when building them. You will quickly find that there are numerous ways to automate one business process; you will also discover that there is usually a best option. To that end, I will dissect each component of this functionality to help guide you through the decision-making process as you automate your own organization's processes.

After going over the workflow rule framework and how to use it effectively, I will examine four scenarios and demonstrate how to take real-world business processes and automate them in Salesforce.com via workflow rules. Knowing how to create a workflow rule is critical, but our end goal is actually satisfying a business need through the workflow rules. By the end of this chapter, you will:

- recognize scenarios warranting business process automation

- know how to properly apply evaluation criteria to workflow rules

- be able to develop rule criteria for workflow rules

- understand how and when to create workflow actions, including time-based actions

- be familiar with key considerations when working with workflow rules

The Elements of a Salesforce.com Workflow Rule

Before you create a workflow rule, you'll need to make sure you clearly understand each piece of the proverbial puzzle. It is very easy to create a workflow that does *not* do what you want it to do, and that is no fault of Salesforce.com. My goal is to prepare you so that you can minimize adjustments and tweaks after you create workflow rules. Once you have an understanding of the workflow rule elements, I will walk you through each step of the creation process for workflow rules. By building upon a solid foundation and delivering your solutions with precision, you can enjoy the lovely silence of satisfied users after putting this chapter into practice.

"Base" Object

The "base object" (my term, not Salesforce.com's) is the object on which the initial, manual (nonautomated) data change will be performed. For example, assume you have a custom object called Property that has a Master-Detail relationship to the Account object. If you wanted to make a change to a Property record to drive an automated, system, you would identify the Property object as your base object. That may seem obvious, but it is important to note that the object that is automatically updated through a workflow rule may differ from the base object. In Figure 4-1, I have identified the object being updated as the "action" object. In other words, a change to Object 1 may trigger an automated update to Object 2; this is called *cross-object workflow* and will be covered later in this chapter.

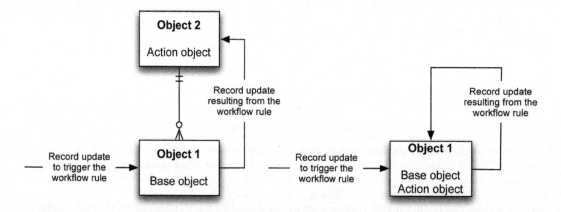

Figure 4-1. *The "base" object can update a Parent record with which it has a Master-Detail relationship (see left side of diagram). Most commonly, workflow rules drive an update of the record that triggered the rule (see right side).*

The *base object* refers to the object where the initial activity occurs, not necessarily where the update takes place. On the left side of the diagram, Object 1 has a Master-Detail relationship with Object 2 that allows configuring a workflow rule to update an object different than the base object.

Navigate to **Setup ➤ Create ➤ Workflow & Approvals ➤ Workflow Rules**. You will select your base object from the available Picklist of objects shown in Figure 4-2.

Figure 4-2. *Base object selection in your workflow rule[1]*

Evaluation Criteria

Once you identify your base object, you will need to configure its evaluation criteria. By establishing the evaluation criteria, you are setting the conditions in which the workflow rule should be considered or evaluated. You can think of it as the first "gate" that needs to be passed through for your automated business process to occur. The choices are fairly straightforward; you must select one of the three available evaluation criteria options identified and described in Table 4-1.

Table 4-1. *Evaluation Criteria Options Within a Workflow Rule*

Workflow rule: evaluation criteria	
Criteria	**Description**
Created	The workflow rule will be evaluated *only* at the point of record creation. Regardless of the rule criteria you specify, the rule will never fire for an existing record.
Created, and every time it's edited	The workflow rule will be evaluated upon every single change to the record, whether at the time of creation or after.
Created, and any time it's edited to subsequently meet criteria	The workflow rule will be evaluated at record creation. It will be evaluated for existing records only when the new/current state of the record satisfies the rule criteria *and* the previous state did not.

The "Created, and any time it's edited" option in Table 4-1 trips some people up. Table 4-2 and Figure 4-3 exemplify real-life scenarios and the resulting outcomes when using this option.

Table 4-2. *A Workflow Rule Using the "Created, and Any Time It's Edited" Option. (Bolded field labels and values signify that the value has been modified from the previous state)*

Workflow rule example

Evaluation criteria: "Created, and any time it's edited to subsequently meet criteria"

Rule criteria: Status = "New" *and* Owner = "John Smith"

Scenario	Previous State	Current State	Evaluated	Details
1	Status = "New" Owner = "John Smith" Product SKU = "A1A"	Status = "New" Owner = "John Smith" **Product SKU = "B2B"**	No	Only Product SKU changed. The rule criteria was already satisfied before update to the record.
2	Status = "Working" Owner = "John Smith" Product SKU = "A1A"	**Status = "New"** Owner = "John Smith" Product SKU = "A1A"	Yes	Update to Status causes rule criteria to be satisfied as a direct result of the change.
3	Status = "New" Owner = "John Smith" Product SKU = "A1A"	**Status = "Closed"** Owner = "John Smith" Product SKU = "A1A"	No	Update to Status causes rule criteria to no longer be satisfied.

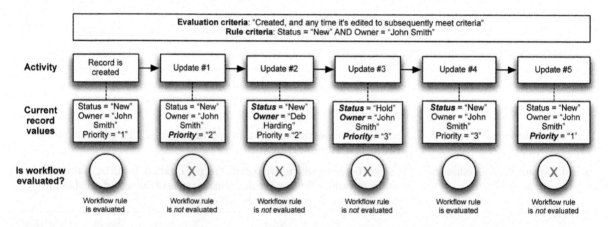

Figure 4-3. *Because the evaluation criteria setting includes "Created, and any time it's edited to subsequently meet criteria," the workflow rule will only be evaluated if the rule criteria are satisfied AND they were not already satisifed before the most recent update*

Figure 4-3 looks at a different scenario than Table 4-2 but also uses the same evaluation and rule criteria. Note that bolded text signifies a field that's value changed in the current step.

■ **Note** Depending on what you want to do with your workflow rule, you may not actually have a choice of your evaluation criteria. For example, if you plan to incorporate time-based actions into your workflow rule, you must select "Created, and every time it's edited." Although Salesforce.com forces you to select this option when using time-based actions, knowing this in advance will help you build solutions via workflow rules more quickly and efficiently.

Rule Criteria

Unlike evaluation criteria, which are comprised of three predefined options, rule criteria are completely wide open and allow for significant flexibility and creativity. Rule criteria equate to the second "gate" in Figure 4-4, which provides an overview of whether corresponding workflow actions are fired by a particular record update.

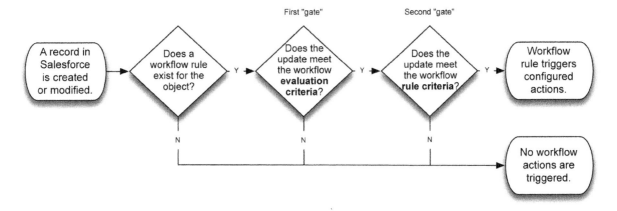

Figure 4-4. *The multiple "gates" that the creation or modification of any record has to pass through before a workflow action will occur*

The rule criteria come into play if and only if one or more active workflow rules exist for the object of the record being updated *and* the evaluation criteria of the workflow rule(s) have been met. The rule criteria that you configure will then be evaluated; if the evaluation deems them to be true, the associated workflow actions will be triggered. Rule criteria can be built by using one of the following tools:

- criteria builder
- formula editor

Criteria Builder

The first and probably most commonly used tool available to you when establishing your rule criteria is the standard "criteria builder." There is actually no official name for this element; I am coining the term for the purpose of quickly identifying this option in the workflow rule creation process. You will find the criteria builder used throughout Salesforce.com, not just in workflow rules. You will see this criteria builder reappear in upcoming chapters for such topics as list views, assignment rules, and escalation rules. This tool allows you to create one or more statements that can be evaluated as true or false. Figure 4-5 is a view of the criteria builder within the workflow rule framework.

Rule Criteria

Run this rule if the following [criteria are met   ▲▼] :

Field	Operator	Value	
--None-- ▲▼	--None-- ▲▼		AND
--None-- ▲▼	--None-- ▲▼		AND
--None-- ▲▼	--None-- ▲▼		AND
--None-- ▲▼	--None-- ▲▼		AND
--None-- ▲▼	--None-- ▲▼		

Add Filter Logic...

Figure 4-5. *Salesforce.com's framework for building your set of rule criteria*

The following sections review the three primary elements within the criteria builder tool: *field, operator,* and *value.* These will come together to establish one or more statements that will ultimately determine whether or not the workflow actions should occur.

Field

There is more to a rule criteria field selection than you might think. You would be correct to assume that all of the fields on the workflow rule's object would be available for selection. For example, if you are creating a workflow rule for the Opportunity object, you could choose Amount as your field; you could also choose any of the other standard or custom fields on the Opportunity object.

However, there are a number of additional fields that may be available depending on your object and your organization's data model. When creating a workflow rule for a standard object, you may use fields from any objects to which your workflow rule object is related via relationship fields. For example, the Contact object has a standard field (Account Name) that is a Lookup relationship from Contact to Account. As a result, you may use an Account field for selection in your rule criteria statement. Figure 4-6 shows the lookup objects fields available for some of the most commonly used standard objects in Salesforce.com.

Workflow rule object	Lead	Contact	Account	Opportunity	Case
Lookup objects available for field selection within rule criteria	Lead User Campaign	Contact Account User	Account User	Opportunity Account User Price Book	Case Contact Account User Asset

Figure 4-6. *Lookup objects available for standard objects. Depending on the object you are using for your workflow rule, you may be able to establish rule criteria from fields on related objects.*

The selection availability differs for custom objects. When creating a workflow rule for a custom object, you may use fields from:

1. the object selected for the workflow rule

2. the User object

3. any object that is the Master object in a Master-Detail relationship with the object selected for the workflow (#1)

■ **Note**   The User object is available for selection as the field when using the workflow rule criteria builder. In this context, User represents the Current User (i.e., the User making the actual change to the record).

When you select a field from the same object used for the workflow rule in the criteria builder, the mode of operations is straightforward. Assume you are using the Opportunity object, you would select "Opportunity: Amount" in the Field column and establish that the amount of the Opportunity is less than 100. Your workflow actions will fire if the evaluation criteria are met and the Opportunity amount in the most recent update is less than 100.

However, the flow is not quite the same when you are dealing with related objects, and it is critical to understand the difference. If you select a field from a related object for the field in the workflow rule criteria builder, you are now no longer dealing solely with the workflow rule object. Again, I will use a hypothetical scenario for you to create a workflow rule for the Opportunity object. This time, however, assume your field is the Annual Revenue field on the (Parent) Account object and that your rule criterion is (Account) Annual Revenue > 1,000,000. Obviously, an update to the Account record must take place for the workflow rule to fire. Unlike in the last example, the update to the Field object (in this scenario, Account) will *not* cause the workflow rule to fire. To complete the process, the Opportunity record itself will need to be updated to pick up the change to the Parent record. Take a look at the flow diagram in Figure 4-7 to help understand the process.

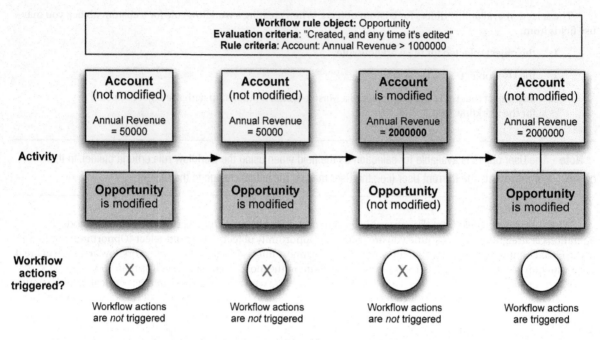

Figure 4-7. *An opportunity workflow rule based on the Annual Revenue field. It is important to understand how a workflow rule operates when the rule criteria involves a field on a related object. Here, we see that the Opportunity's rule criteria is based on an Account field. Although the rule criteria is technically met when the Account field value is edited accordingly, the workflow actions will not fire until those changes are picked up via an edit of the Opportunity record itself.*

The Child Opportunity record does not "know" that the Parent Account record has been updated. As a result, there must be a subsequent update to the Opportunity record to pick up the relevant changes to the Parent Account record. The workflow actions will be triggered at that point.

■ **Note**   One difference between the available fields for standard and custom objects in the workflow criteria builder (but not the formula editor) is that Lookup relationship objects on custom objects are *not* available for use; these are only available on standard objects. For example, Account is available in the criteria builder tool when creating a workflow rule for the Contact object; however, Account would not be available in the criteria builder for a workflow rule on a custom object if the Account were related as the Master in a Master-Detail relationship.

Operator

When using the criteria builder, you are provided with an operator list and must select one value from that list to build out a given statement to be evaluated as part of the rule criteria. The list generally overlaps with the operators found within the formula editor with five exceptions: **Starts With**, **Contains**, **Does Not Contain**, **Includes**, and **Excludes**. These operators can be found in the criteria builder but are not present in the formula editor as operators.

However, these operators do have equivalents with the formula editor if you take into consideration individual formula functions and combinations of formula functions. The five exceptions previously mentioned can be represented in formulas. Here is a mapping of the criteria builder operators that are listed above and the formulas that can be used in place of them:

- **Starts With:** `BEGINS()`
- **Contains:** `CONTAINS()`
- **Does Not Contain:** `NOT(CONTAINS())`
- **Includes:** `INCLUDES()`
- **Excludes:** `NOT(INCLUDES())`

See Chapter 2 for more detail on formula functions. Table 4-3 is a breakdown of operators available in the Picklists in the formula editor and the criteria builder tools.

Table 4-3. *Operators for Building Workflow Rule Criteria Available via the Formula Editor and Criteria Builder*

Comparison of operator availability		
Operator	Formula editor	Criteria builder
Add	+	
Subtract	-	
Multiply	*	
Divide	/	
Exponentiation	^	
Open Parenthesis	(	
Close Parenthesis	)	
Concatenate	&	
Equal	=	✓
Not Equal	<>	✓
Less Than	<	✓
Greater Than	>	✓
Less Than or Equal	<=	✓
Greater Than or Equal	>=	✓
And	&&	
Or	||	
Starts With		✓
Contains		✓
Does Not Contain		✓
Includes		✓
Excludes		✓

Value

Once you have selected your field and operator, you'll need to enter a value to complete your statement, which will be evaluated in your evaluation criteria. There are a few considerations you will need to keep in mind when you complete your statement:

1. You do not need to include quotes around text if the string itself does not include a comma, as shown in Figure 4-8.

Figure 4-8. Proper use of quotes in the value field when commas are not present. Quotes around text are unnecessary, unlike within the formula editor, where they are required

2. Text is not case sensitive—that is, typing in "Mgr" will also match "mgr," as shown in Figure 4-9.

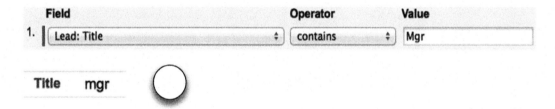

Figure 4-9. Evaluation of "mgr" is identical to "Mgr" within workflow rule criteria

3. Date format is MM/DD/YYYY (leading zeroes are not required), as in Figure 4-10. The Date/Time format is MM/DD/YYYY HH:MM AM/PM; however, HH:MM AM/PM can be omitted and 12:00 AM will be used.

Field	Operator	Value
Lead: Date Field	equals	10/8/1979

Figure 4-10. Formatting a date in the criteria builder

4. Comparative operators (e.g., Greater Than) will work with text (e.g., "zebra" would satisfy "greater than aardvark"). Figure 4-11 shows a similar statement applied to the Lead Description field.

Field	Operator	Value
1. Lead: Description ⬍	greater than ⬍	a

Description b ◯

Figure 4-11. *Comparative operators will work with text*

5. You can use commas to evaluate multiple values in one statement. When used with positive operators (e.g., Equals, Contains, Includes), a comma-separated list of values actually causes the statement to behave differently. For example, take this statement: Last Name = Moore. If I change Moore to Moore,More the statement is not actually evaluated as Last Name = "Moore,More". Instead, it is evaluated as Last Name = Moore OR Last Name = More. Figure 4-12 displays three statements that use commas and their equivalents.

Field	Operator	Value
1. Lead: Rating ⬍	equals ⬍	Hot, Warm
2. Lead: Description ⬍	contains ⬍	Urgent,Critical
3. Lead: Country ⬍	not equal to ⬍	United States,Canada

Figure 4-12. *Criteria with a comma-separated list of values. Omitting quotes evaluates the comma-separated values as a list; including quotes evaluates the string as one value, even if it includes commas.*

The following statements are pseudo code equivalents for the criteria statements shown in Figure 4-12. Note: "*" is a wild card.

1. Rating = "Hot" OR Rating = "Warm"

2. Description = "*Urgent*" OR Description = "*Critical*"

3. Country <> "United States" AND Country <> "Canada"

You can and should use quotes within your value in some situations. If you are trying to evaluate a text string that contains a comma, you must surround the full string with quotes. For example, take a hypothetical status field with two values: "Submitted" and "Submitted, Awaiting Payment". Using an input of "Submitted, Awaiting Payment" (in quotes) would only pick up the second of the two values. To consider both Picklist values, you would enter Submitted, "Submitted, Awaiting Payment" in the Value column. This highlights the need to be very careful with your syntax and pay close attention to detail.

In addition to understanding how the field, operator, and value work together, you should be aware of two additional features: First, you may add rows to the default five that are displayed. You may have up to 25 rows of criteria, although this number may increase at some point in the future.

Next, Salesforce.com offers "filter logic" to provide even more granularity to your criteria. By default, you are creating AND statements. For example, if you create five criteria, they behave as 1 AND 2 AND 3 AND 4 AND 5. If any of the statements is not true, then the workflow actions will not be triggered. However, with filter logic, you can replace the ANDs with ORs and combine the statements in logical groupings for evaluation. Figure 4-13 applies filter logic to these criteria.

Filter Logic:

(1 AND 3) OR 2

Figure 4-13. *Filter logic applied to rule criteria*

Figure 4-14 shows the criteria in Figure 4-13 from a visual perspective.

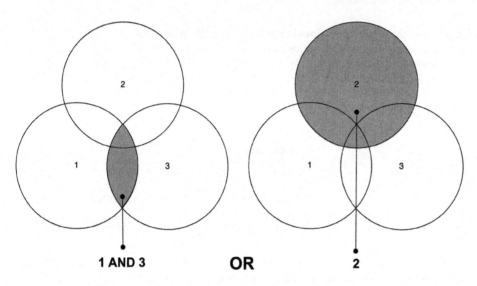

Figure 4-14. *A visual interpretation of rule criteria in Figure 4-13: (1 AND 3) OR 2*

Formula Editor

Workflow rules are one of many features that utilize the formula editor that was covered in previous chapters. All of the fundamentals about formulas and the corresponding formula editor apply to the formula editor associated with workflow rules, although there are some differences between what is available in this tool for formula fields and workflow rules. When building a formula for a workflow rule, you may only use what the previously mentioned Advanced formula editor; the basic formula editor is not an option. Additionally, some functions that are available for formula fields are not available for workflow rules.

By switching to the formula editor, you potentially gain access to additional fields. If you use the criteria builder, you cannot access fields via Lookup relationships from standard to custom objects, or Lookup relationships from custom objects to any other objects. There is no way around this restriction and that factor could be fairly limiting depending on what you need to include as criteria. Fortunately, you can access both if you decide to use the formula editor.

Another significant difference in how the formula editor is used for workflow rules (and many other areas of the platform) compared to formula fields is that the formula you build here *must be a Boolean statement*; the evaluation must produce a true or false result. If your formula evaluates to true, your workflow actions will be triggered, but they will not be triggered if your formula evaluates to false. You cannot select from the slew of return types that are available when creating a Formula field; you are essentially forced to select "Checkbox," which is the only Boolean option. For example, if you tried to create a non-Boolean formula with a return type of Text, you would see this error message:

```
Error: Formula result is data type (Text), incompatible with expected data type (true or false).
```

The following formula *would not* be valid for use as the criteria in a workflow rule:

```
IF(
 Account.AnnualRevenue > 1000000 && Amount < 100,
 "Review Opportunity for potential upsell",
 ""
)
```

The following formula *would* be valid for use as the criteria in a workflow rule:

```
IF(
 Account.AnnualRevenue > 1000000 && Amount < 100,
 true,
 false
)
```

Once you understand how to create your criteria for a workflow rule, you will need to decide whether to use the criteria builder or the formula editor. Part of the decision will be based on your comfort level, as the criteria builder is definitely easier to use. However, since formulas are such an integral part of Salesforce.com development without code, creating a workflow rule may be a good opportunity to explore the formula editor. Take a look at Table 4-4 for suggestions on which tool to use to develop criteria.

Table 4-4. *Guideline for Selecting Which Tool to Use for Developing Workflow Rule Criteria*

Tools for developing workflow rule criteria		
Criteria characteristics	**Criteria builder**	**Formula editor**
Statements/conditions are simple and clear	✓	
Statements include a list of values for the same field/operator	✓	
Requires access to a field via Lookup from a standard to custom object		✓
Requires access to a field via Lookup from a custom object		✓
Data manipulation/transformation required		✓
Use of Salesforce.com functions		✓

Criteria developed via the criteria builder are generally easier to maintain; however, your decision should be primarily based on your ability to meet business needs, not the ability to easily maintain the solution. If your solution does not achieve what your business requires, the ease of maintenance becomes irrelevant.

Workflow Actions

The last, but certainly not least, element of workflow rules is the resulting action or actions that occur. Everything you have done up to this point has determined whether an action will be triggered. Workflow actions determine what will actually occur; these handy helpers give you the automation in business process automation. Like with so many other features, Salesforce.com provides options and significant flexibility here, as well. You can configure what type of action is automated, when the action will occur, and where in the data model it will take place.

Action Types

When you build a workflow rule, you have the option of creating any of a few unique types of actions:

- Field Update
- Task
- Email Alert
- Outbound Message

Field Update

Based on my personal experience, I would say that the Field Update action is undoubtedly the most commonly utilized workflow action type. From a development perspective, you have the most to gain by learning about this type of workflow action; as a result, I will spent much more time diving into the details of Field Updates than I will the details of the other action types. A Field Update allows you to automatically modify a newly created record or an existing record based on the state of the record data and your workflow rule criteria. Figures 4-15 and 4-16 are examples.

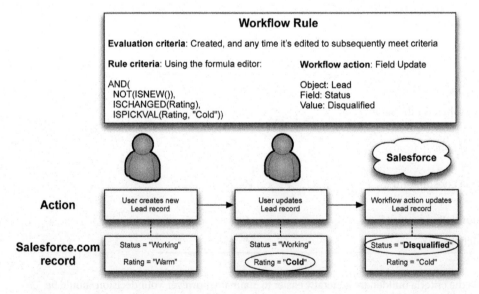

Figure 4-15. *An example of the Status field being updated automatically via a workflow rule*

Figure 4-16. *In this example, the criteria were partially met upon creation (Status = "New"), but failed to trigger the workflow action because the formula excludes new records: NOT(ISNEW())*

Selection of Object

You may notice in Figure 4-16 that "Object" is shown as part of the Field Update details and wonder why it is present since we have created this workflow rule for the Lead object. Recall my terms *Base object* and *Action object* from earlier in this chapter; the selection here is the Action object, not the Base object. In the case of the Lead object, you must select the Lead object; however, for other objects, you may have a choice here. For example, take a look at Figure 4-17 to see what is possible when you create a workflow rule for the Case Comment object.

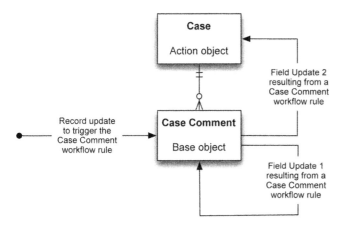

Figure 4-17. *Depending on the object you are using and the relationship fields that exist on it, you may be able to update multiple records within one workflow rule*

Not only can you have multiple workflow actions occur based on the same update, you can actually update two different objects: Case Comment *and* Case. As you would expect, this is only available on objects that have eligible relationships with other objects. Specifically, the base object must have a specific relationship with the Action object. If a standard object is your Base object, certain standard objects may be available, as shown in the following workflows. If a custom object is your Base object, only objects to which your Base Object is related via a Master-Detail relationship are available. This functionality is referred to by Salesforce.com as "Cross-object workflow" and can be extremely powerful in automating your business. Cross-object workflows are available for the following object relationships:

- Case Comment ➤ Case

- Opportunity Product ➤ Opportunity

- Opportunity ➤ Account

- Custom object ➤ any Master object (via Master-Detail relationship)

■ **Note** Since you cannot create a Master-Detail relationship on a standard object, you will not be able to use a workflow rule on a standard object to update a field that resides on a custom object.

Selection of Field

Once you have selected the Action object in your Field Update, you will select the field that you want to modify. There are a few limitations that should be considered. First, you can only update fields that are editable; you would not be able to update a formula field, for example. Second, a workflow rule trumps object and field-level security settings. In other words, a workflow rule configured to update Field B based on a change to Field A will not be prevented if the acting user does not have the ability to directly edit Field B. Likewise, a Read-Only setting on a page layout for a particular field will not prevent a workflow rule from updating that field if that page layout is invoked.

Configuration of Field Value

This is where things get very interesting. In Figures 4-15 and 4-16, I used simple scenarios to show how a Field Update could be used to change the Status field on the Lead object from "New" to "Disqualified" or "Working." In those examples, I would set one of the Picklist values as the value for the Field Update and be done. As you previously learned, there are numerous field types in Salesforce.com; each of these has its own particular behavior when it comes to Field Updates. Field update options differ by field type. Table 4-5 conveys the type of updates that are possible for each field type.

Table 4-5. *Field Update Options by Field Type*

Field type	Ways to update
Numeric (all)	Set the field as blank OR Update via formula.
Text (all)	Set the field as blank OR Update via formula.
Date (all)	Set the field as blank OR Update via formula.
Phone	Set the field as blank OR Update via formula.
Email	Set the field as blank OR Update via formula.
Checkbox	Set the field to True or False.
Picklist	Select the preceding or following value in the list OR specify a value from the list.
Picklist (Multi-Select)	Cannot update.
Formula	Cannot update.
Owner	Specify the Owner.
Lookup	Cannot update, with the exception of Owner.
Master-Detail	Update a field on the Master object according to the previous update options.

Reevaluation of Workflow Rules

Selecting "Reevaluate Workflow Rules After Field Change" will cause Salesforce.com to reevaluate your workflow rules. You will first want to check if one of your workflow rules is dependent on a workflow action from another workflow rule. In that scenario, leaving this field unchecked will prevent the dependent workflow rule from meeting the configured criteria. "Workflow #2" in Figure 4-18 shows an example of what can result from checking off this field.

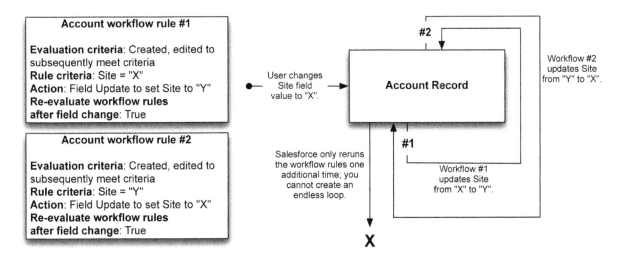

Figure 4-18. *Although it may seem like creating an endless loop is very simple with workflow rules, Salesforce.com has built-in protection against doing so. Workflow rules can be reevaluated only one additional time based on the original event or action. The figure shows an example*

Additional Thoughts on Field Updates

As you take in an inordinate amount of information related to Field Updates, it may be a challenge to see how powerful your options really are. The fact that you can use a formula to set a number of the field types gives you extreme flexibility in your business process automation, and you don't need a line of code to make it happen. Think about this: you can determine if an automated action occurs based on the state of your record and then you can configure a dynamic update based on a formula. You have already seen what formulas can do—they allow you to pull from other fields or even other objects and return a value based on a defined condition. Put this all together and you can perform quite a bit of automation in your Field Update.

New Task

The second type of automated action you can create via workflow rules is significantly different than the Field Update I previously discussed. Here, you can trigger the creation of a new task record, as shown in Figure 4-19. This is fairly straightforward: you specify the values of a number of task fields to be populated in the new task record. There are a couple fields worth calling out, specifically:

- **Due Date:** Like a Time Trigger, you can set the Due Date relative to any Date or Date/Time field on the record.

- **Protected Component:** Selecting this field prevents the component from being referenced or linked to by components created in a subscriber org. It allows a developer to delete the component in a future release without adversely affecting any Apex test results.

Figure 4-19. *Options when creating a new task via a workflow rule*

Email Alert

The Email Alert action allows you to automate the sending of an e-mail to one or more recipients within a workflow rule. This is a simple, but very useful, feature to utilize within Salesforce.com. You will find that modifications to your records will often require notifying someone of the change. One aspect of Email Alerts that is particularly beneficial is that you can send an Email Alert to an e-mail address directly; in other words, the recipients do not have to be Salesforce.com Users. To build out your Email Alert, you'll have to create your Email Template in advance. Once it's completed, you can configure an Email Alert to be triggered as part of your workflow rule. Figure 4-20 shows the Email Alert configuration screen.

Edit Email Alert

Description	Lead Notification
Unique Name	Lead [i]
Object	Lead ⬍
Email Template	Marketing: Product Inquiry 🔍
Protected Component	☐

Recipient Type   Search: User ⬍ for: [   ] [Find]

Recipients

Available Recipients   **Selected Recipients**

User: Jake Jingleheimer   User: Phil Weinmeister

Add
▶
◀
Remove

You can enter up to five (5) email addresses to be notified.

Additional Emails

john.smith@g.mail.com.1

From Email Address   Current User's email address ⬍

☐ Make this address the default From email address for this object's email alerts. [i]

Figure 4-20. *Screen options for creating an Email Alert via a workflow rule*

Outbound Message

Outbound Message is a workflow action type that allows you to send data from your record to an outside system for processing. From a Salesforce.com perspective, this is essentially a "send and forget" function; the actual processing of the sent data, including any responses, acknowledgements, logs, and so on, will be developed outside of your Salesforce.com org. Here, we decide whether an outbound message will be sent (via the evaluation and rule criteria) and what the content of that message will be. To complete the loop of what you can do with outbound messages, you will need to understand how to develop web services that can process SOAP (simple object access protocol) messages. Figure 4-21 shows the Outbound Message configuration screen.

Edit Outbound Message: Lead

Name	
Unique Name	ⓘ
Description	
Endpoint URL	
User to send as	Phil Weinmeister 🔍
Protected Component	☐
Send Session ID	☐

Lead fields to send

Available Fields		Selected Fields
AnnualRevenue		Id
Case__c		
City		
Company	Add	
ConvertedAccountId	▶	
ConvertedContactId	◀	
ConvertedDate	Remove	
ConvertedOpportunityId		
Country		
CreatedById		
CreatedDate		
CurrentGenerators__c		
Date_Field__c		
Date_TIme__c		

Figure 4-21. *Screen options when sending an outbound message via a workflow rule*

■ **Note** A "Flow Trigger" is an additional type of workflow action that is being developed. Be on the lookout for Salesforce.com to make this feature generally available.

Action Timing

So far, I have spoken about field updates in the context of immediate activity: A record is modified and that modification triggers a system update that immediately follows the original action. However, there is another option called "time-based workflow actions" that completely changes that paradigm. Time-based workflow actions allow you to control *when* your configured actions occur; this is defined as your "time trigger." You can configure the following within a time trigger:

- Any Date or Date/Time field

- Whether the action will occur before or after the corresponding Date or Date/Time field

- The time gap between the Date field value and the action; from 1 hour to 999 days

Figure 4-22 explains each of the available time trigger options.

Time Trigger Options

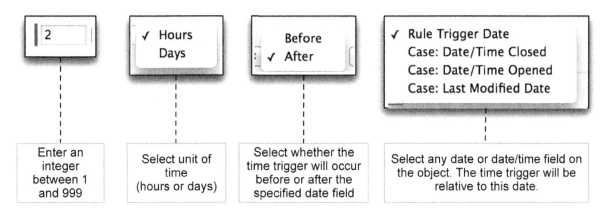

Figure 4-22. You can configure four settings that establish how your time triggers will behave

---

▰ **Note** A time-based workflow action will not be created if the time trigger is based on a Date or Date/Time field that is blank on the modified record. For example, let's assume I have a time trigger that performs an action five days before my custom "Expected Completion Date" field value. If the Expected Completion Date field value is blank, no action will be created.

In the example shown in Figure 4-23, one workflow rule has three resulting actions taking place: field update #1 immediately, field update #2 an hour after the action, and email alert #1 three hours after the original action.

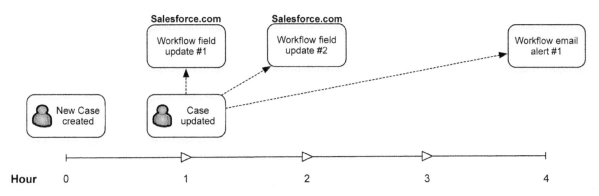

Figure 4-23. Three Workflow actions from a single workflow rule that are set to occur at three different times

Figure 4-24 shows what the updated time-based workflow actions queue would contain immediately after the workflow rule in 4-23 was triggered.

	Record Name	Object	Workflow Rule Name	Scheduled Date	Created By	Created Date
☐	00001032	Case	Case Workflow with Time Triggers	5/14/2014 7:02 PM	Weinmeister, Phil	5/14/2014 6:02 PM
☐	00001032	Case	Case Workflow with Time Triggers	5/14/2014 9:02 PM	Weinmeister, Phil	5/14/2014 6:02 PM

Figure 4-24. *Time-based workflow actions queue where a Case workflow rule has been triggered on 5/14/14 at 6:02 PM*

Figure 4-25 also has multiple future updates. However, in this case, they are not based on the time of the update; they are based on a Date/Time field on the object, which takes place one hour and one day before the corresponding Date/Time value.

Figure 4-25. *This workflow rule uses a time trigger based on a Date/Time field that is on the record instead of the Rule Trigger Date value.*

Figure 4-26 shows what the time-based workflow queue actually looks like while the actions are pending.

	Record Name	Object	Workflow Rule Name	Scheduled Date	Created By	Created Date
☐	00001034	Case	Case Workflow Rule with Time Triggers	2/16/2015 2:00 PM	Weinmeister, Phil	5/10/2014 10:55 AM
☐	00001034	Case	Case Workflow Rule with Time Triggers	2/17/2015 1:00 PM	Weinmeister, Phil	5/10/2014 10:55 AM

Figure 4-26. *Time-based workflow queue showing the pending actions from the example in Figure 4-22*

You have seen what happens initially with a time-based workflow rule; the corresponding time-based actions are created and scheduled relative to the time trigger. However, you should also be familiar with the rule's behavior after the actions are first created. Table 4-6 presents an example of a time-based workflow rule that goes through multiple modifications.

Table 4-6. Breakdown of How Changes to a Record Are Handled by a Workflow Rule

Example of opportunity workflow rule with time-based workflow action

Workflow rule name: Big Opportunity

Evaluation criteria: Created, and every time it's edited to subsequently meet criteria

Rule criteria: Amount > 1000

Time trigger: 5 Days before Close Date

Time-based workflow action: Update next step to "Review Amount with VP of Sales"

Assume current date on which all events occur is **7/4/2015**.

Event	Record field values	Time-based workflow queue
1. An Opportunity record is created. The workflow rule's evaluation criteria and rule criteria *are not* satisfied.	**Amount** = 500 **Close date** = 7/31/2015	No entries
2. The Amount on the Opportunity record is modified. The workflow rule's evaluation criteria and rule criteria *are* now satisfied.	**Amount** = 3300 **Close date** = 7/31/2015	Automatically added entry: **Workflow rule name:** Big Opportunity **Scheduled date:** 7/26/2015 12:00 AM
3. The Close Date on the Opportunity record is modified. The workflow rule's evaluation criteria and rule criteria *are still* satisfied.	**Amount** = 3300 **Close date** = 8/31/2015	Automatically updated entry: **Workflow rule name:** Big Opportunity **Scheduled date:** 8/26/2015 12:00 AM
4. The Close Date on the Opportunity record is modified. The workflow rule's evaluation criteria and rule criteria *are still* satisfied.	**Amount** = 3300 **Close date** = 7/6/2015	Automatically updated entry: **Workflow rule name:** Big Opportunity **Scheduled date:** 7/1/2015 12:00 AM
5. The Amount on the Opportunity is modified. The workflow rule's evaluation criteria and rule criteria *are no longer* satisfied.	**Amount** = 800 **Close date** = 7/6/2015	Entry removed

To explain why the time-based workflow queue was updated as described in Table 4-6, here are some additional details:

1. The created Opportunity does not meet the workflow rule criteria, so no action is triggered.

The created Opportunity now meets the criteria. Since this workflow rule has a time-based workflow action, the corresponding action is added to the time-based workflow queue based on the configured time trigger (five days before Close Date, or "7/31/2015 12:00 AM—5 days")

2. Since the time trigger's Date field was modified, the entry in the time-based workflow queue is also updated accordingly. The entry will now be set to five days before 8/31/2015, instead of five days before 7/31/2015.

3. Since the time trigger's Date field was modified, the entry in the time-based workflow queue is also updated accordingly. The entry will now be set to five days before 7/6/2015, instead of five days before 8/31/2015. Note here that the time trigger is actually in the past (current date is assumed to be 7/4/2015). The action will occur the next time a batch is executed (see "Note" for additional details).

4. If a record with a pending time-based workflow action is modified and no longer satisfies the original evaluation and rule criteria, the corresponding time-based workflow queue entry will be removed completely and the previously pending action will not occur.

■ **Note**   It is critical to be aware of how time-based workflow actions are processed. These actions are executed in batches, not individually. This means that your time-based workflow actions will likely *not* occur precisely at the configured time. Salesforce.com does not publish how frequently batches are processed. In my experience, batches have been executed every 15 minutes starting on the hour (that is not official and may change at any time). Consider the practical impact to your rules. If you have an action queued for 1:14 PM, it would occur one minute later at 1:15 PM. However, if you have an action queued for 1:16 PM, it will likely not occur for 14 additional minutes, until 1:30 PM. Make sure to thoroughly test what you've built and do not use time-based workflow rules if absolute precision is a business requirement.

Building a Workflow Rule and Actions: Step by Step

You have learned the low-level details of workflow rules, but the main goal is to put this knowledge into practice. To help you piece it all together, I will provide a quick recap of the steps to create an effective workflow rule.

Preparation Step: Create Relevant Custom Fields

As is the case with formula fields, you will need to have your data model properly established before you begin creating workflow rules. Most important, any relevant Lookup or Master-Detail relationships fields will need to be created. Additionally, you will need to create any custom fields that you want to update via workflow actions or use as part of your criteria. As a reminder, you'll need to use the following navigation path:

- **For standard objects**: Setup ➤ Customize ➤ [Your Object]} ➤ Fields ➤ New

- **For custom objects**: Setup ➤ Create ➤ Objects ➤ [Your Object] ➤ New Custom Field

It's time to create the actual workflow rule. Navigate to **Setup ➤ Create ➤ Workflow & Approvals ➤ Workflow Rules ➤ New Rule**. The process is as follows:

1. *Create the workflow rule.* To do so, you'll need to take four additional steps:

   a. Identify the Base object.

   b. Provide a name and description for the workflow rule.

   c. Select the evaluation criteria.

   d. Establish the rule criteria, whether via the criteria builder or the formula editor.

2. *Add time triggers.* Do you plan on having any actions that occur at some point in the future? If so, you'll need to create the corresponding time triggers. If you're still in the workflow rule creation process, you'll simply need to click "Add Time Trigger." Create one or more of these time triggers and proceed.

3. *Add workflow actions.* Add your desired workflow actions to your workflow rule. You'll first need to determine whether the actions need to be immediate or time based and then click on the corresponding button. From there, you'll need to select which type of workflow action you want to create. Select your action and follow the steps to completely build it out.

■ **Note** Once you have created a Field Update, New Task, Email Alert, or Outbound Message action, you can reuse it in future workflow rules. To do so, select "Add Existing Action" for your action type and select your desired action.

4. *Activate.* Click on the Activate button to make your workflow rule live!

Workflow Rules: Real-World Examples

Let's look at some hypothetical real-world scenarios in which you might want to utilize workflow rules.

Scenario 1: Lead Assessment (Marketing Cloud)

Let's say your organization sells consulting services and manages its business through Salesforce.com, and some of your leads come in from the web. Since web leads are manually qualified before they are created, they do not initially have a rating value. However, say you wanted to automatically set the rating on certain leads that come in through the web; specifically, to identify web leads that communicate a near-future project start. The following components would be needed:

- **Custom fields**

  - *Projected Project Start (Picklist)*

  - *Picklist values*: 0–1 month, 1–3 months, 3–6 months, 6–12 months, 12–24 months, 24+ months.

  - You create the "Projected Project Start" field to convey the likely timing of the need for consulting services.

- **Evaluation criteria:** Evaluate the rule when a record is: Created

- **Rule criteria:** Run this rule if the following criteria are met:

  - Lead: Lead Source *equals* Web

  - Lead: Projected Project Start *equals* 0–1 Month

- **Immediate workflow actions**

  - *Field update*: Update Rating

  - *Object*: Lead

  - *Field to update*: Lead: Rating

  - *New field value*: Hot

- **Time-dependent workflow actions:** None

Summary

You just created a workflow rule that looks for any web-sourced leads that inquire about engaging your consulting services in the next few weeks. If a lead meets the specified criteria, the rule automatically increases the rating to "Hot"; this will allow users to see this new lead via a list view of open leads with a rating of "Hot" and take action quickly.

Scenario 2: Opportunity Probability (Sales Cloud)

Say you have configured your sales process and set an appropriate Probability percentage for each corresponding Opportunity Stage. However, you feel that some sales situations warrant a higher probability than what you have assigned. One scenario in particular is an open Opportunity associated with an Account within a certain industry (government) with which an Opportunity has closed in the past year. These variables point to a higher probability of closure. As a result, you set up a custom field to track your "True Probability" and update it based on a workflow rule.

This Opportunity Probably scenario involves multiple objects, so read carefully. Both workflow rules are based on the Opportunity object. The first workflow rule updates the Parent Account record and the second rule includes the related Account record in the rule criteria. The following components apply:

Part I: Workflow Rule to Update Custom Date Field on Account

- **Custom fields**

    - *Last Won Opportunity Date (Date)*: You create this field to capture the date of the most recent Closed/Won Opportunity. NOTE: This custom field should be on the Account object, not the Opportunity object.

- **Evaluation criteria**: Evaluate the rule when a record is: Created, as well as any time it's edited to subsequently meet criteria

- **Rule criteria**: Run this rule if the following criterion is met:

    - *Opportunity*: Won **equals** true

- **Immediate workflow actions**

    - *Field update*: Update Last Won Opportunity Date

    - *Object*: Opportunity

    - *Field to update*: Account: Last Won Opportunity Date

    - Use a formula to set the new value: CloseDate

- **Time-dependent workflow actions:** None

Part II: Workflow Rule to Update True Probability on Opportunity

- **Custom fields**: *True Probability (Percent)*: You create this field to convey a more accurate probability of the Opportunity (without overwriting or removing the standard Probability field).

- **Evaluation criteria**: Evaluate the rule when a record is: Created, as well as any time it's edited.

- **Rule criteria**: Run this rule if the following formula evaluates to true:

```
AND(
 ISPICKVAL(Account.Industry, "Government"),
 Amount > 1000,
 (TODAY() - Account.Last_Won_Opportunity_Date__c) < 365
)
```

- **Immediate workflow actions**
  - *Field Update*: Update Last Won Opportunity Date
  - *Object*: Opportunity
  - *Field to Update*: Opportunity: True Probability
  - Use a formula to set the new value: MAX(0.9, Probability *1.2)

■ **Note**   In Scenario 2, assume that you don't want the probability of an open Opportunity to exceed 90 percent so you cap it accordingly. You can achieve this limit by utilizing the MAX() function in your workflow action.

- **Time-dependent workflow actions**: None

Scenario 3: Case Escalation (Service Cloud)

Perhaps your customers do not always accurately communicate the real reason for submitting a Case and your organization has, unfortunately, had an issue with certain urgent Cases slipping through the cracks as a result. You have noticed a correlation between the presence of a few certain keywords in the Description field and requests for subscription cancellations. To address the issue, you want to escalate Cases with any of those particular keywords in the Description field. Additionally, you want to provide a custom visual indicator to appear on the Case Detail page that will show a different image for Open/Non-Escalated, Open/Escalated, and Closed Cases. Additionally, if the Case is still open, you want an e-mail to be sent out two hours after the Case is created as a follow-up to make sure that the Case is closed promptly. The following elements apply

- **Custom fields**: Health Status Indicator (formula):

```
IF(
 IsClosed,
 IMAGE("img/msg_icons/confirm32.png", "Closed"),
 IF(
 IsEscalated,
 IMAGE("/img/msg_icons/error32.png", "Escalated"),
 IMAGE("/img/msg_icons/warning32.png", "Open")
 )
)
```

This formula will display a visual indicator to represent Case status, as in Figure 4-27.

Health Status Indicator

Figure 4-27. *Your Health Status Indicator field*

■ **Note**   You may notice that the images in your formula are not external. They are actually from a little-known library of built-in icon images that you can use. However, the images are not guaranteed to always be around, so keep that in mind.

- **Evaluation criteria**: Evaluate the rule when a record is Created, as well as any time it's edited to subsequently meet criteria.

- **Rule criteria**: Run this rule if the following criteria are met:

  - Case: Description *contains* Cancel,Quit,Sue,Refund.

  - Case: Closed *equals* false.

- **Immediate workflow actions**

  - *Field Update*: Update Escalated

  - *Object*: Case

  - *Field to Update*: Case: Escalated

  - *Set to*: True

- **Time triggers**: Two hours after rule trigger date

- **Time-dependent workflow actions**

  - *Email alert*: Alerts escalations team

  - *Email Template*: Potential Cancellation Case

  - *Recipients*: Director, Customer Service AND Escalations Queue

Recap

In this chapter, you have learned how to automate your business processes within Salesforce.com. As you can see, you have a significant amount of flexibility to build efficiency and productivity into your system using "Clicks, not code." With the right preparation, some creativity, and a little hard work, you can ease the burden on your employees and make your system data much more meaningful. Make sure to plan out your workflow rules carefully and test them extensively and you'll be able to move your business forward with a notable degree of efficiency.

■ ■ ■

CHAPTER 5

Enforcing Your Business Rules with Salesforce.com Validation Rules

To be a successful system administrator, consultant, analyst, or developer, you must keep the needs of your users at the forefront of your decision-making and provide them with the ability to effectively carry out their job. However, while users should retain a critical position in your thought process, they are not perfect, either. A reality with which you are probably all too familiar is that the users of any system, including Salesforce.com, don't always follow the rules. Whether purposeful or not, users' actions within the system sometimes fail to align with their expected behavior. Fortunately, Salesforce.com provides validation rules to support a meaningful, synergistic existence of users and the real-world system that they use. Validation rules are specified conditions that allow you to enforce your business rules of operation and guide your users to interact with the system in a beneficial way.

Thus far, I have discussed a number of possibilities and tools available to you when building solutions within Salesforce.com; I've covered objects, fields, relationships, functions, formulas, and workflow rules and the role they play in declarative development. Now it's time to shift gears and discuss how to keep your users on the right track when using the system. When you don't use validation rules, you grant your users the ability to openly create and modify records without restriction, within the parameters of their configured security and system settings. When you do use validation rules, you can enforce your business rules and provide helpful feedback to users along the way. By the end of this chapter, you will:

- understand the basics of validation rules and why they are valuable

- know when to apply validation rules to your business processes

- be able to create relevant and effective validation rules within your Salesforce.com org

- be familiar with various considerations that should be made when creating validation rules

A Clear Definition of Validation Rules

Before diving into the details of creating effective validation rules, I want to help you understand exactly what they are . . . and what they are not. Validation rules are criteria-based error conditions of your data that you define. When configured as a validation rule, a once-allowed data state immediately becomes invalid. Take a look at the following example (Figure 5-1). We see a sequence of actions, including the creation of a validation rule with the following criteria: Field X = "ABC." At first, Field X on the Contact object does not have a validation rule; this allows for a field value of "ABC." However, once the validation rule is created for Field X, the field value is restricted across all Contact records. In this case, the rule prevents a value of "ABC."

Figure 5-1. *Here, the addition of a validation rule to the Contact object prevents an action that was previously allowed by identifying a particular field value as invalid*

Figure 5-1 shows a simple validation rule that identifies one specific value as invalid for a particular field. This is about as basic as it gets; as you'll see, the formula editor can be used to define your criteria, significantly opening up your options when creating rules.

You may be wondering about the format of the validation rule in the figure: Shouldn't it be `Field X <> "ABC"` to capture the fact that Field X should not equate to the banned value of "ABC"? This observation leads us to the first key takeaway in understanding validation rules: They are error conditions and define the *disallowed* "space" within your system. They are not a description of your proper business modus operandi. Figure 5-2 shows a comparison of two similar validation rules and how they correspond to a real-world business rule.

Figure 5-2. *Two opposite validation rules for the same business rule. While the second may appear to be what is desired, as it mirrors your business rule, the first is correct. You define the error condition, not the business rule*

To solidify this concept, I'd like to take a step back and look at your Salesforce.com org as a whole and how validation rules come into play. Take a look at the image in Figure 5-3. The squares contain all possible states of your data based on the data model that you have created. The inside of the circles represent the desired states of your data based on your business processes, and the outside represents the undesired states of your data that go against your organization's business rules. The validation rules you build will allow you to prevent those undesired states by invalidating them with applicable criteria.

Adding Validation Rules to Your Business

Figure 5-3. *The presence of effective validation rules can help ensure data integrity within your organization*

Validation rules should be the foundation for any systematic effort to support and maintain data integrity within Salesforce.com. In a previous chapter, I commented on how migrations frequently become a simple mapping exercise and result in unused or irrelevant fields being incorporated into your data model. Along with the extraneous fields that can come with a data migration, you run the risk of ingesting a significant amount of irrelevant, incorrect, or unproductive data in the process. Properly created validation rules can prove extremely valuable when importing data. While it may increase the effort required to carry out the import process, having clean data in your Salesforce.com org will pay off in spades for your users and for you.

Using Validation Rules in a Data Migration Process

Figure 5-4. *In this scenario, an organization is migrating data from a system to their Salesforce.com org. The presence of validation rules can serve as a filter to prevent bad data from being transmitted*

Building an Effective Validation Rule

Before I break down some key considerations that warrant your attention when establishing validation rules within Salesforce.com, I will cover the steps involved in creating a validation rule. If you have read the chapters on formulas and workflow rules, you have a great head start. There's actually a fair amount of overlap between how validation rules and some other Salesforce.com elements are created. Following are the steps to create a validation rule.

Step 1: Define the Scenario and Corresponding Business Rules

For this exercise, I will use a specific scenario to illustrate how to create a relevant validation rule for your business. Let's say your business sells subscription-based software services to medium-to-large corporations in a highly competitive space. The sales life cycle typically lasts months and requires a number of conversations in order to come up with an agreed-upon set of features and a corresponding price. You use the Salesforce.com Marketing Cloud to capture incoming Leads via telephone and the web; qualified, converted Leads then enter the Sales Cloud as Opportunity records, which the sales team utilizes in the hopes of generating eventual subscriptions.

The VP of Sales has noticed a recent drop-off in Opportunity win percentage coupled with an increase in Opportunities being closed as a result of the potential client being a poor fit. Although these clients have an initial interest, they rarely end up signing a deal, finding the price tag, large scope, and maintenance needs that come with the software subscription to be overwhelming. After a few discussions, the VP of Sales agrees to a new business rule that would aim to increase the quality of Opportunities, specifically those that are created via a Lead conversion. This new business requirement indicates that for *converted Leads*:

1. The Annual Revenue field must be populated.

2. The Annual Revenue field value must be greater than or equal to $100,000.

3. The Number of Employees field must be populated.

4. The Number of Employees field value must be greater than or equal to 50.

5. An exception process will exist to allow circumvention of the rules, represented by a custom Checkbox field called Approved Exception.

Step 2: Enter Basic Rule Information

You'll need to navigate to **Setup ➤ Customize ➤ Lead ➤ Validation Rules**. As a side note, you would need to navigate to **Setup ➤ Create ➤ Objects ➤ Object Name ➤ Validation Rules** if this applied to a custom object. Click the **"New"** button to get started. You'll begin by identifying information, as shown in Figure 5-5. Like always, put some thought into the rule name and description to facilitate a quick understanding of the rule and expedite future knowledge-transfer requirements.

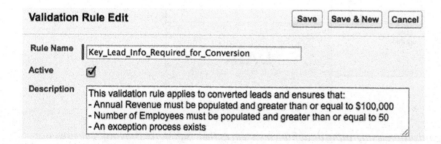

Figure 5-5. It's important to enter a meaningful name and description for your validation rule

Step 3: Establish the Error Condition Formula

The core tool of the validation rule process is the formula editor that was covered in detail in Chapters 3 and 4. With this editor, you will establish the error condition that will be prevented within your Salesforce.com org. It is critical to understand that you are defining the invalid or disallowed state here; you are not simply translating real-world business rules into a Salesforce.com-friendly format. For example, if your business rules required the standard

Opportunity field **Quantity** to be less than or equal to 50, the corresponding Error Condition formula would be: `Quantity > 50`, not `Quantity <= 50`. You'll need to translate each of your business rules into error conditions in a similar fashion. Table 5-1 lays out the requirements for creating error conditions for specific business rules.

Table 5-1. *Requirements for Creating Error Conditions for Specific Business Rules When Building Your Overall Error Condition Formula*

#	Business rule	Error condition (description)	Error condition formula
1	**The Annual Revenue** field must be populated.	**Annual Revenue** is not populated.	`ISBLANK(AnnualRevenue)`
2	The **Annual Revenue** field value must be greater than or equal to $100,000.	**Annual Revenue** is less than $100,000.	`AnnualRevenue < 100000`
3	The **Number of Employees** field must be populated.	**Number of Employees** is not populated.	`ISBLANK(NumberOfEmployees)`
4	The **Number of Employees** field value must be greater than or equal to 50.	**Number Of Employees** is less than 50.	`NumberOfEmployees < 50`
5	Exceptions can be captured via custom Checkbox: **Is Approved Exception**.	**Is Approved Exception** is false.	`NOT(Is_Approved_Exception__c)`

When establishing your error condition criteria, you may feel more comfortable combining the NOT() function with the allowed condition instead of explicitly defining the error condition, as shown in Table 5-1. The fourth rule requires that the Number of Employees field value must be greater than or equal to 50. To achieve this, I have built the following statement for my formula: `NumberOfEmployees < 50`. However, it is completely valid to use the following format instead: `NOT(NumberOfEmployees >= 50)`. Ultimately, this is your choice and should reflect the factors impacting your personal situation (e.g., how you most effectively read code, the likelihood of a future handoff or knowledge transfer). I take and recommend the approach of building a cleaner, simpler formula. That means avoiding the extraneous NOT() in this case. Table 5-2 points out alternative approaches for two of the error conditions from the previous table. The fifth rule is another good example of where an alternative approach can be used. With Booleans (Checkboxes), there is no need for "= true" or "= false", although using each will work. In this case, you could use `Is_Approved_Exception__c = false` instead of the `NOT(Is_Approved_Exception__c)` that I produced.

Table 5-2. *Alternative Approaches for Two Error Conditions from Table 5-1*

#	Business rule	Error condition formula	Alternative approach
1	The **Number of Employees** must be greater than or equal to 50.	`NumberOfEmployees < 50`	`NOT(NumberOfEmployees >= 50)`
2	Exceptions can be captured via custom Checkbox: **Is Approved Exception**.	`NOT(Is_Approved_Exception__c)`	`Is_Approved_Exception__c = false`

You now have the components to use within your error condition formula representing a failure to satisfy a required business rule. The next step is to establish the logic that will allow you to complete the formula. Since you know that the error condition only applies to converted Leads, you know that the system field Converted must be present and must be true. Since this is a Boolean field, the starting point is simply the field name:

IsConverted

Next, you'll need to augment the formula to ensure that the Is Approved Exception field is FALSE. This will prevent circumvention of the business rules:

IsConverted **&& NOT(Is_Approved_Exception__c)**

Third, you'll need to address the error conditions that were established in Table 5-1 to systematically capture unsatisfied business rules. You will want to build your validation rule to halt activity in which *any* of these error conditions are found. In other words, you want to display an error message if error conditions 1, or 2, or 3, or 4 occur. Add the following to the current formula:

IsConverted && NOT(Is_Approved_Exception__c) **&& (ISBLANK(AnnualRevenue) || AnnualRevenue < 100000 || ISBLANK(NumberOfEmployees) || NumberOfEmployees < 50)**

Figure 5-6 gives a view of the formula in the error condition formula screen.

Figure 5-6. *Completed Error Condition Formula screen for our Lead qualification validation rule scenario*[1]

I previously discussed the options available when establishing AND/OR logic within formulas. You have the AND() and OR() functions as well as the && and || operators at your disposal. Either approach is acceptable when building validation rules. The decision whether to select the functions or the operators is up to you. Figure 5-5 shows how this validation rule would appear if you were using the AND() and OR() functions.

---

[1]All Salesforce.com screenshots in this chapter © copyright Salesforce.com, Inc. Used with permission.

Figure 5-7. *An alternative approach for building your error condition formula using AND() and OR()*

Note One notable omission in the validation rule creation process is the criteria builder that is offered when building workflow rules in Salesforce.com. Although it is handy for establishing simple criteria, it does not offer any capabilities beyond what can be done within the formula editor. Ultimately, it's not a loss. Once you get used to using the formula editor, you may end up using it across the board.

Step 4: Formulate the Error Message

Once you've completed the formulation of your error condition, you will need to determine what message will be displayed when that condition is encountered. While this is admittedly straightforward, you may be surprised at the prevalence of error messages present in Salesforce.com orgs today that are ambiguous or simply not useful. If you've ever asked something along the lines of, What in the world does that mean? when running into a system error, you can relate. Here are few suggestions of content to include in your error messages:

    a.   the business rules that are being broken

    b.   the fields at play in the error condition

    c.   the objects at play in the error condition if multiple objects exist in the criteria or update

    d.   the actions required to proceed without triggering the error condition again

    e.   the individuals (e.g., system administrator, developer) needed to resolve the issue if the condition can't be fixed by the end user him or herself

That may seem like it adds up to a verbose error message, but that's typically not the case. You should be able to capture these items within two or three sentences. In this case, you have multiple business rules involved. An effective error message might look like this: "Qualified Leads typically require at least $100,000 of annual revenue and at least 50 employees. If you feel that this Lead is validly qualified, request that "Approved Exception" is checked by the VP of Sales and retry once the exception is granted."

Error Message

Example: | Discount percent cannot exceed 30% |

This message will appear when Error Condition formula is **true**

Error Message | Qualified Leads typically require at least $100,000 of annual revenue and at least 50 employees. If you feel that this Lead is validly qualified, request that "Approved Exception" is checked by the VP of Sales and retry once the exception is granted. |

Figure 5-8. *Provide an error message that has sufficient meaning to your users*

Step 5: Determine the Error Message Location

Now that you have put together a meaningful error message, you'll have to determine where it will be displayed when invoked. As shown in Figure 5-9, Salesforce.com gives you two choices: **Top of Page** or **Field**.

This error message can either appear at the top of the page or below a specific field on the page

Error Location | ⦿ Top of Page ◯ Field ⓘ

This error message can either appear at the top of the page or below a specific field on the page

Error Location | ◯ Top of Page ⦿ Field | Phone ⬍ | ⓘ

Figure 5-9. *Choice between the top of the page or a specific field for the location of the error message*

Both options in the figure will show an error message such as, "Error: invalid data. Review all error messages below to correct your data." However, the field choice will result in the specific validation rule error message appearing just below the selected field instead of at the top with generic error text.

Lead Edit

⭐ **Miguel Jordan**   Help for this

Lead Edit   [Save] [Save & New] [Cancel]

Error: Invalid Data.
Review all error messages below to correct your data.
Phone area code cannot be equal to "123". Please double-check the area code and retry.

Lead Information   ▮ = Required Info

   Lead Owner   Phil Weinmeister   Phone   (123) 123-1234|

Lead Edit

⭐ **Miguel Jordan**   Help for this Page

Lead Edit   [Save] [Save & New] [Cancel]

Error: Invalid Data.
Review all error messages below to correct your data.

Lead Information   ▮ = Required Information

   Lead Owner   Phil Weinmeister   Phone   (123) 123-1234
                                       Error: Phone area code cannot be
                                       equal to "123". Please double-check
                                       the area code and retry.

Figure 5-10. *The different potential locations of your error message*

Salesforce.com recommends that you use the Field option if your validation rule includes only one field; otherwise, it suggests that you choose Top of Page. For the most part, that is the right approach. However, there may be occasions where multiple fields are involved, yet only one of those fields would require a modification by the end user. In that case, you may decide to break from the official suggestion and show the error message next to the corresponding field.

In the case of the Lead qualification example being used in this chapter, the selection of the location is actually irrelevant. If the record update occurs anywhere other than the detail page of the validation rule's object, you will have no control over its display. In the Lead qualification validation rule, we are dealing with the conversion of a Lead, which will occur via the Lead conversion page and not on the Lead detail page itself, as shown in Figure 5-11.

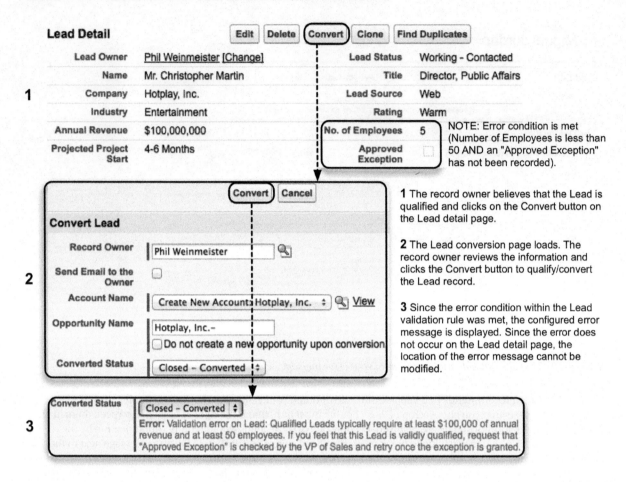

Figure 5-11. *Lead qualification example in which the error message does not appear on the Lead detail page but rather on the Lead conversion page*

A similar situation occurs if a validation rule includes a related object in its error condition formula. Take Figure 5-12, an example that uses the Opportunity Product object, on which the rule criteria exists. However, the Opportunity field included in the criteria (Quantity) is directly impacted by the Opportunity Products that have been added to the corresponding Opportunity record. If we have a validation rule that limits the Opportunity Quantity to one, we will encounter the error condition when trying to add a second Opportunity Product record. Like in the example from Figure 5-11, the error message does not appear on the detail page of the validation rule's object.

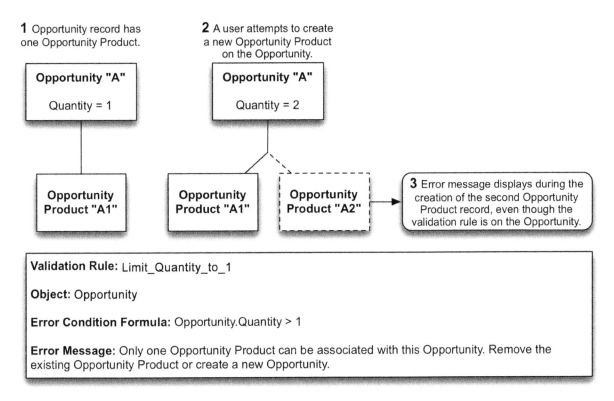

1 Opportunity record has one Opportunity Product.

2 A user attempts to create a new Opportunity Product on the Opportunity.

Opportunity "A"

Quantity = 1

Opportunity "A"

Quantity = 2

Opportunity Product "A1"

Opportunity Product "A1"

Opportunity Product "A2"

3 Error message displays during the creation of the second Opportunity Product record, even though the validation rule is on the Opportunity.

Validation Rule: Limit_Quantity_to_1

Object: Opportunity

Error Condition Formula: Opportunity.Quantity > 1

Error Message: Only one Opportunity Product can be associated with this Opportunity. Remove the existing Opportunity Product or create a new Opportunity.

Figure 5-12. *An Opportunity validation rule for Opportunity Products displayed on the "Add Product(s) to Opportunity" page*

Considerations When Building Validation Rules

There are a few additional factors to take into account when constructing validation rules, and I will go over the important considerations here.

Security Model Impact

While validation rules are not typically heralded as a Salesforce.com security feature, they may impact some of your security-related requirements. It is critical to understand that the error conditions present in an active validation rule cannot be circumvented. They apply to all users, including those with a system administrator profile, they are invoked via all interfaces (i.e., through actions occurring via the standard user interface or API calls), and they are never trumped by any traditional user permission setting. Any exceptions have to be directly established in the validation rule itself. For example, if you want to exempt a User or Profile from being impacted by a validation rule, you would have to include something like, `&& $User.Username <> "bunker.jones@salesforce.com"` or `&& $Profile.Name <> "System Administrator"`. This is not a suggested best practice, but rather an extreme way to handle a specific situation that has no other feasible or quick solution.

Updates to Related Criteria Records

Like you've seen with workflow rules, validation rules allow fields on related objects to be included in the formula. When you have a validation rule that references a Lookup or Master-Detail object, you'll want to be familiar with how the rule is typically invoked. Assume you have a custom Checkbox field called Suspended (API name of "Suspended__c") on the Account object to denote an account that is frozen and cannot be involved in any sales opportunity or interaction. You would create the following conditions for the validation rule:

- **Validation rule:** Prevent_Opportunities_on_Suspended_Accts

- **Object:** Opportunity

- **Error condition formula:** Account.Suspended__c

- **Error message:** You may not add an Opportunity to a suspended Account. Please contact the Finance Manager for additional information.

In this case, the only field included in the error condition formula is a field on a related object (Account). This changes the order of operations to invoke the validation rule. Unlike a rule that only includes fields from the "base object," the error condition can be satisfied on the related object. Here, an Account can have its Suspended flag updated to true and be saved successfully. Don't miss this key point: an Account can have its Suspended flag set to true, but an Opportunity *cannot be added* to an Account with a Suspended flag set to true. This can occur because the validation rule is not on the related object (Account). The validation rule only fires when a record of the object type identified in the rule validation rule's object is created or edited. In this example, that would have to occur on the Opportunity. Figure 5-13 shows this series of events.

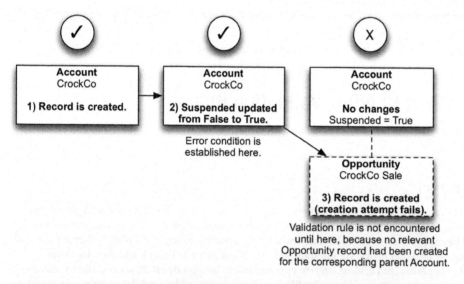

Figure 5-13. *An error condition that is satisfied before a validation rule is encountered*

It is important to understand the difference between this scenario and the one referenced in Figure 5-12. In Figure 5-12, the creation of a Child Opportunity Product record is prevented as a result of a validation rule on the Parent Opportunity record. In that case, the creation of the Opportunity Product directly updates a field on the Parent Opportunity record ("Quantity"). When the Quantity field's value changes on the Opportunity record and satisfies the error condition, the validation rule fires and produces an error message for the user. Since the action originated with an attempt to create an Opportunity Product record, the error will appear on the "Add Product(s) to Opportunity" screen.

Coexistence of Workflow Rules and Validation Rules

You will need to give special attention to your workflow rules when validation rules are present. It is very easy to build workflow rules and validation rules in silos and fail to foresee how they overlap and impact each other. In Figure 5-14, you can see an example of a conflict between a workflow rule and a validation rule.

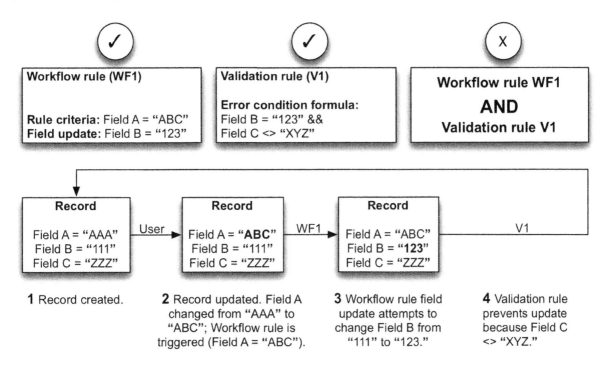

Figure 5-14. *Proceed with caution when you combine validation rules and workflow rules. It is easy to encounter an overlap where a validation rule unexpectedly prevents a Field Update. Make sure that you thoroughly test everything you develop*

In this case, the workflow rule and validation rule "collide." Fortunately, you do have options, and you'll need to decide which route you want to take. To minimize the deviation from the original intention of your workflow rule and validation rule, you may want to consider one of the following approaches:

- Add an additional Field Update to WF1 that sets Field C to "XYZ."
- Leave WF1 and V1 as is but communicate in the error message that Field C will need to be manually updated to "XYZ" before Field A can be set to "ABC."

Error Condition Grouping

When you build validation rules, you have the ability to group error conditions together. This can very beneficial, as it potentially minimizes both the initial development effort and the effort required to modify each of the individual error conditions. However, as you add specific error conditions into your overall error condition formula, keep in mind that the granularity of your error message will inevitably decrease. Take a look at Figure 5-15 to see how this can happen. Here, three fields are included in corresponding error conditions. You can choose to group these into one larger validation rule or to break them out as individual rules. The decision is not one to be made according to a broad generalization. You'll need to review your particular situation and consider your development and maintenance costs and your users' needs as well.

Balancing Development and Maintenance with User Experience

Figure 5-15. *When building validation rules, you can group the rules together (top) or separate them (bottom)*

Existing Error Conditions

It is critical to understand that a newly created or activated validation rule will not directly modify a record that already satisfies the error condition. In other words, validation rules only prevent configured error conditions that exist in updates that occur after that validation rule is in place. In the example in Figure 5-16, an Account was created before a corresponding validation rule was created. The Account record actually satisfies the validation rule's error condition; however, since the Account already existed, it remains intact after the rule is created and activated. The key here is that any *subsequent* modifications to the Account will take the validation rule into consideration, which means that in the next update, the record will need to be modified to *not* meet the error condition.

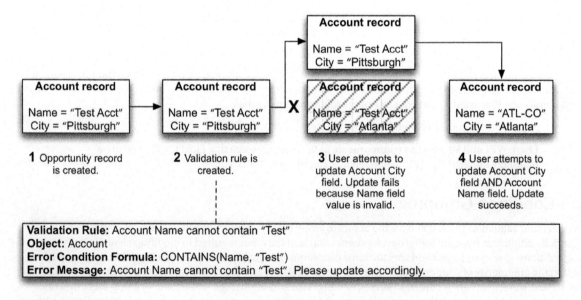

Figure 5-16. *A validation rule that is created when an error condition already exists only impacts the affected records on subsequent updates*

Unavailable Functions

Not all formula functions are available when using the formula editor for validation rules. The following functions cannot be used with validation rules:

- HYPERLINK
- IMAGE
- URLFOR

Note   While there are some unavailable functions within validation rules, VLOOKUP is one function that is *only* available within validation rules. See Chapter 2 for details on this function.

Recap

In this chapter, you have delved into the world of validation rules, and gained an understanding their value for your organization, their relation to business rules, and when to utilize them. You have walked through each step of the rule creation process and identified how to build rules to satisfy related requirements within your organization. To achieve success through creating effective validation rules, make sure that you weigh the key considerations in this chapter and test everything you build thoroughly.

CHAPTER 6

Building Effective Approval Processes for Your Business

When I introduced the previous chapter on validation rules, I made the shocking statement that users of your system are not always perfect. Like you and me, they make mistakes. To help combat a loss of data integrity and prevent general, widespread chaos throughout your org, you learned how to build validation rules to disallow error conditions. Kudos to you on the new skill! However, the scenarios you'll encounter in the real world are not always so cut and dried. While certain conditions can be established in advance as invalid and blocked via validation rules, some conditions still require that special human touch. That's where approval processes come into the picture.

At the most basic level, approval processes allow for the review of a particular state or condition. Excluding a possible "recall" of the review request, the outcome of that request must ultimately emerge as an approval or a rejection. Various real-world scenarios exist that may warrant an approval process. Here are a few examples:

- a sales opportunity that bears an elevated discount beyond a preapproved level

- a new product that is added/submitted and is pending public visibility/consumption

- a support case in an industry with valuable and highly sensitive clients that is pending closure

- a contract that is compiled and prepared for a client's signature

- a new account that is added with certain financial information that warrants confirmation

Like many other facets of Salesforce.com, approval processes can be deceptive because of the speed with which they can be assembled. It's true that Salesforce.com has done an outstanding job of building a framework that significantly eases what could be an overwhelmingly burdensome process. However, your burden still remains—to build an approval process that accurately and efficiently addresses a corresponding business need. You have a number of options when developing an approval process, and I want to make sure you understand all of them clearly. Even for those of you who have experience in this arena, by reading this chapter you'll likely pick up something new that you can bring to the table when working with your customers or fellow employees. By the end of it, you will:

- understand the guiding metadata that serves as the "wrapper" for an approval process

- be familiar with how to limit who can invoke an approval process and under what circumstances

- know how to build a dynamic approval process that is relationship based, not person based

- have learned how to establish a proper flow of the approval process routing

- have walked through a fully detailed, end-to-end review of each step in the creation of an approval process

- comprehend the considerations that should be made when building approval processes

The Flow of a Salesforce.com Approval Process

Before I jump into Salesforce.com-specific terminology and configurations, let me break down the general flow of a Salesforce.com approval process. You should understand each step of the process in detail in order to assist in making it accurate and thorough for your business or your clients. A few questions to ask yourself might be, What am I trying to prevent from occurring by implementing this approval process? and What am I trying to automate as a result of this approval process? Figure 6-1 gives a visual overview of this flow.

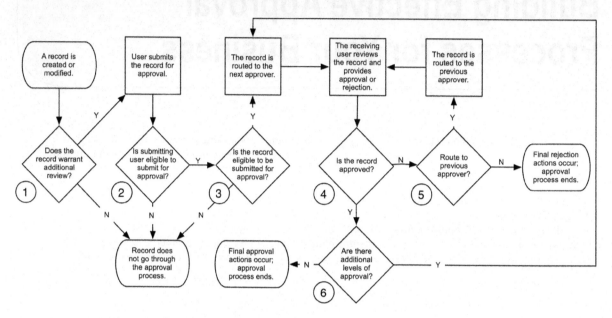

Figure 6-1. *Visual interpretation of flow of general approval process*

I should clarify some considerations about the decision points in Figure 6-1. For each decision point:

1. This decision point should determine whether the record needs to be reviewed (i.e., whether it should be submitted for approval).

2. The user manually submitting the record for approval must be eligible to do so based on the configured criteria. For example, it may be required that the User has a specific Role or is a part of a configured Public Group.

3. The record itself that is submitted for approval must be eligible for submission. The eligibility will be determined based on whether the record meets the configured criteria or, if a formula is used, whether the evaluation for the formula shows that it is true.

4. Once the record is submitted to an approver, that approver will need to make a decision to approve or reject the request.

5. If the request is rejected, the request will either "roll back" to the previous approver or exit the approval process with an ultimate rejection.

6. If a request is approved, subsequent approvers may come into play. If so, the routing process must repeat based on configured settings. Each of the following approvers will review the record and approve or reject the request.

Building a Complex Approval Process

With so many elements making up the overall approval process framework, the variety in the processes that you will create can be extreme. It wouldn't take long to fill up a separate book strictly covering the possible processes that could be built across standard and custom objects. I will set the stage with one specific scenario that could be analogous to what you might encounter in the real world. This will keep the volume of information palatable while avoiding a purely theoretical understanding of approval processes.

Brokerage Support Scenario Overview

Say you work for a brokerage that handles extremely wealthy (and demanding) clients. These clients have a significant amount of money to invest and they do not have the time or patience to deal with ongoing or repeated issues related to their investments. As a result of their sensitivity, improperly or partially resolved issues are seen as completely unacceptable. A Case that is closed without being fully resolved could potentially cost your brokerage millions of dollars. To ensure that Cases are properly resolved, they must go through an approval process immediately preceding their closure. Throughout the chapter, I'll refer to this scenario as the "brokerage support scenario."

Scenario Requirements

In this scenario, I'll assume you've met with stakeholders and gathered the relevant requirements. The following configuration settings establish the primary requirements that will drive the setup of and behavior within the approval process. As I proceed through each key area of the process, I will address a number of other configuration settings not listed here as well.

- **Entry criteria for a Case to be eligible for the approval process**
    - **Status** must equal "Pending Closure Approval."
    - **Type** must not equal "Online Password Reset."
    - **Migrated from Legacy System** (a custom Checkbox field) must not equal TRUE.
- **Initial submitters for Case Closure Approval**
    - The creator of the Case
    - The owner of the Case
    - Users with a Role associated with the customer support organization
    - Users in the Public Group "After-Hours Support"
- **Initial actions**
    - The internal status of a record in the review process will be set to "Closure Review" upon entry into the approval process.
- **Approval steps**
    - The manager of the Case owner (the User identified in the Manager field on the User record associated with the Case owner) must approve the closure of the Case.
    - Case Closure queue members (only if the manager in Step 1 does not have a Role associated with the customer support organization) must approve it.

- Any of the two directors within the customer support organization must approve it.

- Users in the queue containing C-level officers perform the final approval. (Note that if the request is rejected by the chief officers, the Case should be resubmitted to the customer support directors.)

- **Other requirements**

  - A submitted record may not be modified during the approval process, with the exception of changes by Users with the System Administrator profile.

  - Appropriate e-mail notifications will be sent throughout the process.

Initiation of the Approval Process

To start the approval process, you'll first need to kick off its creation. To do so, navigate to **Setup ➤ Create ➤ Workflow & Approvals ➤ Approval Processes**. The first decision you'll have to make when building your approval process will be selecting the appropriate object. Click on "Manage approval processes for:" and select the applicable object (in this example, Case). You can see this drop-down field at the top of Figure 6-2.

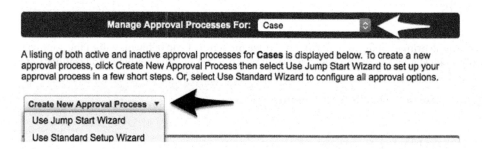

Figure 6-2. After selecting the primary object for your approval process (top), you will be presented with two wizard options (bottom-left) when kicking off the creation of your approval process[1]

Once you have selected the Case, you'll initiate the creation of a Case-specific approval process on the screen shown at the bottom-left of Figure 6-2. Salesforce.com provides two choices: a Jump Start Wizard and a Standard Setup Wizard. For this example, which has a number of intricacies, you will need to use the Standard Setup Wizard.

■ **Note** While the Jump Start Wizard does provide the means to get an approval process up and running very quickly, it is worthwhile to get accustomed to the more robust, thorough Standard Setup Wizard, as a number of settings are not available in the Jump Start Wizard. Ultimately, ensuring that you don't bypass a useful step is preferable to skipping one that you see as unnecessary.

---

[1]All Salesforce.com screenshots in this chapter © copyright Salesforce.com, Inc. Used with permission.

Process Definition Detail

Salesforce.com refers to the primary attributes and metadata belonging to an approval process as the "process definition detail." When you initiate the creation process by selecting the Standard Setup Wizard, you are immediately presented with the configuration settings that comprise the process definition detail. Follow these steps for configuration.

Step 1. Enter Name and Description

As trivial as it may seem, I have to mention that you need to first provide a Process Name (user-facing label), a Unique Name (referenced in the API/Apex), and a Description, as shown in Figure 6-3. As always, resist the temptation to leave the Description field blank; instead, add at least one descriptive sentence that clarifies the process for other users.

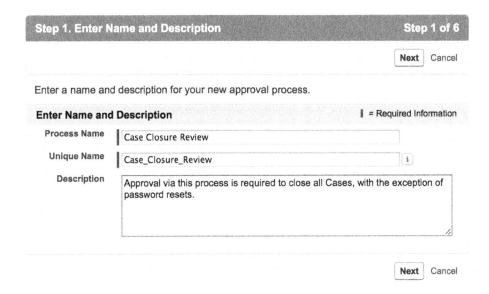

Figure 6-3. *"Enter Name and Description" section for specifying details of your approval process*

Step 2. Specify Entry Criteria

As with the workflow rule criteria, you have a choice of tools when establishing the entry criteria for approval processes: you can use either what I have been referring to as the criteria builder or the formula editor. Many times, the choice comes down to personal preference. However, it may be beneficial to reiterate that the spectrum of criteria combinations you can establish with the criteria builder is only a subset of what can be established with the formula editor. Simple criteria with only a few included statements are best developed with the criteria builder, while anything with complexity is probably best served with the formula editor. I'll go over both options here based on our three requirements for entry criteria. The criteria builder option is shown in Figure 6-4.

Specify Entry Criteria

Use this approval process if the following [criteria are met ⬍]:

Field	Operator	Value	
Case: Status ⬍	equals ⬍	Pending Closure Approval 🔍	AND
Case: Type ⬍	not equal to ⬍	Online Password Reset 🔍	AND
Case: Migrated from Legacy System ⬍	not equal to ⬍	True 🔍	AND
--None-- ⬍	--None-- ⬍		AND
--None-- ⬍	--None-- ⬍		

Add Filter Logic...

Figure 6-4. You can specify criteria to restrict record entry into the approval process in the "Specify Entry Criteria" section

Alternatively, if you wanted to use the formula editor as an option, you could establish the entry criteria via a formula like this:

```
AND(
 ISPICKVAL(Status, "Pending Closure Approval"),
 TEXT(Type) <> "Online Password Reset Request",
 NOT(Migrated_from_Legacy_System__c)
)
```

You may notice that I am not using `ISPICKVAL()` for both Picklists (Status and Type). Since one of the statements involving a Picklist is exclusive, `NOT()` would have to be used in conjuction with `ISPICKVAL()`. To simplify the formula and avoid the function combination, I used `TEXT()` with `<>` instead. For this example, the criteria builder will be sufficient for configuring the entry criteria, so that will be used as the active criteria tool.

Step 3. Specify Approver Field and Record Editability Properties

In this step, you'll need to consider the automated determination of approvers for the approval steps you will create and select a field specifying the appropriate approver, as shown in Figure 6-5. "Automated" corresponds to a relative relationship here. It's one thing to specify a User or a Role for approval; it's another to say that a User related to another User (whether the submitting User of the Case or the Case owner) should be the approver. You don't necessarily know who that individual would be at the time of submission; automated approval configuration allows you to define this relative relationship. In this case, you will want the manager of the Case owner to approve the Case, so you must set the field to "Manager." Additionally, since the manager is relative to the Case owner, not the Case submitter, you'll need to check off the Use Approver Field of Case Owner Checkbox, as done in Figure 6-5.

Select Field Used for Automated Approval Routing

Next Automated Approver Determined By | Manager   ⊕ | i |

Use Approver Field of Case Owner   ✓

Figure 6-5. *In this chapter's example, you want to have the Case Owner's manager approve the request, so select "Manager" for Automated Approver and check the box for Case Owner*

In the same step, you'll determine the "editability" of the record being submitted for approval. You have two choices: Users with a profile of "System Administrator" only, or System Administrators and the current approver. In this example, you want to restrict this to System Administrators only.

Record Editability Properties

◉ Administrators **ONLY** can edit records during the approval process.
○ Administrators **OR** the currently assigned approver can edit records during the approval process.

Figure 6-6. *You may choose whether System Administrators only or both admins and the current approver can edit the record during the approval process*

Step 4. Select Notification Templates

For a truly thorough approval process, you will need to ensure that the proper communication occurs to notify the individuals involved in the process. While I'm not dedicating a unique chapter to creating notification templates in this book, I'll cover them here at a basic level to get you started. In this scenario, you will need to create a custom notification template to be sent to potential approvers that contains key information about the request. Not only does this notification expedite the process by providing immediate awareness of the request, but also it allows the individual to start the decision-making process by conveying the request details via email.

■ **Note** If you decide not to build a custom notification template, a default template will be sent to the approver(s). This template will contain a link that takes the approver(s) to a page where the approval or rejection can be completed.

In order to create a new custom Email template, start by navigating to **Setup ► Communication Templates ► Email Templates** and clicking "New Template." Here, you will be presented with four choices: Text, HTML (using Letterhead), Custom (without using Letterhead), and Visualforce. When done correctly, HTML and Visualforce will always be more aesthetically pleasing than simple text notifications. However, you must weigh your business needs with the estimated level of effort required any time you are building solutions in Salesforce.com. In this case, you're dealing with an internal notification; corresponding beautification of an internal Email template will infrequently be considered a hard requirement. If you already have a letterhead or you are quick with HTML/Visualforce, go for it. Here, you will be creating a simple text-base e-mail notification.

The next part of creating a template is to configure the metadata (Template Name, Folder, etc.). Make sure that the template is marked as "Available for Use" and in a nonprivate folder. Once you've taken care of that, it's on to the Subject and Body of your Email template. To provide the approver with the most relevant information possible, you will want to take advantage of merge fields to pull in information from the Case record dynamically.

The Subject field text should be clear and contain some identifying information. For example, the message "Case 1234 is pending closure and requires your review" provides a unique piece of data and clearly communicates what is needed from the recipient. Since Case Number is Case-specific, a merge field will be needed. Figure 6-7 shows the "Available Merge Fields" section. Select "Case Fields" for the Field Type, then "Case Number" for the Field.

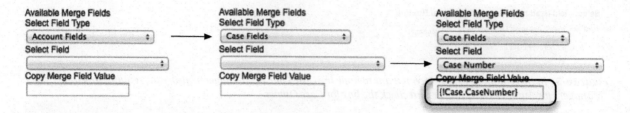

Figure 6-7. *The Available Merge Fields section allows you to select the Field Type and Field to generate a Merge Field value that you will include in your Email template*

Once you've generated the merge field value, you can then set the subject line of your Email to the following: `Case {!Case.CaseNumber} is pending closure and requires your review`. In the Email body, you'll need to provide more detail. You can include the following fields:

1. **Case Owner:** `{!Case.OwnerFullName}`

2. **Case Subject:** `{!Case.Subject}`

3. **Case Account:** `{!Case.Account}`

4. **Case Contact:** `{!Case.Contact}`

5. **Case Type:** `{!Case.Type}`

6. **Case Reason:** `{!Case.Reason}`

7. **Case Resolution Details (custom field):** `{!Case.Case_Resolution_Details__c}`

8. **Case URL:** `{!Case.Link}`

The final template body might look something like this:

```
Case {!Case.CaseNumber} is pending closure and requires your review. Please note the following:

Case Owner: {!Case.OwnerFullName}
Case Subject: {!Case.Subject}
Case Account: {!Case.Account}
Case Contact: {!Case.Contact}
Case Type: {!Case.Type}
Case Reason: {!Case.Reason}
Case Resolution Details: {!Case.Case_Resolution_Details__c}

To further review the Case and provide your approval decision, please click here: {!Case.Link}.
```

Assuming you use a template name of "Case Closure Approval," you will set the Email template as shown in Figure 6-8.

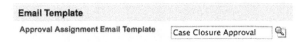

Figure 6-8. *The "Email Template" section allows you to select the template to be used to notify each approver of the pending request*

■ **Note** Salesforce.com actually provides an additional means to notify potential approvers of a pending approval request. A Home Page Component called Items to Approve can be added to the Home Page Layout (**Setup ➤ Home ➤ Home Page Components**). This is a great complement to the Email template, as it does not require any action or visibility outside of Salesforce.com. I would definitely suggest adding this component if you utilize the home page for your users.

Step 5. Select Fields to Display on Approval Page Layout

When an approver initiates the process to approve or reject a request, she is presented with a page that contains information corresponding to the record submitted for approval. While you don't want to add the kitchen sink to the layout of the page, you want to add a sufficient amount of data in order to provide enough information for the reviewer to be able to make a decision on the approval request without having to navigate to the record directly. There's nothing wrong with the reviewer accessing the record directly to gain additional context; however, a streamlined process that does not require her to step outside the intended flow will save time and bring a little happiness to your users. The fields you'll use will closely resemble those included in the Email template you just created. Here is a suggested list of fields you may want to consider including: Case Number, Case Owner, Account Name, Contact Name, Subject, Description, Type, Case Reason, and Case Resolution Details.

Additionally, you will have to decide whether to show the history of all previous approval decisions for this record. Typically, there is no reason to omit this information and it can prove to be helpful. The example shown in Figure 6-9 is set to include the approval decision history.

Figure 6-9. *The "Approval Page Fields" section gives you the option to include the approval history on the approval page layout*

As the final piece in the Definition Detail process, you're required to identify the security settings of the approval page, as shown in Figure 6-10. If you need to provide mobile access, you'll have to select the second option. Do keep in mind that you cannot combine this selection with the ability to manually identify an approver.

Security Settings

◉ Allow approvers to access the approval page only from within the salesforce.com application. (Recommended)
○ Allow approvers to access the approval page from within the salesforce.com application, or externally from a wireless-enabled mobile device. ⓘ

Figure 6-10. *The "Security Settings" section allows you to limit access to the interface to those in the Salesforce.com application or to extend access to wireless devices*

Step 6. Specify Initial Submitters

When building an approval process, a critical question to answer is, Who should be able to submit the record for approval? It's very rare that you will want to grant this ability to all internal users. You may even want to limit the potential users to as few as one (possibly the Case owner). In this case, the requirements listed earlier in the chapter warrant selection of a few different users and groups. Figure 6-11 shows the Available Submitters and Allowed Submitters lists, giving you the option to limit who will be allowed to submit for approval.

Figure 6-11. *Configured list of initial submitters that will be allowed to submit the Case for approval*

You will also have to decide whether to allow recalls of the approval request. Many times, you will want to do this. In this case, the process is tight and there should not be a reason to recall a request once submitted. Do not provide the ability to recall the request in this example; however, this will be driven by your organization's requirements in your own real-world scenarios.

Recap of Process Definition

Let's take a breather and review what you've completed so far. All of the routing and resulting actions are yet to come. Figure 6-12 gives a view of the process definition you just configured.

Process Definition Detail [Edit ▼] [Clone] [Delete] [View Diagram]

Process Name	Case Closure Review
Active	☐ ⓘ
Unique Name	Case_Closure_Review
Next Automated Approver Determined By	Manager of Record Owner
Description	Approval via this process is required to close all Cases, with the exception of password resets.
Entry Criteria	(Case: Status EQUALS Pending Closure Approval) AND (Case: Type NOT EQUAL TO Online Password Reset) AND (Case: Migrated from Legacy System NOT EQUAL TO True)
Record Editability	Administrator **ONLY**
Allow Submitters to Recall Approval Requests	☐
Approval Assignment Email Template	Case Closure Approval
Initial Submitters	Record Creator, Case Owner, Role: Customer Support, International, Role: Customer Support, North America, Role: SVP, Customer Service & Support, Group: After Hours Support

Figure 6-12. *A view of the "Process Definition Detail" screen after configuration*

Initial Submission Actions

Once you have provided what can be roughly interpreted as the metadata of your approval process (the process definition detail), you will start building out the specific individual steps. The first step contains what are referred to as Initial Submission Actions. These actions always occur when the record enters the approval process, with no exceptions.

When building your own process, you'll want to consider adding different types of two high-level features: temporary changes to reflect the state of the record and events to communicate the fact that a review is underway. Some examples may include:

- a field update to a status field

- an Email Alert sent to the Case owner or another interested party

- a call-out to another system to reflect the event

To meet the requirements in the brokerage support scenario previously described, you will be updating the Status field from "Pending Closure Approval" to "Closure Review" to ensure that the current state is clear to all parties. Figure 6-13 shows the initial configuration of the "Field Update Edit" screen, which is followed by "Initial Submission Actions," which comes after the update in Figure 6-14.

Figure 6-13. *Configuration of the "Field Update Edit" screen associated with the Initial Submission action*

Initial Submission Actions ⓘ	Add Existing	Add New ▼	
Action	**Type**		**Description**
	Record Lock		Lock the record from being edited
Edit | Remove	Field Update		Set Status to Closure Review

Figure 6-14. *"Initial Submission Actions" section following completion of configuration*

Approval Steps

Before diving in to the approval steps, I want to point out how much has already been covered before ever touching them. While the approval steps are the crux of the Salesforce.com approval process, there's much more to think about than simply who approves the process and in what order. Without the right foundation for your process, the approval steps won't do you much good. I will walk through each of the previously established requirements to identify the approval sequence and recipients, and explain the configuration approach and reasoning along the way. Figure 6-15 presents an overview of the approval flow.

If manager in step 1 does not have a customer support-related Role, proceed to step 2. Otherwise, skip to step 3.

Proceed to step 4 if Case is escalated. If Case is not escalated, closure is approved.

Figure 6-15. *Approval flow for the brokerage support scenario*

Approval Step 1

The first approval step, based on the criteria described in the "Scenario Requirements" section, involves dynamic routing; you want the Case owner's manager, not a specified individual, to receive the request. To do so, provide the Name, Description, and Step Number for the manager, as shown in Figure 6-16. To navigate directly to this screen, click on the "New Approval Step" button on the main Approval Process screen.

Approval Process Name	Case Closure Review
Name	Manager Review
Unique Name	Manager_Review [i]
Description	Route to Case Owner's manager for review.
Step Number	1

Figure 6-16. *Providing Name, Description, and Step Number for dynamic routing*

When you get to "Specify Step Criteria," shown in Figure 6-17, leave the default setting indicating that all records should enter through this approval step (there are no exceptions).

Specify Step Criteria

- ◉ All records should enter this step.
- ○ Enter this step if the following [criteria are met ↕], else [approve record ↕]:

Figure 6-17. *Specifying step criteria*

Your previous work pays off in the next part of the step. Since you already set the Case owner's manager as the dynamic approver, you simply have to select the provided option for this choice. You don't have any requirements to provide access to delegates so you can leave that unchecked throughout this chapter. This is shown in Figure 6-18.

Select Approver

- ○ Let the submitter choose the approver manually.
- ◉ Automatically assign using the user field selected earlier. (**Manager**)
- ○ Automatically assign to queue. [   ] 🔍
- ○ Automatically assign to approver(s).

- ☐ The approver's delegate may also approve this request. [i]

Figure 6-18. *Selection of approver*

Your approval step is complete. You are then prompted to associate an action with an approval or a rejection corresponding to this step. I'll assume you want to create an action associated with an approval to communicate each of your approval process updates to the Case owner to keep him informed. You can build an Email template to do this and configure it for each approval step by following the prompt in Figure 6-19.

You have just created an approval step. You can optionally specify workflow actions to occur upon approval or rejection of this step. Would you like to do that now?

- ⦿ Yes, I'd like to create a new approval action for this step now. [Email Alert   ⬍]
- ○ Yes, I'd like to create a new rejection action for this step now. [Task   ⬍]
- ○ No, I'll do this later. Take me to the approval process detail page to review what I've just created.

Figure 6-19. *Next steps after creating the approval step*

Your Email Alert settings might look something like this:

- **Description:** "Notify Case Owner of incremental approval."
- **Unique name:** "Notify_Case_Owner_of_Incremental_Approval"
- **Email template:** "Additional Closure approval received."
- **Recipient type:** Owner
- **Selected recipients:** Case Owner
- **From Email Address:** Current User's Email Address

Congrats! Your first approval step is complete (see Figure 6-20).

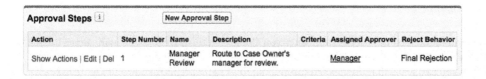

Action	Step Number	Name	Description	Criteria	Assigned Approver	Reject Behavior
Show Actions | Edit | Del	1	Manager Review	Route to Case Owner's manager for review.		Manager	Final Rejection

Figure 6-20. *Approval Step 1 completed*

Approval Step 2

Click on "New Approval Step" to proceed. In this step, you'll first need to filter the records that will be allowed to proceed through this step, routing some of them directly to this step. The criteria established for this step in the "Scenario Requirements" section is that if the Case owner's manager does not have a Role associated with the customer support organization, the Case would need to be reviewed by a User in the Case Closure queue. The format is just like you saw with workflow rules—you have a choice of using the criteria builder or the formula editor. I would suggest using the formula editor here. You can set your formula to this for the brokerage support scenario example:

```
NOT(CONTAINS(LastModifiedBy.UserRole.Name, "Customer Support")) && NOT(CONTAINS(LastModifiedBy.UserRole.Name, "Customer Service"))
```

Once you've determined the criteria, you'll set the queue as the next recipient. Note that a new option, "Reject Behavior," appears. This gives you the ability to send a rejected record back a level. However, based on the requirements, you should leave the default setting set to perform all rejection action and final rejection actions. See Figure 6-21 for a view of the "Select Approver" and "Reject Behavior" sections.

Select Approver

◯ Let the submitter choose the approver manually.

◯ Automatically assign using the user field selected earlier. (**Manager**)

◉ Automatically assign to queue. [Case Closure Queue] 🔍

◯ Automatically assign to approver(s).

☐ The approver's delegate may also approve this request. ⓘ

Reject Behavior

What should happen if the approver rejects this request?

◉ Perform all rejection actions for this step **AND** all final rejection actions. (Final Rejection)

◯ Perform **ONLY** the rejection actions for this step and send the approval request back to the most recent approver. (Go Back 1 Step)

Figure 6-21. Approval Step 2: "Select Approver" and "Reject Behavior" options

Just associate the existing Email alert with Step 2, and you're all done!

Approval Step 3

Step 3 involves routing to two individuals at one time, as outlined in the "Scenario Requirements" section in this chapter. One great option that Salesforce.com provides is the ability to choose whether both of these approvers are required or only one (in which case, the first one to review the record makes the call). Let's go with the latter option and only require approval from one of the two Customer Support directors.

For the "Select Approver" option, select "Automatically assign to approver(s)" and click the lookup icon, as done in Figure 6-22. One at a time, select each director. Since you don't require unanimous approval, you'll leave the default option selected allowing the first response to determine the overall decision for this step.

◉ Automatically assign to approver(s).

| User ⇕ | Richard James | 🔍 |
| User ⇕ | Kelly Medesto | 🔍 |

Add Row Remove Row

When multiple approvers are selected:
◉ Approve or reject based on the **FIRST** response.
◯ Require **UNANIMOUS** approval from all selected approvers.

Figure 6-22. Approval Step 3: Selection of multiple approvers using only one response

Approval Step 4

Step 4 reintroduces the need for prequalification. You want to determine whether the Case is escalated or not; if it is, it requires an additional approval from one of your c-level officers. Since the criterion is singular and straightforward, the criteria builder will be sufficient. Figure 6-23 shows the section in which you will enter the step criteria.

Specify Step Criteria

○ All records should enter this step.

● Enter this step if the following [criteria are met ⬍] :

Field		Operator		Value	
Case: Escalated ⬍		equals ⬍		True	🔍

Figure 6-23. Approval Step 4: Specifying step criteria

While you've seen the queue selection in a previous approval step, you will change the reject behavior here. You will indicate that, if the C-level officers reject this request, it will need to go back down one level for further review. You can configure this by selecting the second option in the "Reject Behavior" section in Figure 6-24.

Select Approver

○ Let the submitter choose the approver manually.

○ Automatically assign using the user field selected earlier. (**Manager**)

● Automatically assign to queue. [Chief Officers] 🔍

○ Automatically assign to approver(s).

☐ The approver's delegate may also approve this request. [i]

Reject Behavior

What should happen if the approver rejects this request?

○ Perform all rejection actions for this step **AND** all final rejection actions. (Final Rejection)

● Perform **ONLY** the rejection actions for this step and send the approval request back to the most recent approver. (Go Back 1 Step)

Figure 6-24. Filling in Approval Step 4: "Select Approver" and "Reject Behavior" sections

You have completed your four approval steps! Figure 6-25 is a view from the approval process detail page.

Approval Steps [i]

Action	Step Number	Name	Description	Criteria	Assigned Approver	Reject Behavior
Show Actions | Edit	1	Manager Review	Route to Case Owner's manager		Manager	Final Rejection
Show Actions | Edit	2	Queue Review	Route to Case Closure Queue if Case Owner's Manager is not in CS	NOT(CONTAINS(LastModifiedBy.UserRole.Name, "Customer Support")) && NOT(CONTAINS(LastModifiedBy.UserRole.Name, "Customer Service"))	Queue:Case Closure Queue	Final Rejection
Show Actions | Edit	3	CS Directors Review	Route to Customer Support Directors		Approval based on first response User: Richard James, Kelly Medesto	Final Rejection
Show Actions | Edit	4	C-Level Review	Route to C-Level Queue if Case is Escalated	Case: Escalated EQUALS True	Queue:Chief Officers	Go Back 1 Step

Figure 6-25. Completed approval steps

Final Actions

It is critical to properly establish the actions that will correspond to specific events in your approval process once it's underway. In specific, there are three actions to consider:

- Final Approval Actions

- Final Rejection Actions

- Recall Actions

For some organizations, the stamp of approval itself may be sufficient. However, I would recommend also considering both status updates and communication via e-mail, at the very least. You will want to clear the Case Resolution Details field we used in this example, since this information is no longer relevant or accurate. Figure 6-26 gives a view of the flow of these final actions and Figure 6-27 shows the configuration steps necessary to implement them. To navigate to the appropriate configuration screen, click on the "Add Existing" button in either the "Final Rejection Actions" or "Final Approval Actions" section on the record detail page of the approval process.

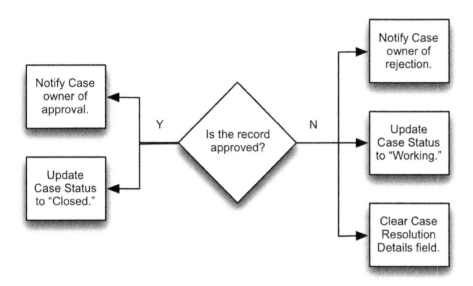

Figure 6-26. *Flow of actions related to final decisions*

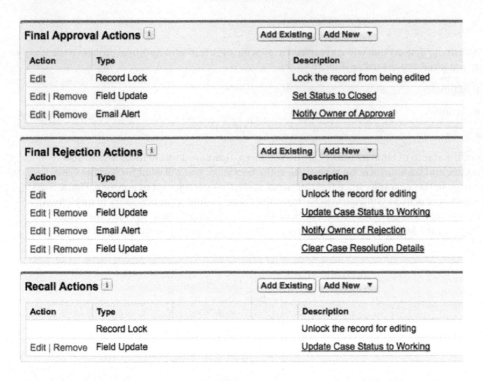

Figure 6-27. *Configuration for final actions*

Once you activate the approval process, it is live and in effect.

Further Considerations

Here are a few additional considerations to keep in mind when creating approval processes.

Submit for Approval Button

When dealing with the approval processes, the "Submit for Approval" button can catch you off guard. Even once your approval process is activated, you must add this button to the corresponding Page Layout(s). Without it, users cannot manually initiate the approval process. To add the button, enter the Page Layout editor, select "Buttons" on the left, and drag the "Submit for Approval" button down to the "Standard Buttons" section, as shown in Figure 6-28.

Figure 6-28. *Adding the "Submit for Approval" button to all applicable page layouts*

Invalid Submission Details

Unfortunately, Salesforce.com does not provide specific instructions for users who submit a record that does not meet the entry criteria. So, if a particular field needs to be set properly, the user would not be told how to do so when encountering an error. To complicate the situation, the error message applies not only to records with invalid entry criteria but also to submitters not included in the valid list of initial submitters. The vague error message you get when the program is unable to submit a record for approval is shown in Figure 6-29.

Unable to Submit for Approval

This record does not meet the entry criteria or initial submitters of any active approval processes. Please contact your administrator for assistance.

Click here to return to the previous page.

Figure 6-29. *Error message that appears when you haven't met entry criteria or when you're not included in the list of allowed initial submitters*

Initiation of Process

With some Apex coding, you can definitely automate the submission of a record for approval within a configured approval process. Since I'm not addressing extensions of the platform via code, I'll assume that you will use the standard manual approach. This means that your users need to understand that an approval will always require the click of a button, without exception. Make sure you communicate the functionality clearly to your audience.

Validation Rules

Status is usually a critical component of any effective approval process. Your entry criteria allow you to restrict the allowed Status field values for users at the time of submission, which is great. However, you'll need to think through the overall process and may need to supplement it with one or more validation rules to ensure proper flow. For example, in the example scenario used in this chapter, you would want to restrict users from manually changing the status to "Closed," as that would defeat the purpose of the approval process. Think through your flow and add validation rules as needed.

Workflow Rules

Since field updates are commonly an element of approval processes, you will want to make sure that any overlaps with existing workflow rules are expected and desired. An approval process may work perfectly as configured; however, if you forget about a workflow rule related to one of the field updates that occurs at the point of final approval, you will likely have some undesired updates and unhappy users.

Recap

In this chapter, you reviewed the bulk of what Salesforce.com offers for declaratively building approval processes for records that warrant some special handling. You walked through a real-life scenario in order to bring some life to the various steps and settings, including: entry criteria, initial submitters, notification Emails, Initial Submission actions, approval steps, implementing approval steps, and final actions. To round out the chapter, I offered you some tips and additional considerations that might come in handy when building out your own approval processes.

▉ ▉ ▉

CHAPTER 7

Use Entitlements and Milestones to Drive Case Automation

Salesforce.com's Entitlement Management feature (utilizing entitlements and milestones) is a bit of an outsider in the world of Salesforce.com configuration and development. While it's likely that most of you familiar with the power of the Force.com platform have heard of entitlements and milestones, it's probably a safer bet that you have not yet touched them from an admin perspective yourself. Unless you're fortunate enough to have spare time to research different areas of Salesforce.com at your leisure, you'll want to know that this topic is relevant to you and can bring potential value when building future solutions. Here's a quick test to see if that's your situation:

- Do you work with Salesforce.com Cases?

- Do you use workflow rules and corresponding actions in your solutions?

- Does your clientele or organization require the precise timing of automated system behavior?

You may be asking why there's no mention of Service Contracts in the previous paragraph, since entitlements and milestones are commonly associated with them and occasionally also Contract Line Items. There's no question that you'll want to take advantage of entitlements and milestones if the products or services you support have different levels of service, either per customer or per product. However, I'm going to look at entitlements and milestones from a different perspective here. They are actually quite analogous to time-based workflow rules, but they have one huge advantage: timing granularity. I can't overstate how valuable this is, but hopefully you'll catch on after reading this.

Action Timing Within Salesforce.com

Before I examine what's so great about entitlements and milestones for Case Management, let me describe the shortcomings of related Salesforce.com functionality in regard to how asynchronous timing is handled. There are two areas in which this applies:

- escalation rules

- time-based workflow rules (and corresponding actions)

There are two attributes, in particular, that I would like to contrast with entitlements and milestones:

- the minimum interval between the triggering event and corresponding action

- the potential variance between expected and actual minimum intervals

Minimum Interval Between Triggering Event and Action

The first attribute that warrants a comparison is the minimum amount of time between the event that "kicks off" an escalation rule or a time-based workflow rule and the corresponding action that it triggers. Take a look at how the following three triggered actions compare in terms of timing in Figure 7-1.

Figure 7-1. *The earliest possible action is based on the triggering event and varies by source*

The intervals in the figure speak for themselves. While with escalation rules and time-based workflow rules, you can only configure an action 30–60 minutes out; with entitlements and milestones, you can configure an action to occur literally 1 minute after the triggering event. Simply put, that's awesome.

■ **Note**   Case escalation rules can only trigger owner changes and Email alerts; unlike workflow rules, they cannot drive automated updates of any fields other than the Case Owner field.

Variance Between Expected and Actual Minimum Intervals

The potential disparity between the expected time intervals and the actual timing of the triggered action shown in the previous figure is another critical consideration when automating your business processes. The intervals of 60 minutes, 30 minutes, and 1 minute depicted are what you configure for the corresponding actions. However, the expected time does not always match the actual interval that occurs. Figure 7-2 shows the percentage of potential variance between the actual time it takes to trigger an action and the time that it is expected to take, as it applies to both time-based workflow rules and entitlements and milestones.

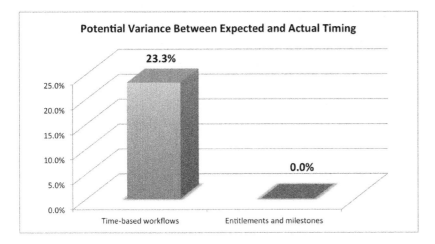

Figure 7-2. *The actual timing of an automated action may vary quite a bit when using time-based workflow rules*

If you're wondering what in the world I'm talking about, let me explain. A subtle, but critical, detail that you need to know about when considering declarative timing is Salesforce.com's "batching" of pending timed actions. All is not as it seems when it comes to action timing. Figure 7-3 shows a Case workflow rule with a time trigger set to fire one hour after the triggering event.

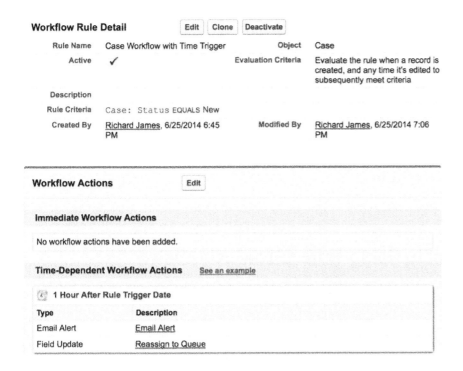

Figure 7-3. *A workflow rule with a time trigger set to fire one hour after the date and time of the triggering event*[1]

---

[1]All Salesforce.com screenshots in this chapter © copyright Salesforce.com, Inc. Used with permission.

Let's say a new Case is created at 3:16 p.m. Based on the workflow rule we just looked at, you would assume that the action would occur at 4:16 p.m., right? Well, think again. Salesforce.com executes these time-based actions only at certain hourly intervals, not in real time as they are configured, as depicted in Figure 7-4. Salesforce.com does not publish these times, but based on my personal experience, they occur at the following times: :00, :15, :30, and :45. To be clear, the times set up are exact times on the hour (e.g., 1:00, 1:15, etc.), not intervals relative to the time at which you input the data (e.g., 1:07, 1:22, etc.). That would mean that this particular Case would trigger actions that would eventually fire at 4:30—which is 74 minutes after the event instead of 60. Again, this is not official information but is what has been observed within Salesforce.com. So, if you're looking for a precise solution, count time-based workflows and Case escalations out.

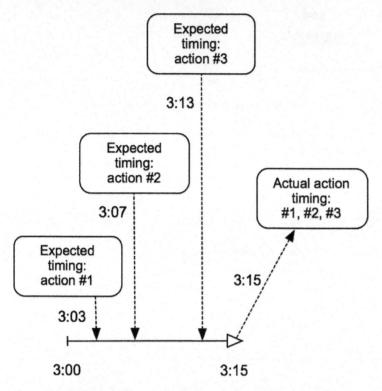

Figure 7-4. *Three pending timed actions will occur at 3:15, not at the exact time between 3:00–3:15 queued by the User*

A Creative Approach to Using Time-Based Workflows

Even though by default, you can only configure an action to take place a minimum of one hour from the triggering event, with a little creativity you can work around that. Using this approach, you can actually configure a time-based workflow to fire an action one minute after the triggering event.

Instead of setting your action relative to a current or future date and time, why not configure it relative to a time in the past? Figure 7-5 shows the creation of a custom Date/Time field with the formula editor that allows setting a default time in the past.

Field Label ┃Workflow Time Reference ⓘ

Field Name ┃Workflow_Time_Reference ⓘ

Description A custom date/time field that will be set to 59 minutes before the creation date/time of the Case

Help Text ⓘ

Required ☐ Always require a value in this field in order to save a record

Default Value Show Formula Editor
NOW() - (59*1/24/60)
Use formula syntax: e.g., Text in double quotes: "hello", Number: 25, Percent as decimal: 0.10, Date expression: Today() + 7

Figure 7-5. *You can create a custom field and use the formula editor to set a default date and time to use in conjunction with a time trigger*

The field shown in the previous figure will always be set to occur 59 minutes before the date and time that the Case is opened. You can then set the field shown in Figure 7-6 to be used for your time trigger.

Workflow Time Trigger Edit

Workflow Rule   Case Workflow w/ Time Trigger

┃1   Hours ⬍   After ⬍   Case: Workflow Time Reference ⬍

Save   Cancel

Figure 7-6. *A new custom field that can be used to retroactively set the time trigger*

While you can decrease the initial interval between event and triggered action, the potential delay does not change. For example, using this custom field, your action would occur one to fourteen minutes after the triggering event, which is a huge variance.

I use all of these examples to set up the argument for using entitlements and milestones for time-based actions that need to occur for your Cases. Remember, you can set an action for one minute after an event and, maybe more importantly, it will actually occur at that minute (or a few seconds after).

Setting up Entitlements and Milestones to Meet Your Action-Timing Needs

Now that I've exhausted the subject of why to consider entitlements and milestones for Case-related automation, I will walk you through how to set up each of the related elements. Navigate to **Setup ➤ Customize ➤ Entitlement Management ➤ Settings** and check off Enable Entitlement Management if you haven't already done so. Once you enable Entitlement Management, you'll be presented with additional settings, as shown in Figure 7-7. For now, you can leave them alone.

Entitlement Versioning   ▌ = Required Information

Entitlement versioning lets you make changes to existing entitlement processes.

> ⚠ Once you enable entitlement versioning, you can't disable it. Entitlement versioning will
> remain enabled even if you disable entitlement management.

☐ Enable Entitlement Versioning

Entitlements-Related Lookup Filters on Cases

Lookup filters help ensure data quality by limiting the items returned in lookup fields. Select the
items you'd like returned in entitlements-related lookup fields on cases.

Asset Lookup - Limit to assets with:
☐ Same account on the case
☐ Same contact on the case
☐ Active entitlements on the case's account
☐ Active entitlements on the case's contact

Entitlement Lookup - Limit to entitlements with:
☐ Active Status
☐ Same account on the case
☐ Same asset on the case
☐ Same contact on the case

Figure 7-7. *You can initially leave the Entitlement Management settings as is (with the default settings in place)*

You will need to create your milestone before getting to the additional settings. To set up the milestone, navigate
to **Setup ➤ Customize ➤ Entitlement Management ➤ Milestones** and click the "New Milestone" button. You will be
brought to the "Milestone Edit" screen, as shown in Figure 7-8.

Milestone Edit   [Save] [Save & New] [Cancel]

Name | 5 Minute Escalation

Description | Milestone to occur at 5 minutes after Case creation

Recurrence | No Recurrence ✦
Type

Figure 7-8. *A new milestone record*

Next, it's on to **Setup ➤ Customize ➤ Entitlement Management ➤ Entitlement Process**. From here, click the
"New Entitlement Process" button and you will get to the "Entitlement Process Detail" screen, as shown in Figure 7-9.
Leave in place the default values for "Case enters the process" and "Case exits the process."

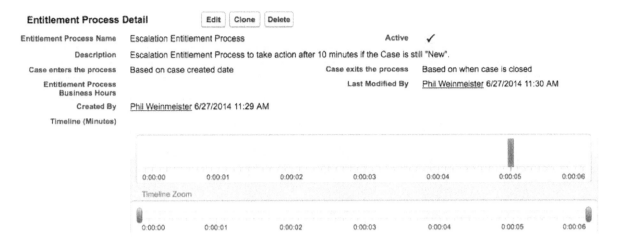

Figure 7-9. *Creating an entitlement process for your milestones*

Once you set up the entitlement process, you'll need to incorporate the milestone that you created. To do so, on the "Entitlement Process Detail" page, scroll down to "Milestone" and click "New." This will bring you to the "Milestone Detail" page (shown in Figure 7-10).

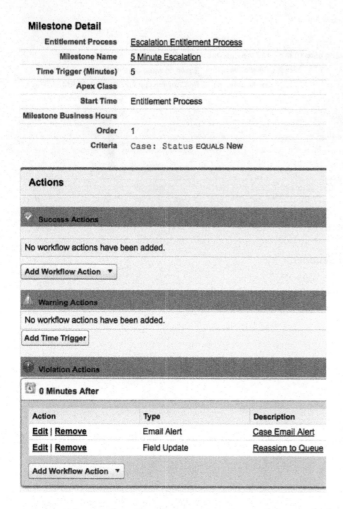

Figure 7-10. *Once you create the entitlement process, you'll need to add a milestone entry within it*

Here, the milestone has been created with criteria of Status EQUALS New. This will result in the milestone being removed from the case when the status progresses past "New," which is what you want. There is no need to trigger an event based on meeting the milestone; it is just necessary when you miss it. In this case, missing the milestone will result in an Email alert and a reassignment. You will need to create those workflow actions after creating the Entitlement Milestone and associate them with Violation Action.

___

■ **Note** You will need to consider Field-level Security settings for a slew of standard case fields that are automatically created when you enable Entitlement Management. For this example, you will need to make the Entitlement Name field editable at the very least.

___

Creating an Entitlement Record

Since in this example we're not concerned with entitlements and milestones from the perspective of applying service contracts or support levels, we want the new Escalation Process record to apply to all records across the board. To make this happen, you'll need to create an actual Entitlement (not entitlement process) record and then associate it with the entitlement process record you created earlier.

This use of Entitlements is an extension of the original intention of entitlements and milestones, so some of the fields don't apply. Even one of the required fields (Account) has no actual bearing on how the functionality works. The main fields you will need to consider are:

- **Entitlement Name**: (Required) Make sure to populate this field with a meaningful description.

- **Account Name**: (Required) This field is actually irrelevant for this example, but you must populate it. Select any account to do so.

- **Entitlement Process**: Select the entitlement process that you created earlier.

- **Status/Status Icon**: This is a read-only formula field.

- **Start Date**: Set the date to a current or earlier date to activate the process.

Figure 7-11 shows a condensed page layout with the key fields populated.

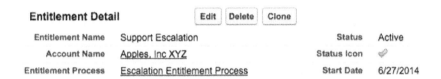

Figure 7-11. *"Entitlement Detail" screen allowing you to create a new Entitlement that is associated with the Entitlement Process*

Case Page Layout Considerations

Each Case will need to be associated with an Entitlement record. While this can be done with a "before insert" Apex trigger that updates the Entitlement Lookup field to the Entitlement record you previously created, I will continue to avoid using code and instead suggest simply adding the Entitlement Name field to your page layout. To do so, you will need to set the Entitlement Name as required within your page layout. This will ensure that the proper Entitlement is created each time a Case is created. Of course, if Cases are created through other interfaces, you'll need to think through that, as well. A validation rule may also be helpful to ensure that no Case is created with a blank Entitlement Name field. Overall, using an Apex trigger is ideal if it's feasible.

Additionally, you may want to drop the related "Case Milestones" list onto your Case page layout. However, consider this option carefully, as the related list doesn't perfectly correspond to what you are building here. The list is more for the traditional use of Entitlement and Milestones, showing whether each milestone has been met or not. If a milestone has been met in this scenario, you don't need to see the detail; it only helps if the milestone has not been met. The list is useful for seeing the remaining time, but having it could also confuse users. Make sure it will make sense to your audience if you do place it on the page layout.

Your Entitlement and Milestone: Live and In Effect

The next step is to create a new Case. Whether you wrote a trigger to handle the Entitlement Name update on your Case or you wrote it to handle the required entry via the UI, you will be able to see the milestone associated with your Case. Just make sure to leave Status EQUALS New in place when creating the Case. The Entitlement record, which is associated with your entitlement process, is also associated with your Case. The corresponding new Case screen is shown in Figure 7-12.

Figure 7-12. *Creating a Case with the newly built entitlement process*

Once you've created your Case, you'll see the corresponding milestone in the related Case Milestones list, as shown in Figure 7-13.

Action	Name	Target Date	Completion Date	Time Remaining (Min:Sec)	Violation	Completed
Edit	5 Minute Escalation	6/27/2014 12:02 PM		4:59		

Figure 7-13. *The Case milestone after it has been applied to the Case upon Case creation*

At this point, the milestone will trigger the configured violation actions as long as the status is still set to "New." Once the status is changed, the milestone will be removed and no pending actions will exist. Do keep in mind that if the status is changed back to "New," the milestone will reappear.

Your new entitlement and milestone are now in place and working. Make sure to adjust the criteria, timing, and actions to meet your own needs when building this out. Because the relationships involved in this development can be a little hard to follow, Figure 7-14 provides a visual to help clarify the connections between the pieces you've created.

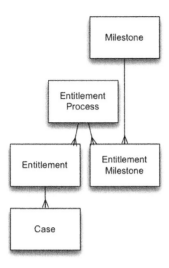

Figure 7-14. *Quite a few elements go into building out entitlements and milestones for the purposes of Case automation*

Recap

In this chapter, you looked at entitlements and milestones as a potential tool for automating Case Management processes. While other features such as workflow rules and Case escalation rules overlap with entitlements and milestones, they fall short in the area of time-based actions, both in regard to the minimum interval and the potential variance between the expected and actual timing. A number of steps are required to complete the build-out for entitlements and milestones. However, once you get the process down, you'll be able to apply it to a number of scenarios to help the service-oriented area of your organization.

■ ■ ■

CHAPTER 8

Producing Advanced Automation with Visual Workflow

If you are getting the sense that Salesforce.com has a strong focus on business process automation, you are absolutely correct. I have dedicated separate chapters to automation via the utilization of workflow rules and entitlement and milestones, yet another key automation tool still needs to be discussed: Visual Workflow. Visual Workflow has had quite a history and has had a variety of titles. It resides in a space that offers significant value for developers and nondevelopers alike: no coding is required, yet it allows for significantly more intricacy and complexity than the other automation solutions I have discussed. Visual Workflow is not simply a different means to achieve the same results that you saw with workflow rules and entitlements and milestones; it covers starkly different use cases. It is critical to understand when and why you would choose to use Visual Workflow to create flows for your business before getting into the details of how it works.

Flows, the output of the Visual Workflow tool, can involve a large number of components and can be extremely complex. This chapter is not intended to be a complete resource on every aspect of flows but instead to provide guidance and walk you through a real-life business scenario for which a flow can be developed. Salesforce.com offers some solid resources on Visual Workflow, and those can serve as an excellent supplement for those of you looking to go even deeper into the world of this tool.

In this chapter, you will:

- understand the differences between flows and workflow rules

- learn when Visual Workflow can be used to effectively solve a business need

- become familiar with the Flow Designer tool

- build your own flow from the ground up

Why Visual Workflow?

While Visual Workflow clearly offers more functionality than workflow rules, it would be shortsighted to always use it in place of workflow rules. Workflow rules allow you to create event-triggered actions that occur immediately or at some specified point in the future. While they may possess some level of complexity, managing and/or enhancing them is often a relatively straightforward task. Although possible, using Visual Workflow instead of workflow rules to update Field B when Field A changes would be overkill. While I feel obliged to provide this warning to not exclude workflow rules, it is true that Visual Workflow does cover a number of scenarios that cannot be satisfied by workflow rules alone. We will look at some of these scenarios in the following sections.

Event-Triggered and User-Triggered Flows

Until recently, a primary factor in the decision between using workflow rules and using Visual Workflow in order to employ an automated solution was whether you wanted an action to be driven by an event (as it would be with workflow rules) or by a user (as happens with flows). In the absence of writing custom code to supplement a configuration-based solution, actions resulting from workflow rules continue to be limited to event-triggered activity. A user doesn't manually make the decision to "activate" a workflow rule; rather the user's behavior is subject to the configured business rules and his system actions determine whether or not automation occurs.

Visual workflows can be triggered by either a system event or a user action. Previously, visual workflows sat opposite from workflow rules, requiring the user to initiate the process. However, Salesforce.com has delivered the "trigger-ready flow," changing the game quite drastically. Along with the traditional types of actions that can be driven by a workflow rule (e.g., Email Alerts, Field Updates, Tasks, and Outbound Messages), the trigger-ready flow provides a configuration-based means to kick off a visual workflow with no human intervention. The main example I'll use in this chapter is a user-triggered flow, but I would definitely recommend researching *flow triggers for workflow* if you have the opportunity.

■ **Note** Although this book focuses on development without code, it must be pointed out that the capabilities with Visual Workflow can be significantly extended using Apex and Visualforce.

User Input and Decision Points

With workflow rules, once the initial user input kicks off a rule, all remaining actions are automated; no additional user input will be elicited. One powerful feature of Visual Workflow is the ability to capture user input *during* the workflow process. The input can be tied to a particular field or not. For example, you could use a flow to "fill out" a customer's Contact record in a logical or strategic sequence that differs from the standard Contact detail page. Alternatively, you could ask questions that would help determine how to handle a particular customer situation. Specifically, these questions could be associated with one or more decision points, another standout feature of Visual Workflow. Using either existing data or data captured during an executed workflow, you can configure different outcomes to occur.

Additionally, the data captured as input from a customer could then be used as query criteria to identify additional details specific to the customer or her situation. Figure 8-1 shows a short flow that involves both input and output on each page.

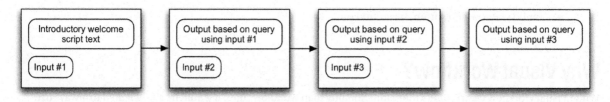

Figure 8-1. *You can capture input and display output on flow screens*

Screen Output and User Interface Impact

With workflow rules, the only notable impact on the user interface has been the automated changes made to the modified record. However, with Visual Workflow, new custom pages showing customized combinations of text and existing data can be displayed to the user through the Salesforce.com user interface. These pages could be used capture user input, as I previously mentioned, or depending on your organization's needs, they could instead be used to display useful information to the user. For example, a customized set of fields showing key contact, account, and subscription information could be displayed to aid the user in confirming a customer's identity.

Multiple Steps / Cohesive View of Process

Although it is possible to "chain" more than one rule to trigger an action when using workflow rules, doing so adds significant risk and complexity to your system's behavior. While some use cases may exist that could benefit from chaining workflow rules, the sensitivity of this approach prevents me from recommending it as a broad approach for a solution. The fact alone that your chained rules have no direct association that is visible within the Setup menu is a potential challenge that warrants thinking twice before utilizing that approach.

Visual Workflow, on the other hand, is ripe for multiple updates or steps within an automated process. The "Visual" aspect of this tool provides a major boost. If you create a sequence of updates within a flow, you can get a visual representation of the process and see what happens along the way. Additionally, the flow is designed for these sequential updates. Workflow rules are very limited in this regard, in that a workflow rule-driven action that modifies the originally updated record can't trigger a second update to that same record. With Visual Workflow, you can update the same record multiple times without an issue. Figure 8-2 gives a look at a completed end-to-end flow that we will create in this chapter.

Figure 8-2. *A look at a finalized flow[1]*

Effective Application of Visual Workflow

Visual Workflow applies to a number of applicable real-life scenarios. Generally, it is most valuable when those scenarios involve interaction between the user and the presented interface. You can build workflows that have no user-facing components once kicked off; however, depending on the exact requirements, a solution based on Visualforce, Apex, and/or other code may better satisfy your organization's needs. Some examples of when it is most effective to apply Visual Workflow include:

- **Lead qualification:** Visual Workflow allows you to walk a potential contact through a series of questions to determine his qualification level. Newly captured data will be saved to the Lead record, and data you have already captured can be displayed on the screen to help reassure the individual that you know him and have listened to him during what can be a fairly cold and impersonal process. Ultimately, you can have the Lead marked as unqualified or follow up the call with a conversion to an Opportunity for qualified Leads.

- **Sales strategy/methodology:** The tool enables you to provide your sales team with a script to guide them through the ins and outs of the sales process by allowing you to display content and questions based on existing Opportunity data. You can remove any potential obstacles in that process by having salespeople step through a series of questions to capturing key, corresponding information along the way. You can also update the Probability and even Amount fields, if applicable.

- **Product or service configuration/sales quotations:** The idea of selecting various options for a service or product plays very well in Visual Workflow. Whether dealing with a service or a product, your reps can walk existing or potential customers through the setup and configuration steps, providing detailed feedback to confirm the current progress. Similarly, high-level quotes can be provided on the fly by easily moving through questions and displaying the calculations you arrive at from the from the flow.

- **Triaging:** Visual Workflow allows reps to ask a series of questions to better understand and address a customer's needs. Based on the customer input, the rep can appropriately send the customer to the right individual or team for additional assistance. Of course, Salesforce. com offers assignment rules, but there may be circumstances where user input is needed to accurately determine the assignment.

- **Product or service troubleshooting:** A flow could be developed with a decision tree that would provide both the scripting to ask the right questions and the potential answers that could resolve a customer's issue with her product or service.

- **Form population:** Any general data entry process that is used on a regular basis could be inserted into a flow to make the process more efficient. Only the necessary input fields would be displayed and dependencies and decision points could be handled in a multistep process.

The Cloud Flow Designer

Salesforce.com provides a tool called the Cloud Flow Designer to create visual workflows. The "cloud" might seem redundant, with Salesforce.com being a fully cloud-based platform, but it makes sense when you know that the only tool originally able to create flows was a desktop application. I will cover each key component of the Cloud Flow Designer here and briefly explain how and when it can be used.

Button Bar

The button bar allows you to perform certain key administrative actions for your flow:

- "Save"/"Save As"

- "Run"

- "Close"

- "Back"/"Forward"

- "Copy"/"Paste"

- "Edit Properties" (*editing properties*: "Name," "Description"; *viewing properties*: "Unique Name," "Version," "Created by," "Modified by")

While building out your flow, some of the buttons on the bar may be grayed out depending on certain factors (e.g., "Paste" will not be available until you copy something). The button bar is shown in Figure 8-3.

Figure 8-3. *Button bar within the Cloud Flow Designer*

Palette Tab

The "Palette" tab contains a variety of elements that can be added to your flow by dragging and dropping them onto the canvas on the right side of the screen. The tab organizes the elements and actions under the following sections:

- **Draft Tools:** The Step element included here can be used as a placeholder when designing your flow. It will need to be replaced before the flow is activated.

- **User Interface**: In this section, you will find the Screen element, which allows the creation of a screen to capture data input and/or display specified text.

- **Logic**: This section includes Decision, Assignment, and Loop elements. The Decision element allows the creation of a decision point to allow for different workflow behavior based on either input or existing data. Assignment is used to update variables you have created in the flow. With Loop, you can "loop" through values in a collection.

- **Data**: The Data element included here allows you to look up, create, update, or delete a record. Standard and Fast options are provided for each function.

- **Email Alerts**: This section contains preset (Case) Email Alerts that can be used in the flow.

- **Other Actions**: In this section, you will find actions that closely map to the list of available Global "Publisher" actions (**Setup ➤ Create ➤ Global Actions ➤ Actions**), with one additional item: Case.NewChildCase.

- **Static Actions**: The actions in this section allow you to send a custom Email that is not based on a specific Email template.

Figure 8-4 shows a partial view of the "Palette" tab.

Figure 8-4. "Palette" tab within the Cloud Flow Designer

Resources Tab

The elements under the "Resources" tab are distinctly different from those under the Palette tab. While Palette elements are focused on system actions, logic, or display behavior, Resource elements represent actual values that can be referenced, manipulated, displayed, or reused in your flow. The elements in Resources include:

- **Variable**: a value that can be updated or referenced in the flow (note that this value is not tied to a specific record or object)

- **SObject Variable**: a record that can be updated or referenced in the flow

- **SObject Collection**: a collection of SObject Variables

- **Constant**: a fixed value that can be referenced in the flow

- **Formula**: a calculation of a value that can be referenced in your flow

- **Text Template**: formatted text that can include any other created resources and can be referenced in your flow

- **Choice**: a selection option that can be set when a choice is presented

- **Dynamic Choice**: dynamic options from an object

A view of the Resources tab is given in Figure 8-5.

Figure 8-5. Resources tab within the Cloud Flow Designer

Explorer Tab

In the Explorer tab, you can access any elements you have created from either the Palette tab or the Resources tab.

Status Indicator

At the top right of the Flow Designer screen, you'll notice some text in the navigation bar. You should see "Draft," "Inactive," or "Active." These are overall flow status indicators.

Flow Administration Options

Navigate to **Setup ➤ Create ➤ Workflow & Approvals ➤ Flows** to view and/or manage existing flows. Your options here are:

- **Open**: Launches the corresponding flow for editing of the flow itself
- **Edit**: Allows you to edit the Name and Description of the flow (not the flow itself)
- **Del**: Deletes the flow
- **Flow Name**: Displays all versions of the flow; provides you with the ability to run/execute it

In Figure 8-6, you can see existing flows and available administrative options.

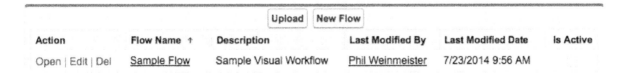

Figure 8-6. Your administrative options with a flow

When you click on a flow's name, you will be taken to its corresponding detail page, as shown in Figure 8-7. Here, you will see the "Run" button. This button executes the flow as a user would experience it.

Flow Detail [Edit] [Open] [Run] [Delete]

Flow Name	Sample Flow	Unique Name	Test
Description	Sample Visual Workflow	Namespace Prefix	
		URL	/flow/Test
Active Version		Activated/Deactivated By	
Created By	Phil Weinmeister, 7/20/2014 2:40 PM	Modified By	Phil Weinmeister, 7/23/2014 9:56 AM

Flow Versions

Action	Name	Version	Description	Created Date	Status
Open	Run	Test	1		7/20/2014 2:40 PM	Draft

Figure 8-7. *Flow Detail page*

Flow Scenario: Customer Service Product Troubleshooting and Resolution

The best way to get acclimated to the world of Visual Workflow is by creating a flow. Visual Workflow is commonly put to use in the customer service arena, so I'll use a corresponding customer support example for this chapter's real-world scenario. Specifically, you'll be creating a flow to assist reps with handling an inbound call regarding a purchased product that is not functioning as expected. Your guiding requirements will be to:

- **provide an initial welcome script for the agent**
- **gather identifying information about the customer to confirm his identity**
- **review/confirm purchased product in question**
- **determine issues that may exist with the product**
- **provide appropriate resolution steps**
- **send an e-mail to initiate the replacement process (if the issue is not resolved)**

■ **Note** Although this example specifically provides a real-life scenario, a full build-out could potentially feature many more elements. Do keep in mind that the example is somewhat simplified to keep the scope at a manageable level for the purpose of learning.

Developing Your Visual Workflow

It's time to build out your flow based on the customer-service-product troubleshooting scenario.

First, let's create the flow. Navigate to **Setup ➤ Create ➤ Workflow & Approvals ➤ Flows**. Click the "New Flow" button. You will be immediately launched into the new flow. Each of the following steps will represent one "box" within the Visual Workflow. Figure 8-8 shows the location of the "New Flow" button that is used to start this process.

Figure 8-8. *"New Flow" button for creating a flow*

1. Contact Record Lookup

When you are designing your flow, it's critical to know exactly where it will fit within your business process. For the customer service troubleshooting scenario, you'll need some information from the Contact record that is associated with the Case, so you'll start with the Case object. This will allow you to quickly access key data quickly and output it onto the screen.

General Settings

Navigate to the "Palette" tab and double-click "Record Lookup." Set Name, Unique Name, and Description to something relevant to looking up the Contact object. The "Record Lookup" screen is shown in Figure 8-9.

Figure 8-9. *Part of the "Record Lookup" window*

Filters and Assignments

In the subsection of the "Variable" window, "Filters and Assignments," select "Contact" as the *Lookup* object, "Id" for the *field,* and "equals" for the *operator.* Doing this bit of work to complete the record lookup allows you to identify the Contact record based on the Contact Id. If you're wondering where that Contact Id is coming from, good thought. As of now, you don't have access to the Contact Id from within the flow. However, you will actually end up passing it in via a custom button as a parameter ("ContactId").

Click "CREATE NEW" under Value and select "Variable." Name your variable "ContactId," enter a description, select "Text" for *Data Type,* and select "Input Only" for the Input/Output Type since you'll be passing in the Contact ID from the custom button/link URL. "Private" indicates a variable that won't receive input from or provide input to

171

anything outside the flow. "Output Only" allows output/use outside the flow but no input. Overall, the least restrictive setting option is "Input and Output" and the most restrictive option is "Private." Figure 8-10 shows a view of the "Variable" edit screen.

Variable

Create updatable values that can be used throughout your flow.

Unique Name *	ContactId
Description	Contact Id to be set from passed parameter on the Case record.
Data Type	Text
Input/Output Type	Input Only
Default Value	Enter value or select resource

Figure 8-10. *Creating a variable to store the Case's ContactId in your flow on the "Variable" edit screen*

Save your new variable from Figure 8-10. Figure 8-11 shows the "Filters and Assignments" screen section once the value has been set to "ContactId."

▼ Filters and Assignments

Look up * Contact that meets the following criteria:

Field	Operator	Value
Id	equals	{!ContactId}

Figure 8-11. *"Filters and Assignments" section within the "Variable" window*

Since you'll want to display some of the Contact's info on a screen, repeat the previous steps for three additional variables, ContactEmail, ContactName, and ContactPhone, using a Data Type of "Text" and Input/Output Type of "Private." You'll then set these three variables by looking up the appropriate (standard) field on the Contact object in the "Field" drop-down list. Figure 8-12 captures the assignment of three fields to different variables within the flow.

Assign the record's fields to variables to reference them in your flow.

Field	Variable
Email	{!ContactEmail}
Name	{!ContactName}
Phone	{!ContactPhone}

Figure 8-12. *Once you've identified the Contact, you can populate related variables in your flow*

Start Element

After saving your Record Lookup, click the down arrow icon in the upper right-hand corner to set the element as your Start element. Figure 8-13 gives a snapshot of the flow after creating the Record Lookup.

Figure 8-13. *Example flow, version 1*

2. Initial Screen

After you name your screen (e.g., "Initial Screen"), you'll want to cover the following items on this first screen to be displayed to the user:

- general welcome script

- confirmation of contact information

- capture of product serial number

You'll need to create the output text to be shown to users. To add display text for the agent, click on the "Add a Field" tab and select "Display Text." Provide a unique name ("WelcomeScript") and enter the following text:

```
Hello <1> and thank you for contacting us. How are you today?

Before we get started troubleshooting your product, can you please confirm your contact information:
Name:  <1>
Email: <2>
Phone: <3>

Thank you. May I have the serial number of your product?
```

If you want to replace the placeholder numbers with the variables you created in our first step ("Contact Record Lookup"), click "Select Resource," then select "VARIABLES," and then replace the numbers and surrounding brackets with the appropriate variables as shown in the following list:

- <1> → {!ContactName}

- <2> → {!ContactEmail}

- <3> → {!ContactPhone}

Although you can place your serial number question in the display text, you cannot capture it in a Screen Output field. Instead, click the "Add a Field" tab again. This time, select "Textbox" in the Input Type field and populate the other fields as shown in Figure 8-14.

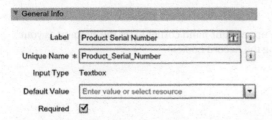

▼ General Info	
Label	Product Serial Number
Unique Name *	Product_Serial_Number
Input Type	Textbox
Default Value	Enter value or select resource
Required	☑

Figure 8-14. *An Input field capturing the serial number of the customer's purchased product*

The Input field will allow the agent to capture the serial number and use it to look up the details of the purchased product, or the "Asset," in the next step. Your screen now has the configuration shown in Figure 8-15.

Initial Screen

Hello {!ContactName} and thank you for contacting us. How are you today?

Before we get started troubleshooting your product, can you please confirm your contact information:

Name: {!ContactName}
Email: {!ContactEmail}
Phone: {!ContactPhone}

Thank you. May I have the serial number of your product?

Product Serial Number

Figure 8-15. *Completed version of your first flow screen*

For now, the flow will appear as shown in Figure 8-16.

Figure 8-16. *Example flow, version 2. You may notice the plus-sign marker at the top-right-hand corner of the Record Lookup; this is the "Start element" and must be assigned to the first element in your flow.*

3. Asset Record Lookup

To access and display details about the product the customer purchased, you'll need to create a second Record Lookup element. In this step, you'll use the provided serial number to find the Asset record, create new variables for display, and set those variables based on the identified Asset record that was found. Here are the specific steps:

- Name the Record Lookup "Look up Asset."

- *Set the unique name to "Look*_up_Asset."

- *In the "Look u*p" section, set the object to "Asset."

- In the following row, set *F*ield to "SerialNumber," *O*perator to "equals," and Value to the variable in which the serial number was previously captured ("Product_Serial_Number").

- For the assignment, populate the Field column with three new text variables, "Id," "Name," and "PurchaseDate," and populate the corresponding Variable column with "AssetId," "AssetName," and "AssetPurchaseDate."

Figure 8-17 gives an abridged view of the Record Lookup details.

Name *	Look up Asset
Unique Name *	Look_up_Asset

Look up * | Asset ▾ | that meets the following criteria:

Field	Operator	Value
SerialNumber ▾	equals ▾	{!Product_Serial_Number} ▾

Assign the record's fields to variables to reference them in your flow.

Field	Variable
Id ▾	{!AssetId} ▾
Name ▾	{!AssetName} ▾
PurchaseDate ▾	{!AssetPurchaseDate} ▾

Figure 8-17. *Looking up the Asset record based on the serial number and populating the corresponding fields to display on your flow screen*

Revisit Step 1 (Contact Record Lookup) for any additional details you might need. Figure 8-18 shows a current view of the flow.

Figure 8-18. *Example flow, version 3*

4. Asset Confirmation and Troubleshooting Start Screen

In this step, you'll create a screen with very similar elements to the initial screen in Step 2, but with different content. First, create a Display Text field with the following text and variables:

```
Please confirm that this is your product:

Product: {!AssetName}
Purchase Date: {!AssetPurchaseDate}
Under Warranty: {!UnderWarranty}
```

The data types that should be entered are text for "AssetName," date for "AssetPurchaseDate," and formula (Boolean) for "UnderWarranty." The UnderWarranty category is set to identify products that are a year old or less as under warranty. The formula is (TODAY() - {!AssetPurchaseDate}) <= 365.

The read-only, informational section of the second screen is now ready. However, an input field on the same screen is also needed to capture the type of problem that is being experienced. Follow these steps:

- From the Screen window, lick on the "Add a Field" tab and select "Dropdown List," under "CHOICES."

- Provide a Label and Unique Name (see Figure 8-19 for example values)

- *In the Choice field, under "Choice Settings," we will define what the user can potentially select from the dropdown lists to input the type of issue she is having*. For this example, I'll keep it simple with only two options: the camera's flash is not working and the camera's button for taking pictures is not working. Create two choices of type "Text" to make this happen.

Make sure to refer back to Step 2, if necessary. The one new step here is creating the choices, which were not present on the first screen. Figure 8-19 shows the available choices for all parts of the screen.

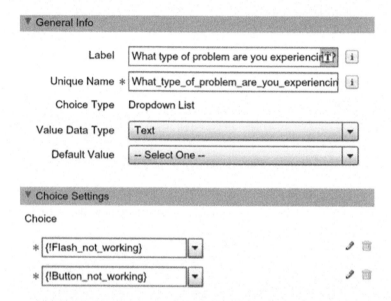

Figure 8-19. Creating choices for the troubleshooting question you are asking your customer. Note the "T" icon on the right-hand-side of the "Label" box; this allows for rich text editing. Rich-text editing allows you to control certain font and paragraph attributes to style your text.

Figure 8-20 gives an updated look at the flow.

Figure 8-20. Example flow, version 4

5. Case Record Update

Once the agent identifies and confirms the asset related to the customer's call, it makes sense to update the Case with that information within the flow. To do this, add a Record Update to your flow by clicking on "Record Update" from the Flow Design palette. You can use CaseId to identify the Case. Then, set the Case Asset Id to the Variable you previously created (AssetId). Figure 8-21 provides the settings that can be used to update the Asset field on your Case.

| Name * | Update Asset on Case |
| Unique Name * | Update_Asset_on_Case |

Add Description

Filters and Assignments

Update * | Case | ▼ | that meet the following criteria:

| Field | Operator | Value |
| Id | equals | {!CaseId} |

Add Row

Update record fields with variable, constant, input, or other values.

| Field | Value |
| AssetId | {!AssetId} |

Figure 8-21. *Using Record Update to populate the Asset field on your Case*

Updating the case record results in the flow shown in Figure 8-22.

Figure 8-22. *Example flow, version 5*

6. Troubleshooting Script

Now that you have identified the customer's product and the issue that prompted his call, you can provide him some troubleshooting steps to potentially resolve the problem. There are a number of ways to develop a solution here; in the following example, a formula will be added to display text based on the reported issue (button or flash). This will allow you to have one screen for both scenarios. Create a variable of "Data" Type formula with the following text:

```
IF(
{!What_type_of_problem_are_you_experiencing} = {!Button_not_working},
"1 - Lightly shake your camera. 2 - Blow on the button to displace any dust or dirt. 3 - Hold the
button down for 5 seconds.",
"1 - Firmly tap the side of your camera. 2 - Blow on the flash to displace any dust or dirt")
```

This formula will display different troubleshooting steps based on the type of issue reported. You will use this formula within your Display Text field on the screen. Here is the text to be used in your field:

```
Let's try a few common fixes to see if we can resolve your issue over the phone.

{!TroubleshootingDetails}

Please try to take a photo now.
```

You'll want your agent to report whether the troubleshooting worked for the customer, so add a Choice field like you did in Step 4, as shown in Figure 8-23.

Figure 8-23. Creating a Choice field to capture whether the troubleshooting was successful or not

The "Troubleshooting Script" screen is displayed in Figure 8-24.

Troubleshooting Script

Let's try a few common fixes to see if we can resolve your issue over the phone.

{!TroubleshootingDetails}

Please try to take a photo now.

Did this solve your
issue?

Figure 8-24. *Screen output for troubleshooting steps*

Figure 8-25 provides an updated view of the flow.

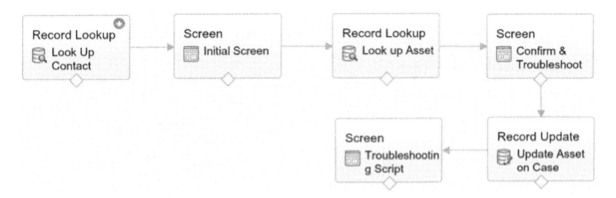

Figure 8-25. *Example flow, version 6*

7. Troubleshooting Decision Point

To set up the final steps, you will need to create a Decision element to drive what the corresponding actions will be for each of the possible outcomes (issue is resolved vs. unresolved). With a decision point, you identify specific outcomes along with one "catch-all" default outcome. In this case, either outcome can be made the default. You will want to associate each outcome with the answer the customer provided to the question "Did this solve your issue?" Configure the Decision element as shown in Figure 8-26.

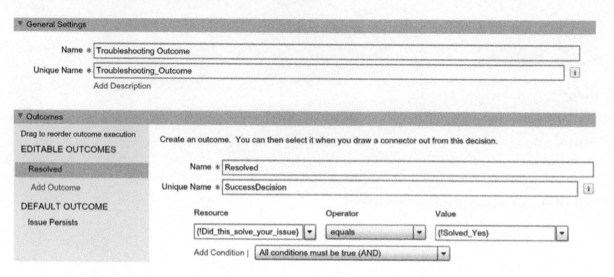

Figure 8-26. *Creating a decision point that has multiple potential outcomes, based on whether the issue was resolved*

Your flow should now look like Figure 8-27.

Figure 8-27. *Example flow, version 7*

8. Success Screen

If the customer lets the agent know that the issue is resolved, no additional action is needed. You can provide a final script for the agent to close the conversation with the customer. Create a Screen element with the following display text:

Dear {!ContactName}, thank you for your time today and we appreciate your continued patronage. Have a great day.

Additionally, you can now associate this new screen with a positive outcome from the Decision element. The flow should appear as shown in Figure 8-28.

Figure 8-28. *Example flow, version 8*

9. Send Email Regarding Replacement Product

If an issue persists, some action will need to be taken. Again, there are many ways to do this. For this example, you will send an Email to the employee responsible for handling replacements. From the Palette tab, drag a Send Email element into your flow and set it up as shown in Figure 8-29.

Figure 8-29. *Configuring an e-mail within a flow*

When you make a connection from the Decision element to this one, the default decision will automatically be applied since the alternate option has already been used. Figure 8-30 gives an updated look at the overall flow.

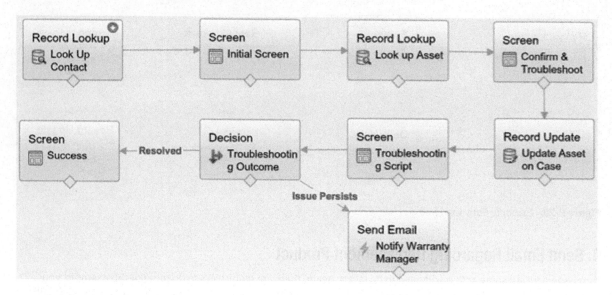

Figure 8-30. *Example flow, version 9*

10. Issue Persists Screen

In the situation that the issue is unresolved, you can provide a different screen for the agent. To do so, create a screen with the following display text:

{!ContactName}, we are so sorry about this issue. We will send you a replacement camera. You should receive it within the next 7-10 business days.

Thanks again for your continued patronage.

Final View of Flow

Figure 8-31 shows the flow after completing all previous steps described in this chapter.

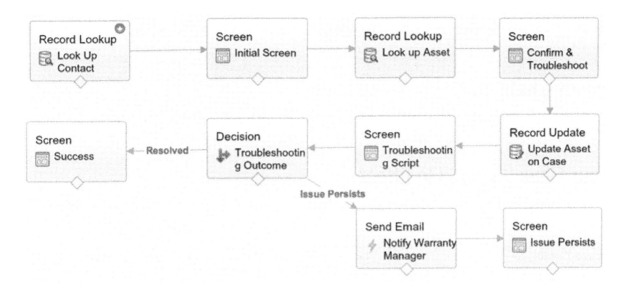

Figure 8-31. *Example flow, version 10*

Creating a Custom Button to Start the Flow

Your flow is now complete, but you must still provide a way to initiate it. In this example, a custom button will do the trick. To create one, go to **Setup ➤ Customize ➤ Cases ➤ Buttons, Links, and Actions**, and click "New Button or Link." Label your button "Troubleshoot Product Issue" and apply the following settings:

- **Display Type**: "Detail page button"

- **Behavior**: "Display in existing window without sidebar or header"

- **Content Source**: "URL"

- **Formula**: "/flow/Product_Troubleshooting?CaseId={!Case.Id}&ContactId={!Case.ContactId}&retURL=/{!Case.Id}" (Omit quotes in formula area)

Next, add your custom button to the applicable Case page layouts. Figure 8-32 shows the Custom Buttons section of the page layout page, where you can drop your custom button onto the applicable page by selecting "Troubleshoot Product Issue" and dragging into the "Custom Buttons" section.

Figure 8-32. *Adding a button to allow a user to start the flow*

■ **Note** The relative URL for any flow is /flow/<flow name>.

Activating Your Flow

The last step is a critical one. Go the correct version of your flow and click "Activate." Once the status appears as "Active," you're ready to go!

Your Flow: Live and In Effect

It wouldn't be any fun to create a flow and leave it there. Let's take a look at it in action! First, click your custom button, "Troubleshoot Product Issue," as shown in Figure 8-33.

Case Detail

Contact Name	Taylor Blankenship	**Status** New
Account Name	Apples, Inc	**Priority** Medium
		Case Origin Phone
Case Number	00001056	**Case Owner** Phil Weinmeister [Change]
Type	Mechanical	**Contact Phone** (555) 867-5309
Case Reason	Breakdown	**Contact Email** tblank12824@gmail.com
Entitlement Name		**Asset**

Buttons: Edit, Delete, Close Case, Troubleshoot Product Issue

Figure 8-33. Initiation of flow

Next, enter your existing product serial number in the area shown in Figure 8-34.

Product Troubleshooting

Next

Hello Taylor Blankenship and thank you for contacting us. How are you today?

Before we get started troubleshooting your product, can you please confirm your contact information:

Name: Taylor Blankenship
Email: tblank12824@gmail.com
Phone: (555) 867-5309

Thank you. May I have the serial number of your product?

Product Serial Number [ ]

Figure 8-34. Completed flow, initial screen (greet customer, confirm info, and capture serial number)

Next, identify the problem type that is being experienced. See Figure 8-35 for the corresponding screen.

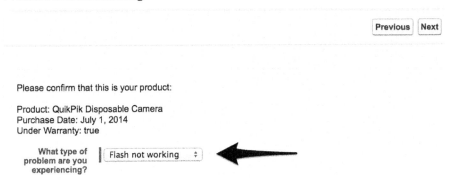

Figure 8-35. *Completed flow, screen 2 (confirming asset and identifying issue)*

Then, confirm whether the provided steps resolved the issue, as shown in Figure 8-36.

Figure 8-36. *Completed flow, screen 3 (troubleshooting steps for nonfunctioning flash)*

Figure 8-37 shows the script to be communicated to the customer that is displayed on the final screen when a successful resolution is reached.

Product Troubleshooting

Previous Finish

Taylor Blankenship, thank you for your time today and we appreciate your continued patronage. Have a great day.

Figure 8-37. *Completed flow, screen 4 (issue resolved)*

Update to Case

If you recall, the flow did trigger an update to the Case itself. Figure 8-38 shows the updated Asset field after the flow is executed.

Case Detail		Edit	Delete	Close Case	Troubleshoot Product Issue
Contact Name	Taylor Blankenship		Status	New	
Account Name	Apples, Inc		Priority	Medium	
			Case Origin	Phone	
Case Number	00001056		Case Owner	Phil Weinmeister [Change]	
Type	Mechanical		Contact Phone	(555) 867-5309	
Case Reason	Breakdown		Contact Email	tblank12824@gmail.com	
Entitlement Name		⟶	Asset	QuikPik Disposable Camera	

Figure 8-38. *Navigate to the Case to see the Asset field that was updated automatically within the flow*

Recap

In this chapter, you learned about another tool for delivering business automation within Salesforce.com. Visual Workflow is more difficult to use than other tools such as workflow rules and escalation rules, but it is significantly more powerful than either. We have covered the key parts of Visual Workflow, including proper application, elements of the Cloud Flow Designer, and the creation of a flow from scratch. At this point, you should be able to clearly see that "development without code" within Salesforce.com is no small topic.

CHAPTER 9

▩ ▩ ▩

Develop Friendlier Solutions with Custom Settings

One of Salesforce.com's most prized qualities is its ability to be tailored to meet an organization's needs to a rather extensive degree . . . without requiring a single line of code. Salesforce.com has built very powerful tools, including workflow rules, validation rules, and formula fields, for the purpose of declarative development. However, with the high level of control that is granted comes a trade-off with configurability. Fortunately, you can mitigate what you have to give up by taking advantage of custom settings in your development.

The best way to explain this trade-off and how custom settings come into play is with an example. Let's say you are creating a workflow rule. You have a choice of using the criteria builder or the formula editor to determine whether the workflow rule should apply to a particular update. The criteria builder has some key limitations (e.g., you cannot choose from the full list of functions), but it's relatively easy to maintain and update. Each criteria entry is distinct and can be modified or removed without a deep knowledge of advanced Salesforce.com functionality.

Assume that a workflow rule needed to be updated and the original developer/administrator was not available for the task. Figure 9-1 shows the criteria for the associated workflow rule. If one of the criteria entries needed to be removed or edited, the task is straightforward: remove the line or change the field, operator, or value, as needed. It's an intuitive interface that can be picked up by others who are not necessarily familiar with the specific workflow rule.

Figure 9-1. *The criteria option typically makes for easy understanding and maintenance of the rule(s)[1]*

When you decide to go with the formula editor, your control over the operations within Salesforce.com significantly increases. However, the speed and ease at which a formula can effectively and accurately be updated decreases. For example, take a look at a formula that serves as workflow rule entry criteria in Figure 9-2. If this formula were not producing the expected results based on current business processes, some analysis would be needed to determine and resolve the source of the discrepancy. The time and effort required to refactor the formula would very likely exceed what might be expected for a reworking of criteria created with the criteria builder.

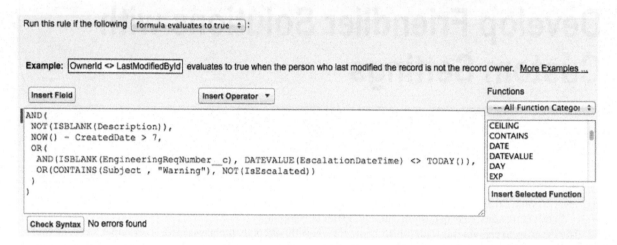

Figure 9-2. *Using the formula editor is not as conducive to simple, quick changes as using the criteria builder*

This is when custom settings come into the picture. They are somewhat analogous to custom objects, and allow you to separate key variables within your business rules and logic from the "code" you have created through configuration. Take a look at the formula editor in the previous figure; it includes the following statement: `NOW()` `- CreatedDate > 7`. This statement establishes whether a Case was created at least seven days ago. With custom settings, you can reference the value in your formula; this allows you to minimize the direct modification to your formulas and make maintenance much easier.

In this chapter, you will learn:

- the basic structure of custom settings
- how to create custom settings
- how to reference them in your formulas

Custom Setting Type

Custom settings provide a means to manage and access your custom data. There are two types: List and Hierarchy. Both have a number of applicable use cases. However, I will only focus on the Hierarchy custom-setting type in this chapter, as the List type cannot be used in configuration-based settings (i.e., it requires custom development).

With Hierarchy custom settings, you can manage data at one of three levels: "Organization", "Profile", and "User". This allows you to create different sets of data specific for individual Users or sets of Users. If doing so is not a requirement, you can simply manage the data at the highest level (Organization). In that scenario, the data applies to all Users and Profiles. Figure 9-3 provides an example of a custom setting of the Hierarchy type that has values managed at all three levels.

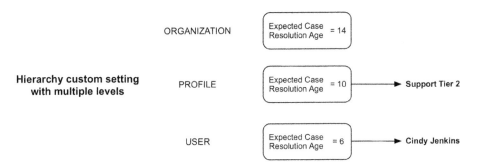

Figure 9-3. *A view of a custom setting (Hierarchy) with settings at three different levels: Organization, Profile, and User*

The lowest, or most granular, setting level always applies when a custom setting is called or invoked. Table 9-1 shows how the values for Expected Case Resolution Age shown in Figure 9-1 would apply would apply to the three Users referenced in Table 9-1.

Table 9-1. *A Look at Three Users and How the Custom Setting Configuration in Figure 9-3 Applies to Them*

User	Profile	Applicable hierarchy level	Applicable hierarchy field value
Cindy Jenkins	Support Tier 1	User	6
Bunker Jones	Support Tier 2	Profile	10
Johnny Smithers	Support Tier 3	Organization	14

The reasoning behind this table is as follows:

- Cindy has a User setting, so any Profile or Organization setting is disregarded. The value associated with her User-level setting is "6."

- Bunker does not have a User setting but does have a Profile setting, since he has a profile of "Support Tier 2" with a value of "10." Any Organization setting will not apply as a result.

- Johnny does not have an applicable hierarchy setting at the User or Profile level. The Organization-level value of "14" will apply to him.

Creating a Custom Setting and Corresponding Fields

To create a new custom setting, navigate to **Setup ➤ Develop ➤ Custom Settings** and click on the "New" button. Figure 9-4 shows the initial screen you will see when creating a custom setting.

Custom Setting Definition Edit

New Custom Setting Definition

| **Custom Setting Definition** | Save | Cancel |

Label		
Object Name		[i]
Setting Type	Hierarchy ⬍ [i]	
Visibility	Protected ⬍ [i]	
Description		

Figure 9-4. A look at the new custom setting screen

When creating a custom setting, the following fields are available to populate:

- **Label**: (Required) The user-friendly name to be used within the Salesforce.com user interface

- **Object Name**: (Required) The name value to be referenced by other applications or formulas within Salesforce.com

- **Setting Type**: (Required) Hierarchy or List. (See previous section for details on the Hierarchy setting.)

- **Visibility**: (Required) Protected or Public. This field impacts the visibility of the custom setting within a managed package. Managed packages are not covered in depth in this book, so this value can be disregarded for now. The default of Protected will be acceptable.

- **Description**: (Optional) Like always, this field is recommended, but not required.

These fields should be populated in with the following information:

- **Label**: "Customer Support Settings"

- **Object Name**: "Customer_Support_Settings__c"

- **Setting Type**: "Hierarchy"

- **Visibility**: "Protected"

- **Description**: "Settings for the customer support organization to be used within various formulas"

Figure 9-5 shows the new custom setting after the initial setup.

Custom Setting Definition
Customer Support Settings

Help for this Page

Create the fields for your custom setting. The data in these fields are cached with the application.

Custom Setting Definition Detail

Edit Delete Manage

Label	Customer Support Settings	**Object Name**	Customer_Support_Settings
API Name	Customer_Support_Settings__c	**Setting Type**	Hierarchy
Visibility	Protected	**Description**	Settings for the customer support organization to be used within various formulas.
Namespace Prefix		**Created Date**	8/14/2014 8:56 AM
Last Modified Date	8/14/2014 8:56 AM	**Record Size**	100

Custom Fields

New

No custom fields defined

Figure 9-5. *A newly created custom setting (fields have not yet been created)*

You can loosely think of your custom setting as an object. Once you create the skeleton of the setting, you'll need to create the corresponding fields. Click the "New" button after the custom setting has been created. It is important to note a limitation here. You cannot create fields with the following types: Lookup Relationship, Roll-Up Summary, or Formula. The values you will store cannot be dependent on Users or other fields in the system. In Figure 9-6, a custom setting field of type "Number" is displayed.

Field Label | Maximum Age at Closure | i |

Please enter the length of the number and the number of decimal places. For example, a number with a length of 8 and 2 decimal places can accept values up to "12345678.90".

Length | 2 | **Decimal Places** | 2 |
Number of digits to the left of the decimal point   Number of digits to the right of the decimal point

Field Name | Maximum_Age_at_Closure | i |

Description | The maximum age at Case Closure, in days. |

Help Text | (In Days) | i |

Required | ☑ Always require a value in this field in order to save a record
Unique | ☐ Do not allow duplicate values
External ID | ☐ Set this field as the unique record identifier from an external system

Default Value | Show Formula Editor
| 7 |
Use formula syntax: e.g., Text in double quotes: "hello", Number: 25, Percent as decimal: 0.10, Date expression: Today() + 7

Figure 9-6. *The new field screen is identical to the new field screen for objects*

Note a couple of the field settings for this custom setting (of the Number type):

- **Required**: This setting is important if you have processes that are dependent on the custom setting. The box should be checked off if that is the case.

- **Default Value**: This setting can provide some peace of mind for future use of the custom setting. If a user is creating a custom setting and she is not aware of the correct value, the default value can be used.

Once you have created your fields, the data model for your custom setting is complete. The next step will be the creation of data that can be referenced.

Managing Your Custom Setting

To use your custom setting, you will need to set up the necessary records based on the fields you just established. Salesforce.com refers to this as "managing" your custom setting. Click the "Manage" button to start the process. Figure 9-7 shows its location.

Figure 9-7. The "Manage" button for creating or editing your custom setting data

I will follow the hierarchical example earlier in the chapter and set up three levels of data for this custom setting. Figure 9-8 shows the placement of the two "New" buttons that will facilitate the creation of the fields for this example.

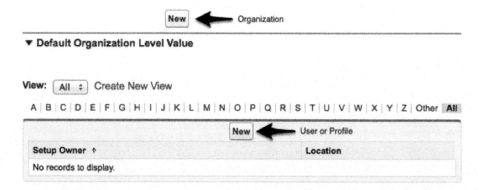

Figure 9-8. The top "New" button is for the organization-wide custom setting; the bottom "New" button is for a setting specific to a User or a Profile

---

■ **Note**   The layout for managing custom settings is not very intuitive. Make sure you pay attention to which "New" button you click to create a record for your custom setting.

Click the "New" button above the "Default Organization Level Value" line to set the custom setting for your entire organization (top of Figure 9-8). Recalling the details from earlier in our example, "Maximum Age at Closure" is required and has a default value of 7. In this case, leave "7.00" as the set value and click "Save." Figure 9-9 shows this screen. Note that "Location" is blank; that is because this is for the user organization as a whole.

Edit Customer Support Settings   Save   Cancel

Customer Support Settings Information   ❙ = Required Information

Location

Maximum Age at Closure ❙ 7.00

Figure 9-9. *Setting the Maximum Age at Closure value at the Organization Level*

Now, move on to the Profile-level setting. Click the "New" button *below* the "Default Organization Level Value" line on the screen we looked at in Figure 9-8. You'll need to configure the location by identifying the level type ("Profile," in this case), and the Profile or User to which you want to apply the setting. You can create a custom Profile ("Custom: Support Profile") and set the Maximum Age at Closure value to "6." Figure 9-10 shows how to set up the corresponding configuration.

Edit Customer Support Settings   Save   Cancel

Customer Support Settings Information   ❙ = Required Information

Location ❙ Profile ⬍ Custom: Support Profile 🔍

Maximum Age at Closure ❙ 6.00

Figure 9-10. *Setting the Maximum Age at Closure value at the Profile Level*

Finally, repeat the steps for creating a Profile-level setting, but this time create a User-level setting instead. Set the custom setting value to "5." See Figure 9-11 for the User-specific setting value.

Edit Customer Support Settings   Save   Cancel

Customer Support Settings Information   ❙ = Required Information

Location ❙ User ⬍ Jerome Walton 🔍

Maximum Age at Closure ❙ 5.00

Figure 9-11. *Setting the Maximum Age at Closure value at the User Level*

You'll end up with three records, as shown in Figure 9-12.

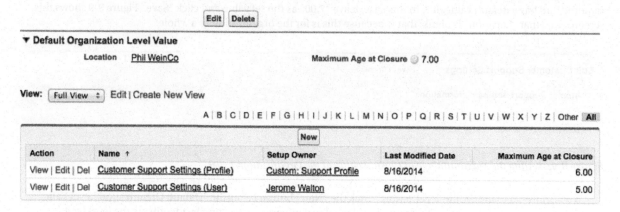

Figure 9-12. A view of the data at multiple levels (Organization, Profile, and User)

Referencing a Custom Setting

Now that you've set up your custom setting, its fields, and the corresponding records, you can put it to work. Take a look again at Figures 9-4 through 9-12; I will use these as your hypothetical scenario. In this case, you have a moderately complex workflow rule that is used to drive business automation for the customer support organization. Let's assume that expectations have changed over time, driving a need to change the associated rule criteria. However, the individuals responsible for making the change have run into some issues with modifying that formula, causing interruptions of the normal business process as a result. You need to come up with a solution to more easily manage the formula. That's where a custom setting comes into play.

To make one, navigate to the relevant object (Case, in this example) and click "Edit" next to the formula field. Once you are in the formula editor, highlight the "7" in this line: NOW() - Created > 7, See below for the full formula:

```
AND(
 NOT(ISBLANK(Description)),
 NOW() - CreatedDate > 7,
 OR(
 AND(ISBLANK(EngineeringReqNumber__c), DATEVALUE(EscalationDateTime) <> TODAY()),
 OR(CONTAINS(Subject , "Warning"), NOT(IsEscalated))
 )
```

Next, replace the highlighted value ("7") with the configurable custom setting. To do so, click on the "Insert Field" button in the formula editor and follow the steps shown in Figures 9-13 and 9-14.

Insert Field

Select a field, then click Insert. Labels followed by a ">" indicate that there are more fields available.

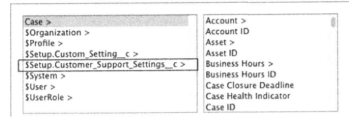

Figure 9-13. *Clicking on the custom setting that you created to find the appropriate field*

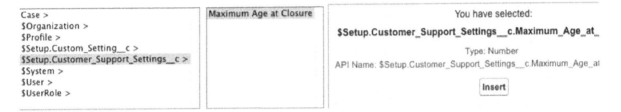

Figure 9-14. *Selecting the corresponding field and clicking "Insert"*

Your end result will be:

```
AND(
 NOT(ISBLANK(Description)),
 NOW() - CreatedDate > $Setup.Customer_Support_Settings__c.Maximum_Age_at_Closure__c,
 OR(
  AND(ISBLANK(EngineeringReqNumber__c), DATEVALUE(EscalationDateTime) <> TODAY()),
  OR(CONTAINS(Subject , "Warning"), NOT(IsEscalated))
 )
)
```

Now the value that is used is configurable. Not only that, but it is configurable at the three levels that were previously created. Find the values for $Setup.Customer_Support_Settings__c.Maximum_Age_at_Closure__c in Table 9-2 based on the applicable User.

Table 9-2. *Values to be Applied Based on the Custom Setting in the Example*

User(s)	Applicable value
User: "Jerome Walton"	5
All Users with "Custom: Support Profile"	6
All other Users	7

It is important to understand the usefulness of custom settings here. Not only do they allow you to store values in a more manageable and configurable location for future maintenance and modifications, they allow you to apply different values across Users or Profiles. This can come in very handy when building formula-based solutions in which different business rules need to be applied for different users.

Recap

In this chapter, we revisited formulas and explored a way to more effectively and efficiently manage the data referenced within them. By utilizing custom settings, you can avoid placing specific hard-coded values within formulas; instead, you can manage the data separately. Custom setting values can be associated with specific users, profiles, or the organization as a whole, potentially simplifying the complexity within your formulas and allowing you to more easily manage formula variables.

CHAPTER 10

Streamline Your Process with Publisher Actions

In the past few years, a key development has somewhat quietly emerged within the Force.com platform. That development is the introduction of Publisher Actions, a truly transformational feature that has significant implications for both developers and users. Historically, the means for a user to manually create a record or activity within the traditional Salesforce.com user interface were limited; you could configure a page layout for a particular object or you could build a completely custom Visualforce page. Of course, using Visualforce dramatically expands your options and doing so is an optimal approach for many projects. However, this assumes that you have the means to write (or pay for someone to write) custom code as well as the capability to maintain it indefinitely.

Salesforce.com has provided some alternative configuration-based options that are specific to service- and sales-oriented use: Case Feed, Service Cloud Console, and Salesforce Console for Sales. Each of these applications has high potential value if configured and applied properly. I won't be covering any of them, but I do encourage you to investigate each of them on your own.

Publisher Actions stands out from the crowd of available interface-related features that allow you to provide more meaningful and efficient ways for your users to interact with data. With Publisher Actions, you can help your users avoid wasteful scrolling, applying unnecessary thought to optional fields, and cumbersome navigation from tab to tab throughout their workday. Actions can be extended with custom Visualforce and Apex. However, they do not require code to perform any of the core functionality. It is important to point out that Chatter must be enabled to fully take advantage of actions. Without Chatter enabled, a limited number of actions can be used and you lose some control over the layout.

I have heard some say that Publisher Actions will become the standard for record creation within Salesforce.com; that hasn't happened yet, but I can absolutely see it as a realistic outcome in the future. In this chapter, you will:

- review the different categories and types of Publisher Actions

- understand where actions can potentially reside

- examine how to configure predefined fields and layouts for actions

- learn how to effectively build and apply actions to meet business needs

- cover certain considerations that should be made when working with actions

Action Categories

There are six primary categories of actions that can be created with Salesforce.com:

- Standard actions

- Nonstandard actions

- Default actions

- Mobile smart actions

- Custom actions

- Record actions

■ **Note** Action types are covered in more detail in the "Nonstandard Actions" section.

Standard Actions

Salesforce.com has created a baseline set of standard actions that are available for all objects. Together, they make up the default Global Action layout that resides within a Chatter feed. These actions cannot be edited or deleted and are specific to their corresponding feed; they include:

- **Post**: Posts a comment

- **File**: Uploads a file from Salesforce.com or your computer and, optionally, an accompanying comment

- **Link**: Posts a URL and, optionally, an accompanying comment

- **Poll**: Posts a description of a poll along with two to ten choices

- **Thanks (if Work.com is enabled):** Posts a note recognizing someone in your organization

Figure 10-1 provides a view of the first four standard actions that are available, even if you do not have Work.com enabled.

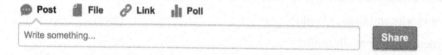

Figure 10-1. *The default set of standard actions in an org when Work.com is not enabled*

You cannot modify how these actions behave although you can reorder them or hide them altogether.

Nonstandard Actions

Nonstandard actions are actions that you can set up for your own organization's or your client's specific needs. There are a few primary types of actions that you can configure within the nonstandard action category:

- Create actions
- Log a call actions
- Question actions
- Update actions

Create Actions

Create actions allow users to quickly create records with a custom abbreviated layout. Related validation rules and required fields still apply, although later in this chapter, I will cover how Salesforce.com has provided a way to minimize their impact on the user's experience by using predefined values. You can develop a Create action for any standard or custom object. For standard objects, default actions and corresponding layouts are available. Alternatively, you can establish a custom layout and modify the displayed fields and their sequence. For custom objects, you'll always have to create the action and the corresponding layout. Figure 10-2 shows a (Create) New Case Action layout.

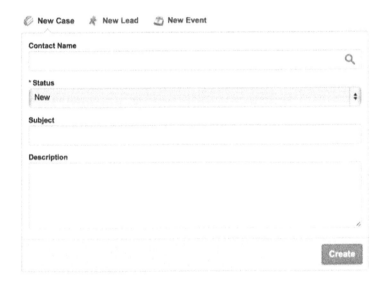

Figure 10-2. *This view shows a layout that contains three Create actions: New Case, New Lead, and New Event. The New Case layout is currently selected/displayed*

Log a Call Actions

The Log a Call action offers a quick way for users to log a call, both with fewer clicks and less fields to fill out. This action allows you to do more than the name suggests. Although it is initially set up to record a Call activity, it can be configured to capture any type of Task (e.g., Meeting, Email, etc.). Of course, you can create any type of Task using the Create action, as well. This action automatically captures the corresponding record and populates the Related To field.

Question Actions

The Question action is a newer action that has been made available that allows the posting of questions that can be answered by other users, essentially incorporating Q&A (Chatter Answers) into a Chatter feed. This is a huge step in consolidating Chatter-relating functionality into one central location (the Chatter feed).

Update Actions

Even if you are already on the detail page of a record you want to modify, it can be a bit tedious to find all of the fields you want to update and then save the record. With the Update action, you can build what is essentially a "light" interface for common updates. Figure 10-3 shows an example Update Contact action.

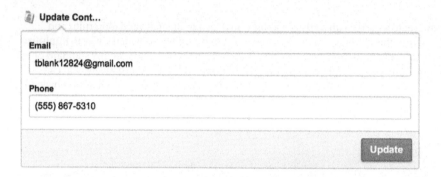

Figure 10-3. *The Update Contact action allows users to update a few specified fields on an existing Contact record*

Default Actions

Default actions are actions that are automatically set up by Salesforce.com. These actions are available for the following objects:

- Custom
- Account
- Case
- Contact
- Lead
- Opportunity

Figure 10-4 shows the default actions that are available for the Opportunity object, as shown from the Opportunity Layout editor.

Figure 10-4. *A number of default actions are created for custom objects and a handful of standard objects; this image shows those associated with the Opportunity object*

Mobile Smart Actions

Mobile smart actions are a bundle of predefined actions that are specifically for mobile users of Salesforce1; they are not shown to users of the full desktop version of Salesforce.com. Mobile smart actions include only required fields and cannot be edited. The only way to change which fields are shown as part of a specific mobile smart action is by changing which object fields are required. Mobile smart actions are only available for the following objects:

- Custom
- Account
- Case
- Contact
- Lead
- Opportunity

Custom Actions

The sky is the limit with Custom actions. Custom actions take advantage of Visualforce pages or Force.com Canvas apps, allowing you to define their behavior with precision. Anything that is not possible via the other action types is likely possible with custom actions. Since these actions require code, I won't be covering them in this chapter. However, I would encourage you to explore Custom actions if the other action categories cannot facilitate your requirements being met.

Record Actions

A few additional object-specific actions are available within Salesforce1 that cannot be modified. These actions may include:

- Send Email
- Log a Call
- Map
- View Website
- Read News

Action Placement

Within Salesforce.com, there are a few locations where actions can be placed for user interaction:

- Home tab
- Chatter tab
- Record detail pages
- Salesforce1 action tray (when using Salesforce1 on mobile devices)

Publisher Layouts

The Home Page, Chatter tab, and all of the record detail pages are associated with a Publisher layout. By default, all pages initially employ a Global Publisher layout. Initially, the Global layout contains the following actions: **Post**, **Link**, **File**, **Poll**, and, if Work.com is enabled, **Thanks**. This layout can be found at **Create ➤ Global Actions ➤ Publisher** Layouts. Like with other entities that have corresponding page layouts, you can customize this layout or create additional Global Publisher layouts to be used for different profiles. Figure 10-5 shows your options for using the Global layout or a custom layout based on the location of the feed.

Figure 10-5. *The Home Page and Chatter Tab can only use the Global layout, but you can create object-specific Publisher layouts for standard and custom objects*

The Home Page and Chatter Tab can only employ the Global layout. However, you can override the Global layout with an object-specific layout for standard and custom objects. Certain actions (e.g., Log a Call) are only available on object-specific layouts.

Publisher layouts are found within traditional record detail page layouts, just below the Highlights Panel section. You'll initially see a note confirming that the object is inheriting the parent Global layout. To override the Global layout, you simply click the wrench icon to the right of the text. Figure 10-6 shows the Publisher Actions section of the "Page Layout" screen when the Global layout default is enabled.

Publisher Actions ⓘ

The publisher actions are currently inherited from the global publisher layout. You can override

the global publisher layout to set a customized list of actions for this layout.   ➡ 🔧

Figure 10-6. *The "Publisher Actions" section on the Page Layout edit screen*

Clicking the wrench will allow you to configure the actions to be displayed on the corresponding record detail page. Figure 10-7 shows what the Publisher Actions layout section looks like after overriding the Global layout default.

Publisher Actions ⓘ

| Post | File | Mobile Smart Actions | Link | Poll | ↩ |

Figure 10-7. *Once an override has been applied, you can click the arrow on the right to revert back to the Global layout*

The actions you select will be displayed in the Publisher Actions menu on the corresponding record detail page. They will display in the sequence you configure. However, if you have more than four actions in your layout, only the first three will be shown on your record detail page. The rest will be available from a drop-down menu in the place of the fourth item. To revert back to the Global layout, click the arrow to the right of the displayed actions.

Action Attributes

When you create an action, the type primarily defines the core behavior. However, some metadata will also contribute to the functionality. All actions require a Label and Name; the Label is what will appear in the Publisher to users. You can use a standard label type for quicker creation of an action; this allows you to use standard language to maintain consistency among your actions. Figure 10-8 shows some of the available standard label types.

Figure 10-8. *You can use a standard label type or use your own custom label when creating an action*

Create actions have a few more attributes to be configured than other action types. One option is Target object, which defines the object of the record to be created. This isn't present for Update actions since those are only associated with the object for which they are created. It is important to understand that the relationships between objects can drive which objects are available for selection. For example, a Create action for a custom object that is the Master with another custom object in a Master-Detail relationship allows the Detail object to be the Target object in the parent's Publisher layout. Another option with Create actions is Record Type; this attribute only appears for Create actions that have multiple Record Types.

Action Layouts

While the Publisher layout defines which actions appear within a given feed, the Action layout defines how a specific action appears to users. The Action layout editor is built on the same framework as record detail page layouts: you have the ability to add fields to and from the layout as well as reorganize them within the layout. Figure 10-9 provides a view of how an Opportunity-related action layout editor would appear.

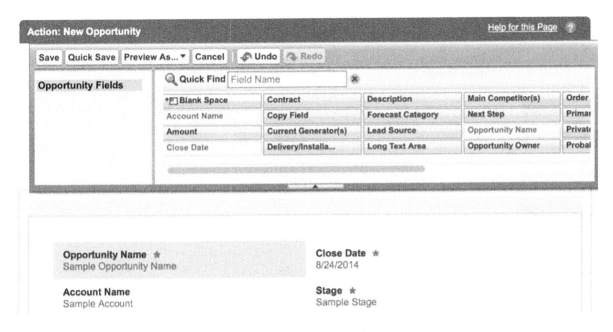

Figure 10-9. *The Action layout editor for configuring a New Opportunity*

Figure 10-10 shows you how the layout configured in Figure 10-9 would appear to a user.

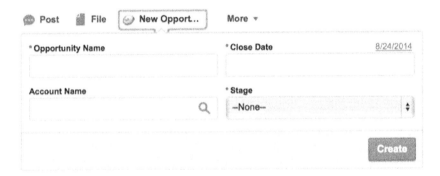

Figure 10-10. *The user's New Opportunity action, as configured in Figure 10-8*

Predefined Field Values

Salesforce.com did us all a favor when it decided to provide the ability to include predefined field values in a Publisher Action. A predefined field value is a configuration record that identifies a default value for a particular field. What makes this particularly valuable is that it applies to all fields, including those that are not present in the page layout. You can use the predefined field value to:

- avoid forcing users to populate required fields
- reduce the time required to fill out the record postcreation
- prepopulate fields with likely/probable values for the particular action scenario

Figure 10-11 shows how an Action layout and predefined field values can be combined in a hypothetical scenario.

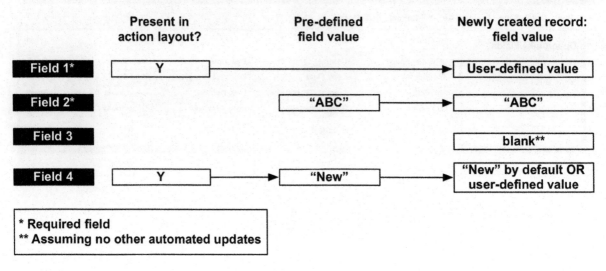

Figure 10-11. *You can place a field on the Action layout and/or create a predefined field value to drive how a particular field is populated through an action*

Creating a Publisher Action

This section offers a step-by-step guide for creating a Publisher action within Salesforce.com.

Business Scenario

In this hypothetical scenario, the sales team at your subscription-based software business is asking for additional efficiency in their sales process. The team feels burdened with the existing page layout, in that they have to scroll considerably to find and update important fields. Additionally, they have one very common Opportunity scenario that they would like to be able to create more quickly. After a detailed assessment of the process, you identify a few actions that would most dramatically aid the sales organization. The first phase of your action implementation is focused on the Account object. You plan on creating two actions: a quick update for the Account and a quick create for Child Opportunities related to software subscription renewals.

Example Action #1: Quick Account Update

This Quick Account Update will provide a "light" page with only minimal fields to quickly update an existing Account.

1. Navigate to the Account object: **Customize ➤ Accounts ➤ Buttons, Links, and Actions**.

2. Click "New Action."

3. Configure the new Account action shown in Figure 10-12 using the following settings:

    a. **Action Type**: "Update a Record"

    b. **Standard Label Type**: "--None--" (you will instead define your own label)

    c.   **Label**: "Quick Update"

    d.   **Name**: "Quick_Update"

    e.   **Description**: A meaningful description for other administrators

Figure 10-12. *Updating the action—main details*

    4.   Configure the Action layout for the new Account update as shown in Figure 10-13. These Account fields are those most commonly updated by the sales team.

Figure 10-13. *Updating the Action layout*

    5.   Click "Yes" when asked if you want to continue saving, as shown in Figure 10-14. This is an existing record and will already have Account Name.

Figure 10-14. *You will be notified of any required fields that you do not have in the Action layout, as in this message*

    6.   No predefined fields will be needed since this is an update to the existing record.

Example Action #2: Creating a Child Opportunity from the Account

This Opportunity Creation action provides a quick way to create a common type of Opportunity from the parent Account page. To configure it:

1. Navigate to the Account object: **Customize ➤ Accounts ➤ Buttons, Links, and Actions**

2. Click "New Action"

3. Configure the new Account action shown in Figure 10-15 using the following settings:

    a. **Action Type**: "Create a Record"

    b. **Target Object**: "Opportunity"

    c. **Standard Label Type**: "--None--" (you will instead define your own label)

    d. **Label**: "Quick Renew"

    e. **Name**: "Quick_Renew"

    f. **Description**: A meaningful description for other administrators

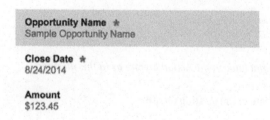

Enter Action Information	Save Cancel
Object Name	Account
Action Type	Create a Record
Target Object	Opportunity
Standard Label Type	--None--
Label	Quick Renew
Name	Quick_Renew
Description	A basic renewal Opportunity with some pre-populated fields.
Icon	Change Icon

Figure 10-15. Creating the action—main information

4. Configure the Create Action layout for the New Opportunity as shown in Figure 10-16. These fields are the minimum set of fields that need to be manually populated for a software subscription renewal.

Opportunity Name ★
Sample Opportunity Name

Close Date ★
8/24/2014

Amount
$123.45

Figure 10-16. Creating the action—layout

5. Click "Yes" when asked if you want to continue saving. We will predefine Stage and a few other fields in the next step.

6. Click the "New" button in the "Predefined Field Values" section. Select "Stage" for the field and "Proposal/Price Quote" for the Value.

7. Click the "New" button in the "Predefined Field Values" section. Select "Type" for the field and "Quick Renewal" for the Value.

Figure 10-17 provides a view of the predefined field values that have been configured for the Child Opportunity example.

Predefined Field Values   [New]

Action	Field Name	API Name	Field Type	Value
Edit | Del	Stage	StageName	Picklist	Prospecting
Edit | Del	Type	Type	Picklist	Quick Renewal

Figure 10-17. Creating the action—setting the predefined field values

Establishing the Publisher Layout

The following steps will allow you to configure your Account object with a customized Publisher layout:

8. If your Account object is not already enabled for Chatter Feed tracking, you'll need to configure the appropriate setting as such: **Customize ➤ Chatter ➤ Feed Tracking ➤ Account ➤ Enable**).

9. Navigate to the Account page layout (**Customize ➤ Accounts ➤ Page Layouts**).

10. After selecting the corresponding layout, scroll down to the "Publisher Actions" section. If you are currently inheriting the Global layout, click the wrench icon to override it and use a custom layout.

11. Remove all actions except for Post from the "Publisher Actions" section by dragging them up to the top layout section.

12. Click "Actions" in the top section of the Account page layout editor.

13. Drag and drop "Quick Update" and "Quick Renewal" down to the "Publisher Actions" section, immediately after "Post."

14. Click "Save."

View New Actions

Now that you've created a few new Publisher actions for accounts, let's take a look at the actions and one of the resulting records. Figure 10-18 shows the "Quick Account Update" screen that were created in the first example.

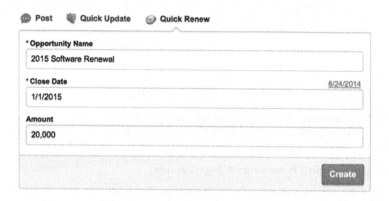

Figure 10-18. *"Quick Update" action from the Account Chatter feed*

Figure 10-19 shows the Creation layout for the Child Opportunity that was built in the second example.

Post **Quick Update** **Quick Renew**

* Opportunity Name

2015 Software Renewal

* Close Date   8/24/2014

1/1/2015

Amount

20,000

Create

Figure 10-19. *Quick Renew (Opportunity) action from the Account Chatter feed*

Figure 10-20 shows the final result of the Opportunity action from the second scenario when the resulting Opportunity record has been created.

Opportunity Detail   Edit   Delete   Clone

Opportunity Owner	Phil Weinmeister [Change]	Amount	$20,000.00
Opportunity Name	2015 Software Renewal	Expected Revenue	$18,000.00
Account Name	Apples, Inc	Close Date	1/1/2015
Type	Quick Renewal	Stage	Prospecting

Figure 10-20. *A look at a record immediately after it was created via the Quick Renew action in Figure 10-19*

Without a significant amount of work, you've just streamlined your sales team's process. With these actions, salespeople can make quicker updates to Accounts and create quick Opportunities for subscription renewals.

Considerations

Here are some important things to consider when Publisher Actions are used:

- A minimal field set should be created for your Action layouts. If you can predefine a field or update it via a workflow rule, do so.

- Your actions should be named clearly, but they should be kept short (under 15 characters, ideally) to show as much of the text as possible.

- Your fields should be kept in one column for mobile views.

- The number of actions you add to a specific layout needs to be taken into account. More than four actions the full site will result in only the first three displaying without an additional click and only the first six appearing on the first page of the actions tray in Salesforce1.

Recap

In this chapter, you learned all about Publisher Actions. Publisher Actions allow for quick, or shortcut, behaviors that "trim the fat" from traditional record creations and updates within Salesforce.com. With control over type, corresponding fields, and layouts, as well as predefined field values, you can configure a tailor-made action to drive user behavior through an extremely simplified process. By developing actions for your firm, you can potentially save your users time and help them to fall (further) in love with Salesforce.com.

CHAPTER 11

Using Web-to-Lead Effectively and Creatively

One of Salesforce.com's core features is Web-to-Lead, a tool that facilitates the capture of sales inquiries from a website outside an organization's instance of Salesforce.com. This offers potentially significant value to those of us who would like to allow individuals without licenses (i.e., the public) to submit data into the system without having to write any code to make that happen. The tool itself is not new and has not been notably modified in years, but it is still a great feature to know. Additionally, there is depth to Web-to-Lead that is not immediately apparent to most users; I will be exploring its multiple levels to add another bow to your Salesforce.com development quiver.

In this chapter, you will:

- understand the purpose of Web-to-Lead

- learn the basics of the out-of-the-box tool

- gain insight into modifying Web-to-Lead HTML to meet your needs

- become familiar with certain considerations when using Web-to-Lead

- explore how to combine Web-to-Lead with custom objects

Note Using Salesforce.com's Web-to-Lead tool does not require any previous knowledge of HTML. In this chapter, I will show you exactly what changes need to be implemented to effectively utilize Web-to-Lead. A basic understanding of HTML will provide you with some additional help when building out this functionality, however.

Web-to-Lead 101

Before I go deeper, I'll start with the basics of Web-to-Lead. There are a few key components to understand:

- **Systems:** There are two systems involved: a client's website and a Salesforce.com org. The only requirement of the website itself is that it contains an HTML form that has Salesforce.com-generated Web-to-Lead HTML. The site can be public or private (e.g., Intranet). *Salesforce.com org* refers to your company's or client's instance of Salesforce.com to which you have administrative control.

- **Actors:** There is one actor involved: a website user. This actor populates and submits the form on the website previously mentioned.

- **Records:** A Lead record in Salesforce.com is created when the Web form is submitted.

- **Data:** The record's fields are populated based on how the Web form is filled out. The Web form fields can be visible to or hidden from the user.

Figure 11-1 provides an overview of how the Web-to-Lead process works.

Figure 11-1. *The Web-to-Lead creation process*

Using the Web-to-Lead Tool

In order to get the most out of the Web-to-Lead tool, let's take a closer look at its various elements.

Web-to-Lead Settings

Once you enable Web-to-Lead functionality, you have two settings to review:

- Default Lead Creator

- Default Response Template

Setting a default lead creator is critical (and required). It refers to the individual who will be shown as creating a Lead generated via a Web-to-Lead form. The selection of your default lead creator may affect assignment rules, triggers, validation rules, and workflow rules that are based on the creator (and possibly owner) of Lead records, so select wisely.

As for the default response template, this is the e-mail template that will be sent if no template is determined based on the configured auto-response rules in the **Lead ➤ Auto-Response Rules** section. The default response template depends on how you have configured your auto-response rules. The template is not required but is a good way to let users know that their submission was successful. Figure 11-2 shows the "Web-to-Lead Settings" screen.

Web-to-Lead Settings   ❘ = Required Information

Enable your organization to receive online leads.
      Web-to-Lead Enabled   ☑

The user who will be listed as Creator when a Lead is created online.
      Default Lead Creator | Phil Weinmeister   🔍

Use Lead Auto-Response Rules to select different email response templates based on attributes of the leads submitted online. Leads not matching any of the rules will be sent the default response template selected below.
      Default Response Template   Leads: Web-to-Lead emai 🔍

Figure 11-2. *"Web-to-Lead Settings" screen*

Selection of Fields / Configuration of Return URL

The fields you select will determine one key to the effectiveness of your Web-to-Lead form. Once you click on the "Create Web-to-Lead Form" button, you will be able to determine the content of your Web form. Include all fields you would like to be populated in the Web-to-Lead process regardless of how those fields are to be populated. Specifically, make sure all hidden and visible fields are selected for inclusion in the form. Figure 11-3 shows the available fields along with the selected fields that will appear in your Web-to-Lead form.

Select the fields to include on your Web-to-lead form:

Available Fields		Selected Fields	
Salutation		First Name	Up
Title	Add	Last Name	
Website	▶	Email	▲
Phone		Company	▼
Mobile	◀	City	
Fax	Remove	State/Province	Down
Address			
Zip			
Country			

Figure 11-3. *Selection of Lead fields for inclusion in your Web-to-Lead HTML form*

Additionally, Return URL (shown in Figure 11-4) is also available for configuration. This is the URL that your users will be directed to after submission of the form.

After users submit the Web-to-Lead form, they will be taken to the specified return URL on your website, such as a "thank you" page.

    Return URL | http://

Figure 11-4. *Return URL configuration*

Generation of HTML

The selection of fields and configuration of the return URL field drive the specific HTML that is generated in the next step of the process. You will be presented with an HTML form that can then be used within a Web page on any site you choose. One key aspect of Web-to-Lead to understand is that the generated HTML is not stored anywhere. It is created once for you to copy and paste somewhere else; its content is unique to your settings at the time.

So, what should you do when changes occur to the Lead object within your internal org? Your first option is to edit the previously generated HTML directly. This does not require any access to Salesforce.com unless your HTML resides within a Visualforce page. If you have highly customized your HTML form, changing it directly may be your best option; however, you do assume the risk of not "picking up" relevant changes that would affect your form. For example, assume an extra Picklist value is added to a field; unless you are aware of that specific change, it would be missed through direct HTML editing. Creating a new Web-to-Lead form would capture that change.

Personally, I recommend a hybrid of the two. If your form is already established, you would typically not want to create it entirely from scratch. At the same time, you would not want to have any inaccuracies. Generate a new HTML form and compare it to your existing HTML form; copy the lines that are different and paste them in, as needed.

When reviewing your HTML, you may notice the difference in how standard and custom fields appear within the HTML form. Standard fields use the field name, whereas custom fields use the actual record ID of the field itself. Standard and custom fields within a Web-to-Lead form might generate output like the following HTML:

Standard

```
First Name Field: <label for="first_name">First Name</label><input  id="first_name" maxlength="40" name="first_name" size="20" type="text" /><br>
```

Custom

```
Twitter ID Field: <input  id="00N40000002Dj7E" maxlength="20" name="00N40000002Dj7E" size="20" type="text" /><br>
```

The HTML that is generated includes all of the details specific to your org to allow a Lead coming through the resulting form to be able to properly route to your Salesforce.com org. Here is an example of generated HTML with commented rows removed:

```
<META HTTP-EQUIV="Content-type" CONTENT="text/html; charset=UTF-8">
<form action="https://www.salesforce.com/servlet/servlet.WebToLead?encoding=UTF-8" method="POST">

<input type=hidden name="oid" value="00DF000000061Hc">
<input type=hidden name="retURL" value="http://www.salesforce.com">

<label for="first_name">First Name</label><input id="first_name" maxlength="40" name="first_name" size="20" type="text" /><br>
<label for="last_name">Last Name</label><input id="last_name" maxlength="80" name="last_name" size="20" type="text" /><br>
<label for="email">Email</label><input id="email" maxlength="80" name="email" size="20" type="text" /><br>
<label for="company">Company</label><input id="company" maxlength="40" name="company" size="20" type="text" /><br>
<label for="city">City</label><input id="city" maxlength="40" name="city" size="20" type="text" /><br>
<label for="state">State/Province</label><input  id="state" maxlength="20" name="state" size="20" type="text" /><br>

<input type="submit" name="submit">
</form>
```

Modifying the HTML for Your Site

It's very likely that the HTML you've generated will require some modification. Unless you have an extremely basic site with no styling, this will be the case. Let's walk through some items that are candidates for tweaking.

Styling

Although I won't be delving in to the world of Web design here, suffice it to say that you will need to ensure that your HTML form renders properly within your site. This may mean employing CSS or identifying font properties within the HTML directly. Either way, you'll need to see how your form looks and update it accordingly. Using the HTML "as is" will not produce very aesthetic results within your site.

Hidden Fields

Just like with any HTML form, you can have hidden fields and input values in the Web-to-Lead form, which is a simple but powerful aspect. The fields are extremely valuable if you want to know the exact source of a Lead. For example, let's say you have ten Web-to-Lead forms spread across your website. Without some specific identification within the form itself, it may be impossible to determine the original source of the Lead. To hide a form field, use the formatting shown in the following code for standard and custom fields:

Standard

```
<input type="hidden" name="fieldName" value="desiredValue">
```

Custom

```
<input type="hidden" name="fieldID" value="desiredValue">
```

The values in the name and value attributes can vary, but type must be equal to "hidden." Hiding fields provides two potential benefits:

- You can set a field to a specific value that cannot be modified by the user.

- You can hide the field from view on your web page.

Picklist Values

Picklist values are automatically generated for you during the process. However, you may want to omit some values or display them in a more user-friendly fashion on your site. Simply edit or remove them as needed. For example, HTML for a Picklist field can be changed from

```
<label for="industry">Industry</label>
<select  id="industry" name="industry">
<option value="">--None--</option>
<option value="Electronics">Electronics</option>
<option value="Government">Government</option>
<option value="Media">Media</option>
<option value="Other">Other</option>
</select><br>
```

to

```
<label for="industry">Industry</label>
<select  id="industry" name="industry">
<option value="">--None--</option>
<option value="Electronics">Electronics</option>
<option value="Media">Media</option>
<option value="Other">Other</option>
</select><br>
```

Here, the "Government" Picklist option was removed from the list.

Validations

Validations are a key and can easily be missed in the process. There are no validations that are automatically built into your generated form HTML. Users can enter whatever they would like in your form fields; it's up to you to restrict and control the information received, as desired. It is true that Salesforce.com will enforce system-level validations (e.g., a field of the number type cannot contain letters), but this will not be visible to the user; the form will "silently" fail. Make sure to work with your Web team to build in form validations accordingly.

Modifications for Sandbox Testing

A simple change that is often missed is the modification of a Web-to-Lead form to work with a sandbox org. If using Web-to-Lead in a sandbox, change the form's action attribute URL to test.salesforce.com as shown:

```
<form action="https://test.salesforce.com/servlet/servlet.WebToLead?encoding=UTF-8" method="POST">
```

Lookup Fields/Campaigns

One valuable feature of Web-to-Lead is the ability to specify a Campaign. The formatting of a Campaign field is a bit different than that of other fields, since it is a lookup field. The values will be the ID of the Campaign records. You can specify the Campaign Member Status as follows:

```
<label for="Campaign_ID">Campaign</label><select  id="Campaign_ID" name="Campaign_ID">
<option value="">-None-</option>
<option value="CampaignID">Campaign 1</option>
<option value="CampaignID">Campaign 2</option>
<option value="CampaignID">Campaign 3</option>
<option value="CampaignID">Campaign 4</option>
</select><br>

<input type="hidden"  id="member_status" name="member_status" value="" /><br>
```

Unfortunately, you cannot follow this same approach for other lookup fields. This is a feature that would be well received if ever offered by Salesforce.com.

Combining Web-to-Lead with Other Functionality

Although the only direct actions you can control with a Web-to-Lead form are creating Leads and Campaign Members, you can pair workflow rules with your generated records to greatly expand the capabilities. Like with standard workflow rules, you can create and assign a task, send an e-mail using a predetermined template, or update a different field on the Lead object. I believe that the most exciting synthesis will be with trigger-ready flows, however. These are the flows that can be kicked off from a workflow rule. It is absolutely conceivable that you could create a very creative solution associated with objects other than the Lead object using a combination of Web-to-Lead and a trigger-ready flow. I would definitely recommend exploring this option when this flow type is fully available to the public.

Other Web-to-Lead Considerations

What follows are some final items to consider when generating Web-to-Lead forms within Salesforce.com.

Debugging

Since failed Web-to-Lead requests do not show up anywhere by default, Salesforce.com has intelligently provided a debugging option for administrators. To do this, simply uncomment the two hidden input fields that follow (make sure to set them with your e-mail address) and you will receive details of failed Web-to-Lead submissions. You will receive a confirmation e-mail after submitting the form. See below for the original and the revised HTML to activate debugging via e-mail. Bolded lines are those that require a modification.

```
<!--  ----------------------------------------------------------------  -->
<!--  NOTE: These fields are optional debugging elements. Please uncomment   -->
<!--  these lines if you wish to test in debug mode.                    -->
<!--  <input type="hidden" name="debug" value=1>                        -->
<!--  <input type="hidden" name="debugEmail"                            -->
<!--  value="pweinmeister@example.com">                                 -->
<!--  ----------------------------------------------------------------  -->
```

should become

```
<!--  ----------------------------------------------------------------  -->
<!--  NOTE: These fields are optional debugging elements. Please uncomment   -->
<!--  these lines if you wish to test in debug mode.                    -->
<input type="hidden" name="debug" value=1>
<input type="hidden" name="debugEmail" value="pweinmeister@example.com">
<!--  ----------------------------------------------------------------  -->
```

Daily Limit

Another consideration you'll need to make when using Web-to-Lead is its daily limit. At the current time, the limit of Leads created using Web-to-Lead is five hundred per day. However, that is subject to change in the future. This limit may not be a concern for your organization, but you should be aware of it when making related business decisions.

Recap

In this chapter, you examined a commonly used tool for capturing incoming Lead records in Salesforce.com from the Web, Web-to-Lead. You went over how to customize the HTML to meet your specific business needs and also reviewed considerations that should be made when using the tool. While this tool has been around for some time, a little extra time investigating its additional layers could potentially prove fruitful for you when working with Leads and the Marketing Cloud in general.

CHAPTER 12

■ ■ ■

Customizing the Look and Feel of Salesforce.com for Your Users

I have spent a considerable amount of time discussing how to configure Salesforce.com to capture and store data as desired, provide users with critical functionality, and drive automated business processes to make your business efficient. However, this could all be for naught if you do not allocate the proper attention to the Salesforce.com user interface. While there are clear limits on what you can do with the interface via declarative methods, the extent to which you appropriately configure it for your organization or client can make a world of difference. Successfully designing and implementing your user interface will bring the following benefits to your organization:

- increased user efficiency/reduction in process "waste"

- proper access and visibility to objects, fields, and data

- minimized need for user training and assistance

- enhanced user experience/increased user adoption

- delivery of additional functionality

As with many other areas in Salesforce.com, you can significantly extend your control with code. You can employ Visualforce pages (and, optionally, Apex classes) to drive a very high level of customization within the user interface. For example, if you want to completely change colors, styles, and page elements (or to eliminate the Salesforce.com look and feel altogether), you'll want to look into using Visualforce and Apex. In this chapter, I will solely focus on the options available to you via "clicks, not code." A number of declarative options are available to you that can have a true material impact on your business. In this chapter, you will:

- become familiar with layout options for various pages, including the home page and record detail pages

- learn how to effectively configure page layouts

- understand how to employ formula fields to present visual elements on a record's detail page

- combine formula functions to increase your control of configurable page layout elements

- review considerations to be made when configuring the Salesforce.com user interface

The Record Detail Page Layout

Since most of your users' time will be spent viewing or acting upon records within Salesforce.com, it makes sense that the biggest bang for your buck in terms of enhancing the user interface can be found in standard page layout editor. This editor allows you to control the layout and the content in the "detail pages" that display the records from each of your objects. The following subsections review the key areas in the page layout that can bring value to your organization.

Fields

When thinking through the layout for your record detail pages, you'll want to make some decisions about the fields you intend to display. Arguably, the most important aspect of the page layout is the selection of the fields that you decide to present to users. If you fail to allow access to a key field, your users' ability to be productive will be avoidably inhibited. Less critically, but still important, is the inverse of that scenario. Littering the screen with extraneous fields will slow progress and potentially cause confusion while users perform standard business operations. If you can combine a thorough-yet-streamlined selection of key selection of fields with a strategic placement of those fields on the page layout, you can make a notable impact on the user experience. Here's a checklist of what to include to help you get started:

- **Required fields**: Add any required fields that are not present on the layout by default.

- **Fields critical for business processes**: Add fields that play a role in operational activities that are performed by your users.

- **Reference fields**: Add fields that may be referenced during operation or for reporting/ analytics even if they are not always critical for viewing or editing.

Of course, there are a number of factors that will come into play when determining exactly which fields to place on your page layout. The main takeaway here is that you should not blindly dump all of the object's fields onto the page layout; you should have a reason for each field being present.

Each field that you place on a record detail page is associated with a section. A section is a group of fields with a shared header and common navigation behavior. Figure 12-1 shows a Contact detail page layout with six sections.

Figure 12-1. *The numbered areas on the Contact detail page layout are field sections[1]*

Here are some options and factors to consider when creating sections:

- **Balance of section count with field density**: You want to find a happy medium between a layout that has a few sections that contain numerous fields and one that is loaded with small sections. You should consider breaking up some of your bigger sections for two reasons: First, a section with a moderate number of fields (five to ten) is easier to mentally digest than one that takes up half a page. Second, the opportunity to collapse a section is diminished as the volume of fields in a particular section increases. Don't forget that your users can collapse/ hide sections. If you limit them to a few large sections, they will likely not be able to collapse these sections due to one or more key fields being included.

- **Section names**: Section names, surprisingly, seem to be overlooked quite often. Adding them is simple and quick, and it provides important context for your users. Carefully consider the fields that will be placed within a section and assess how well they can be logically grouped. Would a user be surprised to see (or not see) a particular field in a certain section based on the section name? If so, handle the field accordingly, either by adding or omitting it to the section.

---

[1]All Salesforce.com screenshots in this chapter © copyright Salesforce.com, Inc. Used with permission.

- **Use of screen space/number of columns**: Typically, page layout sections have two columns. This usually makes sense for minimizing white, or wasted, space. A one-column section is also twice as tall as a two-column section with the same field count. However, trying to force fields with large field values (e.g., because they have a long text area) into a section with two columns can sometimes present an odd look.

- **Header display**: While adding a section name can be very important, sections can be created specifically for layout purposes without needing to display a header. As previously mentioned, a long text field can sometimes look odd in the smaller columns. However, it may make sense to group one-column and two-column sections underneath the same header. To do this, you can create a new one-column section below the related two-column section and simply hide the header of the bottom (one-column) section. See Figure 12-2 for an example of how this looks to an administrator when the page is viewed in edit mode.

Column 1		Column 2	
Additional Information			
Languages	Sample Languages	Level	Sample Level
Description Information (Header not visible)			
Description	Sample Description		

Figure 12-2. *A hidden header (on the bottom) in edit mode. Note that two sections exist in this view: a two-column section at the top and a one-column section at the bottom.*

Figure 12-3 depicts how the screen in Figure 12-2 would appear to a user.

▼ Additional Information			
Languages	Spanish	Level	Secondary
Description	Head of the IT Security group. Has been a part of the organization for over 20 years. Key decision maker and has heavy influence over C-level executives.		

Figure 12-3. *A user's view of the page layout created in Figure 12-2*

Buttons

You have the ability to determine which buttons are present on your page layout. You'll be given an initial default set of standard buttons when your org is set up, but it's highly recommended that you tailor these appropriately to your users' needs. Figure 12-4 shows a potential button layout for a Case object, with three standard buttons and one custom button.

Figure 12-4. *A possible Case button layout that includes a custom button*

The following features should be considered when building your set of buttons:

- **Standard object buttons**: Each standard object has its own unique set of standard buttons. For example, there are some Community- and Partner-related buttons for Contacts that are not present for Cases. The buttons that appear in the standard button list depend on factors such as the data model. A detail object in a Master-Detail relationship will not have the "Sharing" button, for example. In addition to the Sharing button, four other standard buttons can be displayed on custom objects: "Edit", "Delete", "Clone", and "Submit for Approval."

- **Button sequence**: You can only control the sequence of buttons to a degree. Salesforce.com does not allow custom buttons to be placed before (to the left of) standard buttons.

- **Security**: Removing a button is not a security measure that will prevent certain actions from occurring. For example, the removal of the Delete button does not prevent a user from deleting a record; it just prevents him from deleting it via the standard button on the record detail page. If you are concerned about a user performing an inappropriate action, you need to restrict his permissions via their profile or a permission set. If a user is not able to delete a record, he will not see the Delete button even if it is present on the page layout.

Highlights Panel and Mini Console View

Your highlights panel is specifically for the Service Cloud Console and the Salesforce Console for Sales. The panel provides a quick reference to specified fields for use when working with a customer, client, prospect, or related contact. You can add up to eight fields within the highlights panel. Figure 12-5 provides a view of the highlights panel layout.

Figure 12-5. *Edit view of a Highlights Panel for a Case to be displayed within the Service Cloud Console*

Similarly, the mini console view can be configured for the Agent Console. The Agent console is an older console that does not have some of the newer features of the Sales and Service consoles. The editor is very basic, just allowing for the selection of fields to display.

Publisher Actions

The layout of your publisher actions determines which actions appear in a record's Chatter feed at the top of a record detail page. Chapter 10 gives the full scoop on configuring actions for your organization.

Mobile Cards (Expanded Lookups)

With the introduction of Salesforce1 came the introduction of mobile cards, which are mobile-specific layouts that can be accessed from records of configured objects. Mobile cards can be established for Parent records (via Lookup or Master-Detail relationships). I am not covering Salesforce1 in detail in this book, but you'll definitely want to configure these expanded lookups if you are taking advantage of it.

Related Lists

Your setup of related lists, along with field configurations, will likely have the largest impact on the user experience in the page layout editor. Related lists contain sets of corresponding records from Child objects or, in some cases, certain related records (e.g., "Notes & Attachments"). Figure 12-6 shows how different Child objects could be represented as related lists.

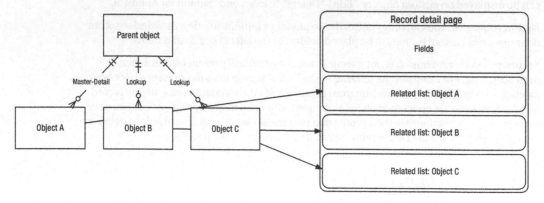

Figure 12-6. *Your Child objects can be represented by related lists on an object's page layout*

Some of the related records that can be represented as related records include:

- Activity History

- Open Activities

- Approval History

- Campaign Influence

- Object Field History

- Content Deliveries

- Notes & Attachments

- Related Content

Although some related lists cannot be modified, the majority of the lists possess a few key elements that can be configured. You can add up to ten fields and assign a sequence to those fields. It's worth mentioning that the standard Name field must be present as the first field in the list of selected fields. Additionally, you may be able to configure the sorting attributes, including the field and sorting direction (ascending or descending). Finally, depending on the Child object and any custom buttons built for it, you can add buttons to the related list. Figure 12-7 provides a view of the related list configuration screen.

Figure 12-7. *The "Related List Properties—Leads" screen allows you to configure certain elements of some related lists, including fields, sorting method, and buttons*

Mini Page Layout

A low-profile but still important tool within the page layout editor is the mini page layout editor. This layout editor determines which fields appear when hovering over a relationship field. When configuring a mini page layout, you will want to keep a minimal number of fields while making sure that you display relevant fields to users. Figure 12-8 shows a possible mini page layout for the Case object. Note that the Web Email field is not displayed on the page layout; Salesforce.com is honoring field-level security by preventing the visibility of that field. Providing the appropriate field-level permission to the applicable user(s) will allow them to have this field displayed.

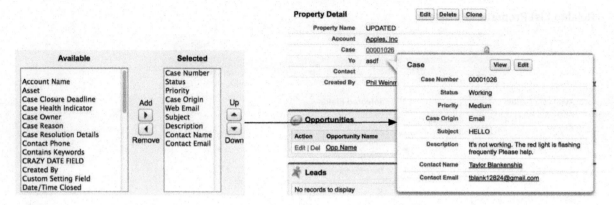

Figure 12-8. *The selected fields in the mini page layout edit screen are displayed when hovering over the related field on a record's detail page*

Properties

Certain standard objects have properties that can be configured in the page layout editor. These properties control key behavior related to your object, so make sure that you review each of them carefully. Here's a breakdown of the properties available for each object:

- **Task** (note that "Enable User Control over Task Assignment Notifications" via **Setup ➤ Customize ➤ Activities ➤ Activity Settings** must be disabled to edit these properties)

  - Email Notification Checkbox: Show on edit page

  - Email Notification Checkbox: Select by default

- **Lead**

  - Lead Assignment Checkbox: Show on edit page

  - Lead Assignment Checkbox: Select by default

- **Case**

  - Case Assignment Checkbox: Show

  - Case Assignment Checkbox: Select by Default (note that the Select by Default checkbox is ignored if the Show checkbox is not enabled.)

  - Email Notification Checkbox: Show

  - Email Notification Checkbox: Select by default

  - Show Submit & Add Attachment Button

▪ **Note** Although I do not cover it in this configuration-based book, Visualforce pages can be inserted into your page layouts. By adding Visualforce to a standard page, you can significantly enhance the look and feel of your page and add custom functionality, as well.

Using IMAGE Within a Formula Field

I have covered formula fields in detail, but I've only touched on the visual impact they can have. Buried in the large list of functions that Salesforce.com provides is the IMAGE function. This function, which can be used in text formula fields, is extremely useful for making simple visual changes to the standard Record Detail page. Figure 12-9 shows an example of a visual icon that can be created with the IMAGE function.

Health Status Indicator

Figure 12-9. An example of an image in a formula field created with the IMAGE function

IMAGE Syntax

IMAGE allows an image to be inserted into a standard detail page. The inserted image can optionally be combined with text. The syntax of the function is: `IMAGE(image_url, alternate_text [, height, width])`. I covered this function in Chapter 2, but will delve a bit further into the details here.

Image_url

`Image_url` contains the URL of the image to be displayed; it can be a relative reference to a file within Salesforce.com or an absolute reference to an image on the Web. If you are using a file in Salesforce.com, you have two options for how to upload and store your image: "Documents" and "Static Resources."

To reference a Document in your IMAGE function:

1. Navigate to the "Documents" tab and upload your image.

2. Once the image is uploaded, get the URL of the image by right-clicking the image and either opening it in a new tab/window or viewing the file properties. You'll see something like this for the URL: `https://c.na12.content.force.com/servlet/servlet.ImageServer? id=015T0000003KLHo&oid=00DF000000063Kc`.

3. Go ahead and remove the `https://` and everything before the next forward slash.

4. You'll end up with something like this: `/servlet/servlet.ImageServer? id=015T0000003KLHo&oid=00DF000000063Kc`.

Documents are handy when some degree of user modification may be needed. However, the URLs do not translate between orgs. Notice `oid` in the URL; this is the org ID. If you deploy something that references a Document record to another org, even if you include the Document, manual updates will be needed after deployment to update the reference.

Most likely, a better option for you when using images within your formula fields would be to take advantage of a Static Resource. A Static Resource can be deployed with its corresponding reference and no further updates will be needed. To upload a Static Resource, navigate to **Setup ➤ Develop ➤ Static Resources ➤ New** and upload your image. Click the "View File" link on the "Static Resource" page. You will see a URL similar to this: `https://na12.salesforce.com/resource/1409553319000/MyPhoto`.

One great thing about using a Static Resource is that you can reference either the most recent version or a specific version (even if a new version is uploaded). To reference a specific version, you will follow a route similar to the one we followed for referencing a Document. Simply include everything after the base domain: `/resource/1409553319000/ MyPhoto`. To make sure that the most recent version is used, remove the unique value between "resource" and your Static Resource's name: `/resource/MyPhoto`.

■ **Note** Make sure to include quotes around your URL within the IMAGE function.

Alternate_text

Alternate_text contains the text value that will be displayed if the image hasn't loaded yet or is prevented from loading. A description of the image is usually what you'll want to include here, but think through your scenario. If the image is critical for understanding the record, you may want to provide some additional detail in your alternate_text string.

Height, Width

Another option is to provide a height and width. Unless your image has been customized specifically for Salesforce.com, you may want to consider setting these dimensions.

■ **Note** Height and width must be set together. Salesfore.com will not resize an image proportionately if you only define one attribute.

Here's an example of what one of the examples I used might look like:

```
IMAGE("/resource/MyPhoto", "My Photo", 50, 200)
```

Combining IMAGE with Other Functions

The real power of using a formula field to display images comes when you combine the IMAGE function with other functions. By doing so, you can further facilitate business processes by injecting additional functionality and conditions into the field. The following subsections cover some examples of potentially valuable combinations.

IMAGE and IF

Combining the IMAGE and IF functions allows you to display different images conditionally. This can be extremely useful if you want to catch a user's eye and communicate key data quickly. The Case Status and Opportunity Stage fields lend themselves to visual representation well. An image can ensure that users clearly understand the state of a particular record. Figures 12-10 and 12-11 provide two examples, both related to the Case record. For each example, I have uploaded the necessary images as Static Resources.

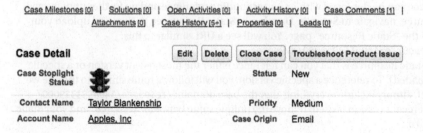

Figure 12-10. Based on the formula, this Case displays a green stoplight for an open Case that is not on hold

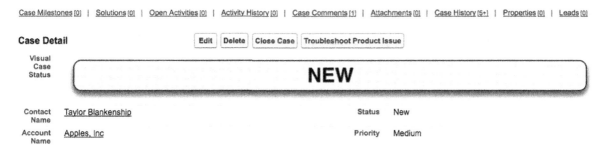

Figure 12-11. *In this example, a banner image showing the status has been created with a formula field*

In the first example, shown in Figure 12-10, I represent different Case statuses with a stoplight theme. For Cases with a Status of "On Hold," I would show a yellow stoplight. For all other open Cases, I show a green stoplight. For closed Cases, I would just show the text "Case Closed." The resulting formula is:

```
IF(ISPICKVAL(Status, "On Hold"), IMAGE("/resource/YellowLight", "On Hold", 32, 32),
IF(NOT(IsClosed), IMAGE("/resource/GreenLight", "On Track", 32, 32), "Case Closed"))
```

In the second example, shown in Figure 12-11, the scenario is similar. However, I map the Case statuses differently. Additionally, I employ a banner instead of a graphic and use a one-column section to show my visual field at the top of the Case page. The resulting formula is:

```
IF(ISPICKVAL(Status, "New"), IMAGE("/resource/YellowNew", "New", 71, 800), IF(NOT(IsClosed),
IMAGE("/resource/GreenInProgress", "In Progress", 71, 800), IMAGE("/resource/RedClosed",
"Closed", 71,800)) )
```

IMAGE and HYPERLINK

The IMAGE function can be combined with the HYPERLINK function to give users the ability to click a button, such as the one shown in Figure 12-12, to link to a web site. True, you could just add links. But an image-based link will stand out and engage your users. In this example, I created a button on the Contact detail page to allow users to view related orders in an external system. The Contact ID is embedded in the URL and the IMAGE function replaces the friendly_name attribute within the HYPERLINK function.

```
HYPERLINK("https://intranet.yourcompanydomainhere.com/orders/" & Id ,
IMAGE("/resource/1409799656000/ViewOrdersButton", "View External Orders", 25, 250))
```

View Related Orders   **VIEW RELATED ORDERS (External System)**

Figure 12-12. *A button created using a combination of the IMAGE and HYPERLINK functions within a formula field that is displayed on the page layout*

IMAGE, IF, and HYPERLINK

If you want to get really creative, you can combine IMAGE, IF, and HYPERLINK to show conditional linked images to your users. In this example, I show an image if the Case is closed and an image hyperlink if the Case is open.

```
IF(
IsClosed,
IMAGE("/resource/CaseClosed", "Case is Closed", 50, 200),
HYPERLINK("https://intranet.yourcompanydomainhere.com/detailednextsteps/" & Id,
IMAGE("resource/DetailedNextSteps", "Next Steps", 50, 200))
)
```

The Home Page

The home page is a two-column page on which you can place certain components to determine their sequence. The home page can significantly impact your users' experience, as it will often be the first page they see when they log in to your Salesforce.com org. You can use some pre-defined components or you can create your own custom components such as the following:

- links

- image/logo

- HTML area

- Visualforce area

You'll want to carefully think through how you approach your layout. The HTML and Visualforce areas are great, as you can create a completely custom look and feel for this page.

Other Considerations

There are a number of other configurations that impact the user interface. While these topics would be more appropriate in a beginner/administrator book, they are still important aspects to consider when building an experience for your users. In particular, make sure to review the following elements:

- **Search layouts**: These layouts control the fields (and corresponding sequence) that are displayed in different search scenarios. Some of the layouts you can modify include: standard search results, a lookup dialog (when populating a record in a lookup relationship field), and tab home pages.

- **Compact layouts**: You can configure compact layouts to drive the display of key fields for your objects within Salesforce1. Compact layouts also affect which fields are displayed in the Chatter feed after creating a record via Publisher Actions.

- **Tabs**: If you plan on navigating directly to or viewing the list views of records of a custom object you've created, you'll want to make sure to create an associated tab for the object. Your interface options will be significantly limited without a corresponding tab.

- **Apps**: You can create apps to present a logical grouping of tabs for a particular set of users. This setup is very straightforward and will notably enhance your users' experience.

- **Record types**: With record types, you can display different page layouts for one object to the same user depending on the underlying record data. This can be valuable if different types of records require different fields to be shown or edited.

- **User interface settings**: The user interface settings (available at **Setup ➤ Customize ➤ User Interface**) include a number of configurable options for controlling the look and feel of Salesforce.com for your users. Setting categories include: User Interface, Sidebar, Calendar, and Setup.

Recap

In this chapter, I took a slight detour from building solutions to focus on Salesforce.com's user interface. If you take some time to familiarize yourself with the plethora of options, you may be surprised how much you can control in the user interface without writing code. In particular, you'll want to methodically review the page layout for each of your objects and set up a streamlined look for each that has everything your users will need. You can use a formula field or two to give your page a bit of flair and engage your users even more effectively.

■ ■ ■

CHAPTER 13

Useful Features and Options for Building Reports in Salesforce.com

If you have any experience with Salesforce.com, it's probably safe to assume that you've created and/or run a few reports as part of that experience. Salesforce.com reporting falls into a different category than many of the other chapters in this book, as it is available to the vast majority of end users and not just a subset of those with administrative permissions. It's also worth mentioning that the A-to-Z of reporting within Salesforce.com could easily provide enough content for a separate book. Considering both of those factors, I will assume a working knowledge of how to create and execute reports. I won't be rehashing core report-builder functionality, such as how to view additional columns or limit by a date range. I will narrow our scope and go deeper in more focused areas, keying in on considerations that you should be aware of when designing and creating reports for your client or organization. We'll cover a few areas in particular:

- report types
- report filters
- summary fields
- bucket fields

Report Types

Report types are fundamental pieces of the overall reporting functionality within Salesforce.com. One way to understand their role is to see them as the framework for the reports themselves. Report types determine a number of key reporting elements, including the available objects, the relationship between objects (for report types with multiple objects), available fields, and categorization. Multiple report types can exist for one object and multiple objects can exist in one report type. Figure 13-1 shows how objects, report types, and reports can relate to one another.

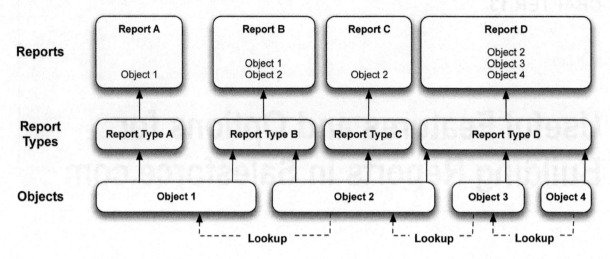

Figure 13-1. *An object can be associated with multiple report types and report types can reference multiple objects. By creating the right report types, you can build reports that show exactly what you want your audience to see.*

A report type exists for each standard object within your org. In addition, a report type is created for most custom objects for which you have allowed reports. Figure 13-2 shows the setting on the custom object that "enables" the report type for use.

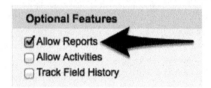

Figure 13-2. *"Allow Reports" must be checked off on a custom object to enable a standard report type that cannot be customized. This setting behaves differently for objects that are the detail object within a Master-Detail relationship; for these, the Master object must have "Allow Reports" enabled to see the detail records.*[1]

In general, allowing reports for a custom object will make the corresponding report type available. However, the visibility of standard report types is impacted by relationships between objects and can sometimes result in a custom object with "Allow Reports" enabled so that it does not have an available standard report type. For example, a Child object with a Master-Detail relationship to another object will not result in an available (standard) report type if the Parent object does not allow reports even if the Child object is set to allow them. Figure 13-3 gives some scenarios of objects with their report setups and the resulting report types that are made available to users.

---

[1]All Salesforce.com screenshots in this chapter © copyright Salesforce.com, Inc. Used with permission.

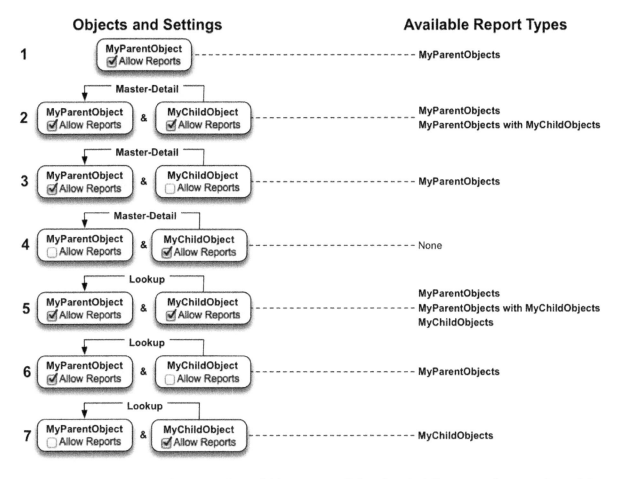

Figure 13-3. *The report types that are made available automatically based on the "Allow Reports" setting value and the type of relationship between objects*

Standard report types will include all standard and custom fields from the corresponding object. If you create a new custom field for the object, it will automatically be added to the standard report type to be used when running reports using that type.

Custom Report Types

You may find that the report types that are available by selecting "Allow Reports" are not quite what you need. Not to worry; you can create a custom report type. Custom report types allow you to configure objects, relationships, and fields, unlike with standard report types that are automatically determined. To create a custom report type, your first step is to identify the primary object for the report type. You can do this by navigating to **Setup ➤ Create ➤ Report Type ➤ New Custom Report Type**. Figure 13-4 shows a report type for which the Case object is being selected as the primary object.

Report Type Focus

Specify what type of records (rows) will be the focus of reports generated by this report type.

Example: If reporting on "Contacts with Opportunities with Partners," select "Contacts" as the primary object.

Primary Object | Cases ▲▼

Figure 13-4. *When creating a report type, you must first identify a primary object. The Case object is used here.*

Object Relationships

Once your primary object is set, you'll need to configure the related object for your report. Salesforce.com has an intuitive interface that conveys the set of data that will be accessible based on your configuration. Assume you want to report on Cases and you would like to include in your report certain Child, Grandchild, and Great-Grandchild records associated with your Case. You can require the Parent object at each level to have at least one Child record or allow Parents without Child records. Figure 13-5 shows an example in which you have four objects in your report (note that it's not required that the Cases in the report actually have any Child, Grandchild, or Great-Grandchild records).

Figure 13-5. *This example shows how you can report on some of the records related to the Case object along with the Case object itself. However, the Case records that are available are not restricted to those associated with Child records.*

Alternatively, you could require Child records at each level, which would potentially limit the set of reportable data. Figure 13-6 shows this different approach to a Case report type.

Figure 13-6. *In this example, the Cases that are available are limited to those with specific related records (as opposed to the full set of all Case records)*

▪ **Note**   You can associate up to four objects with a custom report type.

Fields and Layout

Once you've decided which objects will be a part of your report type, you can configure the fields to include for each of those objects (to do this, go to **Setup ➤ Create ➤ Report Types ➤ [Report Name] ➤ Edit Layout**). While it may work to simply include all available fields, this approach may not always be ideal. If you include all available fields, your users may be overwhelmed and may limit their use of that particular report as a result. I would recommend removing those fields that you know will be not be valuable for any relatively common reporting scenarios. For example, there may be certain fields that are built specifically for a workflow or trigger, but provide no meaning to an end user. You can safely omit those fields.

Field selection isn't just about removing fields. While your initial set will include all fields related to your objects, there are additional fields you can include in your report. Salesforce.com allows upward traversal of your included objects to pull in fields from related objects. Figure 13-7 shows two images, one showing the button for adding these fields and the next displaying the corresponding dialog window that appears.

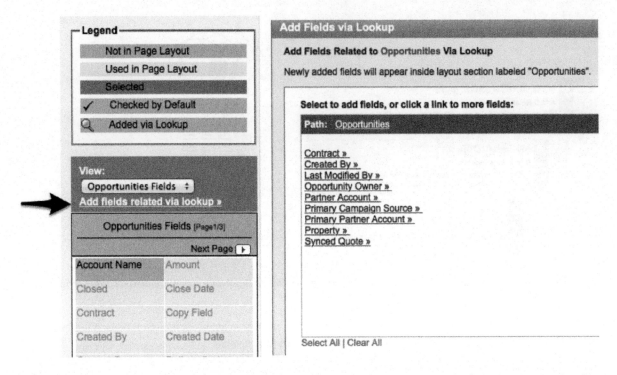

Figure 13-7. *To add related fields to your report type, you select your object and click "Add fields related via Lookup." A window will open from which you can select the desired fields to include in your report.*

You can also select fields from your Lookup objects. Additionally, you can continue to look up other objects. In total, you can have five levels of objects, or four lookups. Figure 13-8 shows an example of some fields you can include in a report type that uses the Account and Opportunity objects.

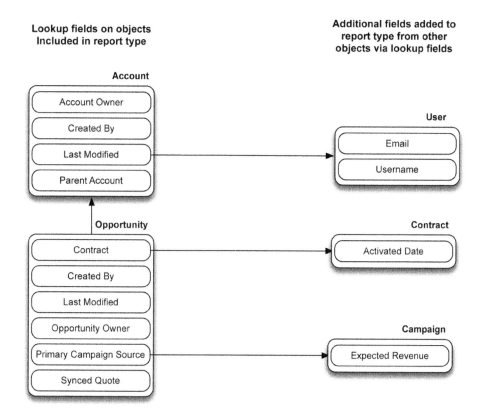

Figure 13-8. *Some possible Lookup fields that could be included in a report that contains both Accounts and Opportunities. Note that the included Lookup fields come from three objects that are not explicitly included in the report type.*

Along with selecting the fields you want to be accessible within your report type, you can configure how those fields are grouped via a layout editor. Although there's no right or wrong way to do this, it is important consider how your users view data and group the fields in a sensible, logical way.

Advanced Reporting Features

Once your report type is in place, you're free to start creating reports. Again, I'm assuming you have an understanding of how to create and run reports at a basic level. In the following subsections, I'll point out some specific reporting components that should be considered when constructing reports for your organization.

Report Filters

A key element of the Salesforce.com Report Builder is the ability to filter results. The primary filtering functionality is the field filter, which can be found in multiple areas within Salesforce.com (e.g., the workflow rule criteria, the list view criteria). See the "Criteria Builder" section in Chapter 4 to revisit the details of how it works. Figure 13-9 shows the filter drop-down in the Report Builder; from here, you can create your filter and, optionally, its related logic.

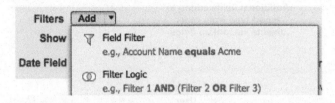

Figure 13-9. *Clicking the "Add"button and selecting an item from the drop-down list within Report Builder allows you to create a field filter or filter logic*

The filters and logic you've created will be displayed clearly below any of the "built-in" filters that appear at the top of Report Builder. Figure 13-10 shows the two filters with filter logic that will display records if either of the two filters is true.

Figure 13-10. *Here, two filters have been applied to the Accounts report. The "OR" filter logic will result in records being displayed if either of the two filter statements are true. Without that logic, only records that meet both statements would be displayed.*

In addition to the standard field filters and corresponding filter logic that you can find in multiple areas within Salesforce.com (refer to Chapter 3 for more details), reports present a few additional filter options for users.

Cross Filters

There may be times when you want to run a report specifically on the subset of an object's records that has one or more Child records from a particular object. For example, let's say you want to report on Accounts as they relate to Child Cases. You have a couple options. You can build a custom report type that includes Accounts and Cases and specify that the Accounts have at least one associated Case. However, if you don't need the data from the Child/detail object, there is a much simpler approach. You can use cross filters to limit the set of returned records to those with at least one record of the specified Child object.

What makes cross filters so valuable is the ability to set more granular filters in addition to the simple filter that requires the presence of a Child record. You can, for example, create a cross filter for Cases and add one that further limits the Accounts shown. Figure 13-11shows a cross filter on an Account report that would only display Accounts that have at least one Case that is not Closed (IsClosed = "False").

Figure 13-11. This cross filter allows you to limit the display Accounts to those with Cases that are not closed

Row Limit

If you are working with a tabular report (with no grouped rows or columns), you can apply a row limit. A row limit will let you restrict the number of displayed records, up to a maximum of 99. Additionally, you can specify the field to sort by, including the sort direction (ascending or descending). Figure 13-12 shows an example of a report with a row limit of five for Account records.

Accounts with Cases
   └ Closed equals "False"
AND Row limit 5, sorted by Billing State/Province, Ascending

Preview	Tabular Format ▼	Show ▼	Remove All Columns	
Account Name		Billing State/Province ↑	Last Modified Date	
GenePoint		CA	3/8/2014	
Burlington Textiles Corp of America		NC	3/8/2014	
Apples, Inc		NY	8/24/2014	
United Oil & Gas, Singapore		Singapore	3/8/2014	
Edge Communications		TX	3/8/2014	

Figure 13-12. The applied row limit restricts the displayed number of rows to five and sorts by Billing State in ascending alphabetical order

    Row limits open up another setting as well. When you set a row, you can optionally update your dashboard settings to configure how a table-based dashboard component will look if it is based on the corresponding report. After clicking the "Dashboard Settings" button, you can set a "Field" and "Value" to be used in your dashboard. Figures 13-13 and 13-14 show the "Dashboard Settings" button and the resulting "Dashboard Settings" window that opens, within which you can configure the Field and Value settings.

Figure 13-13. Once you have added a row limit, the "Dashboard Settings" button will become available

Dashboard Settings   ✕

For tabular reports that have a limited row count, choose a Name and Value to use in dashboard tables and charts. Tables show both name and value. Charts are grouped by name.

Name | Percent Field   ▼ |
Value | Number of Locations ▼ | ⓘ

Figure 13-14. The "Dashboard Settings" window, allowing you to configure the Name and Value for a dashboard to be created

Summary Formulas

To bring more value to your created reports, you can create formula-based Summary fields from within your report. These fields differ from the general custom formula fields on your object in that Summary formula fields can only be based on summarizable fields (number, percent, or currency) and are used for grouping at desired levels. You must be using a report with row or column groupings (i.e., the type of the report must be Summary or Matrix). You can apply a grouping (e.g., Average, Sum, Min, Max) and leave it at that or, apply an additional formula function. Summary formulas help you to avoid creating a large number of custom fields on your object while still being able to output the reporting data you need. Figure 13-15 shows the "Custom Summary Formula" edit screen.

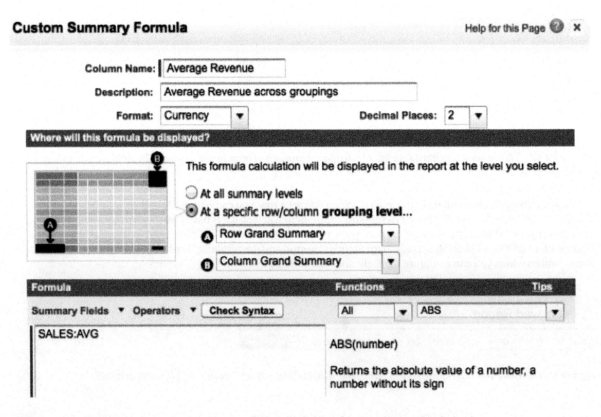

Figure 13-15. You can create a numeric Summary formula field within your report that helps for grouping at certain levels and allows you to minimize the number of custom formula fields on your object

Bucket Fields

Bucket fields allow you to group your data in a way that is not possible based on existing record values. Not only can you "regroup" Picklist values into categories that make more sense for your needs but you can also group non-Picklist fields. For example, you can group the values from a number-based field based on number ranges or you can group specific text values together. Table 13-1 shows examples of possible groupings.

Table 13-1. *Possible Buckets for Two Different Fields*

Grouping	Number field	Grouping	City
Low	< 100	West	San Francisco, Los Angeles, Seattle
Medium	>= 100 AND < 1000	East	New York, Boston, Orlando
High	>= 1000	Other	All others

Note: Number fields are grouped by number ranges and labeled as "Low," "Medium," or "High." An additional text field for cities is grouped as "West," "East," and "Other" based on specific text values.

Once you've grouped your fields, you can then use your bucket field to create a row or column grouping based on each of the corresponding values.

Recap

In this chapter, based on the assumption of readers' existing knowledge of report creation, I covered some key considerations that should be made when building out reports for end users. Specifically, you read about report types, including those generated automatically and those created manually (custom report types). In the scope of report creation, you reviewed some specific report filters (cross filters and row limits). Finally, you examined some field types that can only be created from within reports: Summary formula fields and Bucket fields. These fields can add value to your reports while helping you avoid having unnecessary fields on the object itself.

■ ■ ■

CHAPTER 14

Applying the Proper Security Model to Support Your Solutions

Although one chapter is not nearly enough to cover all of its facets, I would be remiss to completely omit security considerations in this book. The world of Salesforce.com security is vast and involves a number of features and intricacies. However, I believe that I can break down the key security elements, as they relate to Salesforce.com development without code, in a meaningful, understandable way to help you as you build declarative solutions on the platform.

It's hard, if not impossible, to find two organizations with identical security models. Each organization has its own needs, considerations, and concerns, resulting in a unique sharing configuration. It hardly needs to be mentioned that security should be a key piece of any implementation. Even if your client or organization has not presented you with specific security requirements, you will need to ensure that your solution has not put the company at an inappropriate, avoidable level of risk. I am purposefully using the word "inappropriate," as all solutions inevitably carry some security risks (even if the risk is that the system is too restrictive).

In this chapter, I'll walk you through specific security elements that should be assessed and updated, as needed, when developing declarative solutions within Salesforce.com and explain how they can be addressed together to build an effective, reliable security model. In particular, I will focus on those security elements that directly impact your users' ability to access data within the org. This chapter will cover the following topics:

- object and field permissions
- profiles
- permission sets
- organization-wide sharing defaults
- sharing rules

This chapter's primary focus will be on how your users will interact with objects, fields, and records within Salesforce.com. I will not be covering any security topics related to login restrictions, such as IP ranges or login time. Additionally, since this book focuses on configuration-based solutions, I will not be addressing any items specifically related to code (e.g., access to Apex classes, access to Visualforce pages, Apex sharing rules).

Establishing a Sensible Strategy

There is no one-size-fits-all solution that can be assumed to work perfectly across all organizations, even pertaining to those with similar security requirements. To that end, I will not provide a specific approach that you must always follow. However, there are some key considerations that you should review to ensure that you create a successful security component as part of your implemented solutions. The following are some questions you should ask yourself:

- *What permissions will be needed to perform critical or required operational activities?* Each user will need at least the permissions necessary to carry out her responsibilities within Salesforce.com. This may seem obvious, but it is overlooked quite often.

- *Do requirements exist that call for the explicit prevention/restriction of access for specific individuals or groups of individuals?* If so, you must be careful not to establish an oversimplified security model that grants too much access to certain individuals. You should only provide higher levels of access to those required to have it.

- *Does an open-sharing model present notable risk?* Just because there is not a requirement to provide specific field or object permissions, it does not mean that restricting access to the field or objects for the related user(s) is your only option. You may decide that you are willing to allow individuals to have more access than is required per documented business needs. This comes down to an analysis of the potential value in providing the additional access versus the associated risk in doing so.

- *If you are rebuilding a solution from another system in Salesforce.com: were there any security configurations lacking in my previous app that I would have wanted? What about configurations that were present but did not prove helpful or effective?* You may be able to glean significant value from looking at your own past experience to determine specific configurations that should or should not be included in your current solution.

No matter the size or complexity of the solution you are building, you will need to ask these questions and others to have a strong grasp of your organization or client's security requirements. Tread carefully and pay attention to detail. Repeated audits and deep testing of your security configurations are a wise investment.

Understanding the Salesforce.com Security Model

Before I dive into each element that impacts your users' ability to see and/or interact with data within your Salesforce.com org, I want to provide some context around how the security model works overall. There are two high-level groupings that are critical to understand:

- object and field permissions
- record access via sharing

Object and Field Permissions

A user's permission to modify a specific object or field can be broken down to four parts encompassed by CRUD ("Create," "Read," "Update," "Delete"). For standard and custom objects in Salesforce.com, *edit* is the term used in place of *update*. That explains why I previously referred to these permissions as "CRED." Logical rules exist in the program to ensure a sensible configuration of the CRED settings. For example, "Create," "Edit," and "Delete" cannot be granted if "Read" has not been granted, since "Read" is required for any of the dependent actions. Additionally, "Edit" is required in order for the "Delete" permission to be provisioned. Figure 14-1 shows full access being granted for the Account object.

	Read	Create	Edit	Delete
Accounts	✓	✓	✓	✓

Figure 14-1. *Full CRED permissions to Account records enabled for a specific profile in Salesforce.com*

Additionally, special permissions called "View All" and "Edit All" can be granted to ensure the highest-possible levels of "Read" and "Edit" access, respectively. If these permissions are enabled for a particular user, that user can view or edit all records for that object regardless of the organization-wide default setting or any other sharing rules.

Overlaying object permissions are field permissions, known as "Field-Level Security" within Salesforce.com. Two settings are presented at the field level: "Visible" and "Read-Only." These values are represented differently with the newer "Enhanced Profile User Interface" setting enabled. To use that view, navigate to **Setup ➤ Customize ➤ User Interface** and check "Enable Enhanced Profile User Interface." Enabling that setting will make the field-level security setting terms identical to those at the object level. Table 14-1 shows the equivalent object-level permissions for "Field-Level Security" settings.

Table 14-1. *"Field-Level Security" Permissions Translated to the Equivalent Permissions at the Object Level*

Enhanced Profile User Interface	Standard Profile User Interface	
	Visible	Read-Only
No access		
"Read"	✓	✓
"Read", "Edit"	✓	

Figures 14-2 and 14-3 show possible configurations for the Created By field, as presented via the two profile user interfaces that are available within Salesforce.com.

Field Name	Field Type	Visible	Read-Only
Created By	Lookup	✓	✓

Figure 14-2. *In this configuration, the profile has read-only permission for accessing the Created By field. This image shows the original view, in which the "Enhanced Profile User Interface" is disabled.[1]*

Field Name	Read	Edit
Created By	✓	

Figure 14-3. *This image shows how these permissions are displayed when "Enhanced Profile User Interface" is enabled. The profile has read permission for accessing the Created By field.*

---

[1]All Salesforce.com screenshots in this chapter © copyright Salesforce.com, Inc. Used with permission.

Record Access via Sharing

Object permissions are not the only determinant of whether you can view or edit a record. If your org does not have an open-sharing model, the object permissions alone will not necessarily allow you to view or modify any records. In that case, you must also be granted the ability to view or manipulate the desired record via sharing. For example, although you may have the ability to read/view Account records, you will not be able to view those that have not been shared with you through your org settings. Table 14-2 breaks down how the CRED permissions work for record access in terms of allowing a user to view a specific record.

Table 14-2. *Combinations of Object Permissions and Sharing Access and How They Impact the Ability to View Records*

Account read permission	Access to Account record "A"	Able to view Account record "A"?
No	No	No
Yes	No	No
Yes	Yes	Yes

Access to one or more records can be granted to a user a few different ways:

- organization-wide defaults
- sharing rules
- "View All"/"Edit All" permissions

Practical Application of Security Elements

So far in this chapter, we've been looking at a high-level conceptual security framework for field- and object-level security. Now it's time to dive into these areas in more detail and see how to apply these elements within your own org.

Field-Level Security

When you create a new field, you have an opportunity to properly configure the related security settings. Although it might be tempting to rush through the "Field-Level Security for Profile" screen to set up your new field, I highly recommend that you take the time to closely review the access that is granted to each profile and adjust the settings as needed. You might not need to create any new User profiles in conjunction with an implementation of functionality; however, you will need to at least ensure that related permissions have been properly set for your existing profiles. Figure 14-4 shows the screen you are presented with when creating a new custom field.

Field-Level Security for Profile	☐ Visible	☐ Read-Only
Authenticated Website	☐	☐
Chatter Only User	☑	☑
Contract Manager	☑	☑
Cross Org Data Proxy User	☑	☑
Custom: Marketing Profile	☑	☐
Custom: Sales Profile	☑	☐

Figure 14-4. *When you create a new field, you will need to review the security settings associated with existing profiles on the "Field-Level Security for Profile" screen*

Once you have configured the initial settings, you can update them by following these navigation paths:

- Standard objects: **Setup ➤ Customize ➤ [object name] ➤ Fields ➤ Field Label**
- Custom objects: **Setup ➤ Create ➤ [object name] ➤ Field Label**

Once you are on the custom field detail page, click the "Set Field-Level Security" button. The screen format is identical to the screen shown in Figure 14-4.

Object-Level Security

Salesforce.com handles object-level security settings differently from how it handles field-level security. As you saw in Figure 14-4, you are prompted to set the permission level for each profile during field creation. However, no such screen exists to set profile permissions for the creation of custom objects. With the exception of the standard "System Administrator" profile (which has full access to all standard and custom objects), profiles are not initially granted any permission to access a new custom object.

You can establish your object-level permissions in one of two ways: If only a few profiles require permission to access the object in question, you can simply navigate to the profile itself and update the permissions for the specific object. You will need to scroll down to either the "Standard Object Permissions" or the "Custom Object Permissions" section, depending on the type of object. Figure 14-5 shows the "Custom Object Permissions" section in edit mode.

Custom Object Permissions

	Basic Access				Data Administration			Basic Access				Data Administration	
	Read	Create	Edit	Delete	View All	Modify All		Read	Create	Edit	Delete	View All	Modify All
MyChildObjects	☑	☐	☐	☐	☐	☐	MyParentObjects	☑	☐	☑	☑	☐	☐
My Custom Objects	☑	☐	☑	☐	☐	☐	New Custom Objects	☑	☑	☑	☐	☐	☐

Figure 14-5. *The "Custom Object Permissions" section of the "Profile Edit" screen, which allows you to modify object permission for a particular profile*

A valuable option for quickly applying object permissions across multiple profiles is enabling the "Enhanced Profile List View" permission and managing your profiles from the profile list view screen. To enable the appropriate view, navigate to **Setup ➤ Customize ➤ User Interface** and select "Enable Enhanced Profile List Views." This interface will allow you to update profiles with object permissions en masse. Once that is enabled, navigate to **Setup ➤ Manage Users ➤ Profiles**. There, you can create a list view that displays Profile Name and the related permissions. Figure 14-6 shows the desired settings that should be selected to apply permissions for an object called "New Custom Object."

Figure 14-6. *When creating a list view for the enhanced profile list view screen, you can select all permissions related to your new object(s) in order to quickly apply a mass edit*

Once you've created your list view, select the profiles you want to update by checking them and then double-click the permission to be added or removed. See Figure 14-7 for a view of the screen just before double-clicking the permission.

	Action	Profile Name ↑	New Custom Object: Create
☑	Del | Clone	Custom: Marketing Profile	☐
☑	Del | Clone	Custom: Sales Profile	
☑	Del | Clone	Custom: Support Profile	
☑	Clone	Customer Community Login User	
☑	Clone	Customer Community User	

Figure 14-7. *To add or remove a permission to multiple profiles at once, select the applicable profiles and double-click the applicable permission setting*

After double-clicking on the permission, the window shown in Figure 14-8 will appear, allowing you to add or remove individual settings and apply the change to all of the selected profiles.

Edit New Custom Object: Create   ✕

Change the following setting

☑ New Custom Object: Create

These settings will also be enabled

Learn More❓

ℹ️ When New Custom Object: Create is enabled, if any of the following permissions are currently disabled, they will be enabled. <u>Don't show this message again</u>

General User Permissions	Administrative Permissions	Object Permissions
No Impact	No Impact	New Custom Object: Read

Apply changes to

🔘 The record clicked
⚪ All 25 selected records

Save   Cancel

Figure 14-8.   *After selecting multiple rows (profiles) from an enhanced profile list view, double-clicking a field to edit it will bring up the "Edit New Custom Object" window. Here, you can apply the change to the record that was clicked or to all selected records*

Using Permission Sets and Validation Rules

As you've seen thus far, managing your field- and object-level security requirements centers on the configuration of your User profiles. A few other features can be utilized to extend your security configuration further to meet certain requirements. While it is commonly the case that all Users in an existing profile would need the same permissions to access a new field or object, there can be variance within that group of Users. That variance might lead you to consider using permission sets or validation rules in your security model.

Take a User profile called "Tier 1 Support," with 50 Users, as an example. Assume that 10 of those 50 support individuals need the ability to edit records for a new custom object called Asset Warranty; these users need to be able to update a few fields on that record based on customer input. The remaining 40 users within that profile, however, need only to view Product Warranty records. You have three primary options for providing the first group (the 10 Users) with the required "Product Warranty Edit" permission. Figure 14-9 presents a visual representation of these options.

Figure 14-9.   *Three possible options for providing additional permissions to a subset of Users in one profile*

So, which option is the best? As always, it depends on your situation.

- **Option 1**: In this scenario, you grant all of the Users within the group profile the "Account Read" and "Account Edit" permissions. This is the simplest approach and it may be a completely legitimate solution for your organization. However, you are potentially introducing risk by providing 40 individuals the extraneous ability to edit Asset Warranty records.

- **Option 2**: Here, you separate out the 10 higher-access Users and provide only them with "Read" and "Edit" permissions to access the Asset Warranty object. This will definitely meet your needs, although you now have an extra profile to manage. If you frequently were to go down this route for similar situations, you would potentially find yourself with an inordinate number of profiles. Most likely, you would not want to create a completely new profile for minor permission differences.

- **Option 3**: Here, you use a permission set to grant "Edit" access only to specified individuals. This allows you to avoid Option 1, in which users have extraneous permission, and Option 2, in which a second profile must be maintained.

The permission set is an extremely effective feature within Salesforce.com; I highly encourage you to consider using it when it is applicable. Before the days of the permission set, all you had to work with for object and field permissions was the User profile. This required provisioning users a profile for each unique set of permissions; in some cases, those unique sets resulted in an extreme number of profiles (even in some smaller organizations).

Permission sets provide the ability to enforce a "least privilege" model by establishing the minimal number of impactful profiles and giving them the broadest set of permissions. Once the profiles are put in place, you can focus on variances and additional needs by creating and assigning permission sets to users. With permission sets, you avoid the need to create new profiles for minor differences in permissions. Instead, you can create one primary profile for the similar permission groupings and then layer a permission set on top of the profile for each unique group of permissions. Figure 14-10 shows the difference between a profile-only approach and one that uses permission sets.

Without permission sets   **With permission sets**

Figure 14-10. *Without permission sets, each unique grouping of permissions must be assigned its own profile. With permission sets, on the other hand, you can consolidate similar groupings and assign permission sets to handle the variances.*

Another type of exception to the profile-only approach may emerge, as well. Say you have a hypothetical profile of 100 users. If you want 99 of them to have the ability to edit the NewObj object but 1 of them explicitly not to have editing permission, your options differ slightly from the "Tier 1 Support" example I used earlier in which you only wanted to grant 10 of 50 users access to edit records. Here, again, you could move one of the two groups to a different profile or you could add a permission set to grant the additional permission. You could also take a restrictive approach that would basically grant editing permission to the set of 100 users but block that access for that 1 user. Creating a validation rule would prohibit a specific user from editing the field in question. Figure 14-11 shows these two options.

Figure 14-11. *If you have a very small subset of users that require reduced access, you can add a profile or restrict the access by creating a validation rule*

Option 1 or 2 may best meet your requirements. Although it should only be seen as a way to handle outlier scenarios and exceptions, you may also consider looking at Option 3. By taking that approach, you minimize the setup and maintenance required for your profiles and permission sets. Of course, there's a cost (isn't there always?). In the case of Option 3, you have to manage the validation rule itself.

The validation rule can be formulated a few different ways for this example. One way is to construct it to restrict changes to the Name field for *new and existing records* for the user ID "005F0000004gHbf." You would build the following formula for the validation rule:

```
ISCHANGED(Name) && $User.Id = "005F0000004gHbf"
```

To restrict changes to the Name field for *existing records only* for this user ID, the formula would be:

```
NOT(ISNEW()) && ISCHANGED(Name) && $User.Id = "005F0000004gHbf"
```

To apply this to an entire object, you would replace "Name" with "Last Modified Date." For example, to restrict changes to all records for a given object made by the same user, you would use:

```
ISCHANGED(LastModifiedDate) && $User.Id = "005F0000004gHbf"
```

However, going with a validation rule for security elements also has trade-offs. The previous option requires additional administration responsibilities to maintain the security model. You can minimize those responsibilities by creating a custom setting and managing the affected users via a custom setting field (as opposed to hardcoding the User ID), but you'll still need to make sure that your administrators are aware of these exceptions.

■ **Note**   Using validation rules as part of a security model is not intended to be best practice but rather a workaround for very specific, extreme circumstances. An example of a situation in which you might want to use a complex validation rule involving multiple fields and preventing a certain update is if you wanted to exempt your system administrator from a general rule and allow an override.

Record Access Through Sharing

As I mentioned earlier in the chapter, your profile-based permission to access a certain object does not necessarily mean that you can view or edit that particular record. The sharing model must be considered, as well. The following are a few key areas you should review related to record sharing when you are building solutions within Salesforce.com.

Organization-Wide Defaults

When you create a new custom object, an organization-wide default is set to control the sharing behavior for that particular object. These defaults allow you to "shut down" record access for an entire org before you open it back up for specific use cases via other sharing mechanisms. To manage these settings, navigate to **Setup ➤ Security Controls ➤ Sharing Settings**. For each object, you have three main options in terms of settings:

- **"Public Read/Write" (default setting)**: Allows all users *with "Read" and "Edit" permissions for an object* to view and edit all records related to the object. This is known as an "open sharing" model.

- **"Public Read Only"**: Only allows all users *with "Read" permission for an object* to view all records related to it.

- **"Private"**: Restricts all users from viewing or editing an object. This is known as a "closed sharing" model.

■ **Note**   The "Public Read/Write/Transfer" setting is an additional option for Leads and Cases. This is similar to "Public Read/Write" but allows an additional sharing of the ability to transfer record ownership.

It is critical to understand that a user always needs to have the proper object permissions to view or edit a new custom object. Even if you set the organization-wide default to "Public Read/Write," a user without "Read" access for the object will not be able to view it. Figure 14-12 shows how this works.

Figure 14-12. *Even if your organization-wide default is set to "Public Read/Write," individual users will still need to have the proper permissions to read or edit records of that object type*

The obvious exception to the organization-wide default sharing rules is for the owner of a record since the purpose of a sharing rule is to share a record beyond its owner. The owner of a record interacts with it as though the organization-wide default is set to "Public Read/Write." For example, if the user Bunker Jones owns a record that is set to private, he can *potentially* see or edit the record. I say "potentially" because the object permissions still trump everything else. Bunker can only do what his permissions allow, even if he is the record owner. Figure 14-13 shows an object's access to a record when it has a "Private" sharing model.

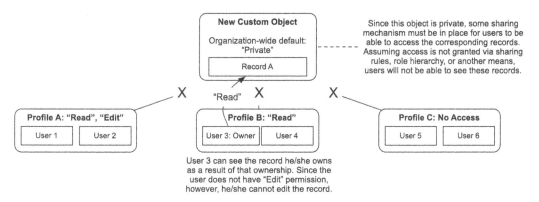

Figure 14-13. *A record owner can view and/or edit the record(s) he owns depending on the permissions granted to him. In this case, the owner does not have "Edit" permission, so he can only view the owned record*

■ **Note**   While you can start with either an open ("Public Read Only" or "Public Read/Write") or closed ("Private") default setting for sharing your object, the related security settings and rules in Salesforce.com are designed to grant additional access, not to restrict it. In other words, you wouldn't share object records with all users and then identify specific users or groups that should be removed from that group. Rather, you would start with a closed sharing model and then grant access to the appropriate users. This is sometimes referred to as the "principle of least privilege."

There are also two additional items related to organization-wide default settings that should be assessed and configured properly: The first is the "**Grant Access Using Hierarchies**" option, which is presented to you when you create a new custom object. When selected, it shares the record with all users who are higher in the hierarchy than the owner. This applies to users in public groups, as well. If a user is granted access to a record via a public group and that group is configured to grant access using hierarchies, that record will only be shared with users who are above the owner in the hierarchy. As with the previously discussed scenarios, for this to apply the impacted users must have the proper object permissions in place; if they do not have "Read" permission for a record that is shared with them, they will be prevented from viewing the record.

Figure 14-14 shows how this feature works. In this example, assume that the record owner has a Role 3c status and that "Grant Access Using Hierarchies" is enabled. Note that although Role 2a is higher than Role 3c, because they are not directly related in the hierarchy. Users in Role 2a are not granted access to the records owned by users in Role 3c when using this setting.

Figure 14-14. *When the "Grant Access Using Hierarchies" setting is enabled for an object, a record owned by a user in Role 3c would be automatically shared with users in Role 2b and Role 1*

The other configuration to take note of when establishing the default settings is the (relatively new) ability to set the **"Default Internal Access"** and **"Default External Access"** separately. This is extremely useful if you have a Portal or a Community associated with your org. You could, for example, set the organization-wide default for your custom object to "Public Read/Write" for internal users and "Private" for external users. Although I am not specifically covering Portals or Communities in this book, I encourage you to assess your internal and external sharing defaults separately and carefully if you are using either external feature.

■ **Note** For custom objects that look up to another object via a Master-Detail relationship, you have the option of inheriting the organization-wide default setting from the Master object or setting it up independently on the Detail object. The selection name is "Controlled by Parent."

Sharing Rules

If your organization-wide default setting for your new object(s) is set to "Public Read/Write," your sharing model is complete. All records for the applicable objects have been shared to the full extent with all users. There is no value in any additional sharing, as it would be redundant.

However, for any objects that have a "Public Read Only" or "Private" sharing default, you will need to review your requirements to determine if the defaults are sufficient. With sharing rules, you can augment the default sharing to create customized access for specific users or users that are members of particular groups or roles. Figure 14-15 shows the type of access that can be provided for different organization-wide defaults via sharing rules for objects.

Figure 14-15. The organization-wide defaults for a given object grant more access than already provided via sharing rules

There are three primary types of sharing rules that you can configure yourself:

- criteria-based sharing rules

- owner-based sharing rules

- manual sharing rules

All three rule types allow you to share records with users who are members of specified public groups or roles. Additionally, there are record-based sharing rules, which allow for more granular sharing made directly to users.

Criteria-based rules can satisfy fairly complex sharing needs. You can use Salesforce.com's criteria builder in the way that was discussed in Chapter 4. Figure 14-16 shows an example of a criteria-based sharing rule for a custom object.

New Custom Object Sharing Rules	New	Recalculate		New Custom Object Sharing Rules Help ?

Action	Criteria	Shared With	Access Level
Edit | Del	(New Custom Object: Number Field LESS THAN 5000) OR (New Custom Object: Percent Field GREATER THAN 50.0)	Role: Marketing Team	Read Only

Figure 14-16. *A criteria-based sharing rule for a custom object*

■ **Note** If you want to venture outside of the "development without code" world, Apex sharing rules can go even further than criteria-based sharing rules in handling complexity.

Owner-based rules have only one criterion, and that is the role or group of the record owner. Records that are owned by a User with an applicable role or public group will be shared with users in one or more roles or groups. Figure 14-17 shows an owner-based rule that shares records with an owner in Role 1 with Users in Role 3a.

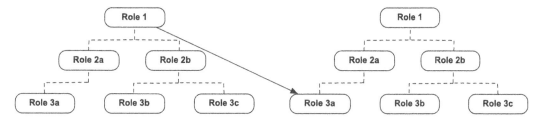

Figure 14-17. *This diagram represents an owner-based sharing rule that shares records owned by users in Role 1 with users in Role 3a*

In addition to identifying a particular role or group to share records with when using owner-based rules, you can include all Users in lower levels of that group by selecting them, either in the criteria or in the "Shared With" assignment. Figure 14-18 shows how records owned by Users in Role 2b or lower-level roles can be shared with Users in Role 2a.

Figure 14-18. *An owner-based sharing rule that shares records owned by users in Role 2b or lower-level roles with users in Role 2a*

Figure 14-19 displays two owner-based sharing rules, each with unique criteria and access levels.

Sharing Rules

New Custom Object Sharing Rules	New Recalculate		New Custom Object Sharing Rules Help ?
Action	**Criteria**	**Shared With**	**Access Level**
Edit | Del	Owner in Role: CEO	Role: CEO	Read Only
Edit | Del	Owner in Role, Internal and Portal Subordinates: CEO	Role: Marketing Team	Read/Write

Figure 14-19. *The "Sharing Rules" screen with two owner-based sharing rules*

Manual sharing rules are rules that allow records to be shared on an individual record basis. They are managed on the record itself, not on the "Sharing Settings" screen. The key difference between manual sharing rules and the other two types is that manual sharing rules allow records to be shared with specific users in addition to users in groups and roles. Figure 14-20 shows the screen that results from creating a record-based rule to provide Read Only access to three users in different categories: users in a public group, users in a role, and individual users.

User and Group Sharing		Add Expand List		User and Group Sharing Help ?
Action	**Type**	**Name** ↑	**Access Level**	**Reason**
Edit | Del	Role	Eastern Sales Team	Read Only	Manual Sharing
Edit | Del	Public Group	After Hours Support	Read Only	Manual Sharing
Edit | Del	User	Jerome Walton	Read Only	Manual Sharing

Figure 14-20. *Three manual sharing rules. Record-based rules can be shared with individual Users in addition to groups and roles*

Let's take a look at a scenario in which all three types of sharing rules are applied to records from the same object. Figure 14-21 shows the different sharing rules and the users that would be given access to the applicable record(s) as a result.

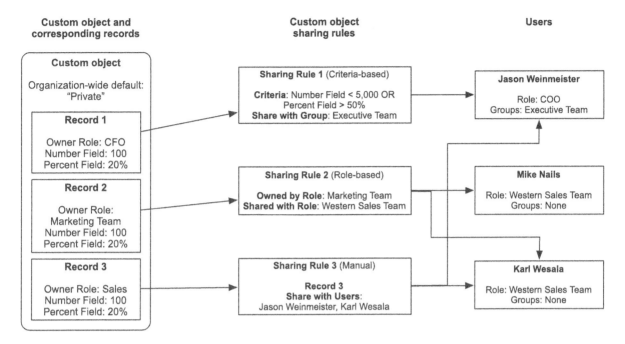

Figure 14-21. *In this example, multiple records for the same object are shared via different types of sharing rules. The users with whom the records are shared are shown on the right*

It is important to understand the reasons why the sharing rules are being applied as shown in Figure 14-20:

- **Record 1** is being shared with Jason Weinmeister through Sharing Rule 1:

  - Record 1 meets the sharing rule criteria.

  - Jason is a member of the public group that Record 1 is shared with.

- **Record 2** is being shared with Mike Nails and Karl Wesala through Sharing Rule 2:

  - The role of Record 2's owner matches the "owned by" role specified in the sharing rule.

  - Mike and Karl are members of the role that Record 2 is shared with.

- **Record 3** is being shared with Jason Weinmeister and Karl Wesala through Sharing Rule 3:

  - Record 2 is being manually shared in Sharing Rule 3.

  - The sharing rule grants access specifically to Jason and Karl.

"View All" and "Modify All"

Special permissions called "View All" and "Modify All" can be granted to ensure the highest-possible respective levels of "Read" and "Edit" access. If these permissions are enabled, the organization-wide default has no impact on these settings and the associated user(s) can view or edit all of the records for the corresponding object. For example, consider an object with an organization-wide default setting of "Private." Typically, access must be granted via ownership or sharing, as described earlier in the chapter. However, "View All" would allow a user to view all records, regardless of what sharing rules exist.

Object Permission and Record-Sharing Overlap

Let's take a look at a few examples to make sure the basic framework is clear before we more closely review the specific functionality that will help you to accurately and reliably satisfy your security-related requirements.

Figure 14-22 shows three different objects and four corresponding records for each of them. A user's "View All/Read" access to each record is indicated by the shading. A white record represents a record that is accessible to the user in question and a shaded record represents a record that is inaccessible to the user. The record access granted via sharing is denoted by a line around the particular record and the object read permission is specified below each object. Each circled number is followed by a corresponding explanation for why the record is or is not accessible to the user.

Figure 14-22. *This diagram shows how sharing and object permission granted for record access impact a user's ability to access (view) a particular set of records*

The records are or are not accessible for the following reasons:

1. **Records 1-A, 1-B, 1-C: Accessible**

   a. User has object "Read" permission.

   b. Access to records has been granted shared via sharing rules.

   c. The user has the ability to view records for this object and these particular records have been shared with her.

2. **Record 1-D: Inaccessible**

   a. User has object "Read" permission.

   b. Access to records has *not* been granted shared via sharing rules.

   c. Although the user has the ability to view records for this object, this particular record has not been shared with him. Therefore, the user cannot it.

3. **Records 2-A, 2-B, 2-C, 2-D: Accessible**

   a. User has object "Read" permission.

   b. Access to records has *not* been granted shared via sharing rules.

   c. User has object "View All" permission.

   d. Since the user has the "View All" permission, she can access these records. This example mirrors number two (Record 1-D) with one key exception: in this case, the user has the "View All" permission. As a result, the user can view all records for this object, regardless of sharing through other means.

4. **Records 3-A, 3-B, 3-C: Inaccessible**

   a. User does *not* have object "Read" permission.

   b. Access to records has been granted shared via sharing rules.

   c. In this case, access to the specific records has been granted to the user. However, the user does not have permission to view/read this object's records. As a result, the user cannot view this record.

5. **Record 3-D: Inaccessible**

   a. User does *not* have object "Read" permission.

   b. Access to records has *not* been granted shared via sharing rules.

   c. In this case, access to the specific records has not been granted to the user and she does not have "Read" permission to access this object's records, so she cannot view the records.

Recap

The most critical takeaway from this chapter is that security requirements and needs must be analyzed as a part of all implementations, even if your security model is well established. Of course, that does not mean that you need to rehash every security-related element across your entire org every time an enhancement or fix is deployed. However, it does mean that any aspects related to permission, sharing, or visibility that pertain to your solution must be updated as needed. In this chapter, the security model was reviewed, specifically in regard to object and field permissions and sharing settings. With the right balance of permissions and access granted via sharing, you can ensure that your users will be able to perform the actions that are needed in their positions while minimizing risk for your client or organization.

■ ■ ■

CHAPTER 15

Managing Your Salesforce.com Data with Data Loader

Once you've built the perfect system using Salesforce.com, you can be assured that you'll have no lack of data to manage. If there's one guarantee with your implementation, it's that you will need to give that data some TLC from time to time. While you should definitely employ validation rules, page layouts, and workflow rules to the fullest in your efforts to achieve and maintain data integrity, you'll also need to extract, transform, and load records to keep your system in tip-top shape. Fortunately, Salesforce.com provides some useful tools to help you with this endeavor. In this chapter, I will focus on one indispensable tool, Data Loader, and how you can use it to manage your data.

Data Loader Overview

Data Loader is a client application that can be downloaded from within your Salesforce.com org (**Setup ➤ Data Management ➤ Data Loader**). It provides the ability to extract, transform, load, and delete large amounts of data by following a simple step-by-step process. Anyone in a developer, consultant, or administrator role should be familiar with this tool. Seven specific functions are available within Data Loader:

- **Insert:** Create new records

- **Update:** Update existing records

- **Upsert:** Create new records and/or update existing records, depending on whether existing records match those included in the input file

- **Delete:** Move existing records to your organization's recycle bin

- **Hard Delete:** Permanently delete existing records

- **Export:** Export records that are not deleted (i.e., not in the recycle bin)

- **Export All:** Export records, including those that were previously deleted and are currently in the recycle bin (permanently deleted records will not be included)

Each function possesses its own unique considerations; I'll walk through each in detail to provide a solid understanding of how you can use the specific function to successfully manage your organization's data. Figure 15-1 shows how each of the available functions is used within Data Loader.

Figure 15-1. *Data Loader allows users to apply seven different functions to a specific set of data*

Setup

Once you download and install Data Loader, you'll need to perform some verification before proceeding. First, you'll need to make sure the proper access is set up. You must have been granted "**API Enabled**" permission, either through your profile or a permission set. Additionally, you'll need the corresponding permissions ("Create," "Read," "Edit," "Delete") permissions for each applicable object. For example, you would need to have "Read" access for Cases to be able to export Case object data. Similarly, you'd need "Create" access on Opportunities to insert Opportunities. Most likely, you have System Administrator access and you don't need to worry about obtaining additional permissions.

The second step is simply making sure you are pointed to the correct server host URL. If you are working in production (i.e., your "live" instance), you'll need to keep the default URL (https://login.salesforce.com). This applies if you're using Data Loader for a trial or development org, as well. However, if you are managing data in a sandbox, you'll need to modify the URL to https://test.salesforce.com.

■ **Note**   One of the most common reasons for encountering login issues is using the wrong URL. Make sure to double-check your URL and adjust it based on your org type. Development/trial/production orgs use https://login.salesforce.com and sandbox orgs use https://test.salesforce.com.

Depending on your org's security settings, you may need to include the security token associated with your user when entering your password. The token is emailed to you when your User record is first activated. If you can't find the token in your e-mail inbox, you can reset your token and have it e-mailed to you by navigating to [**Your Name** (Top Right)]" ➤ **My Settings** ➤ **Personal** ➤ **Reset My Security Token** and clicking on the "Reset Security Token" button. If you had a password of "a1b2c34R" and a token of "79xyz22," you would enter the following for your password within Data Loader if a token was required: "a1b2c34R79xyz22."

Exporting Data

Exporting data via Data Loader is simple and straightforward. The application is your best friend if you need to manipulate a large number of Salesforce.com records quickly. First, I need to reiterate the difference between the "**Export**" and the "**Export All**" options. "Export All" includes records that are in the Recycle Bin; "Export" does not. Typically, you'll want to use the "Export" feature, not "Export All." Of course, if you do need deleted records, you'll be very happy that the "Export All" feature exists.

To start the export, you'll need to select one object; you cannot export data from multiple objects simultaneously. By default, you'll see a list of the available standard and custom objects. It's key to pay attention to the "**Show all Salesforce objects**" checkbox at the top of the dialog window. If it is checked off, a number of additional objects will be exposed to you, including but not limited to objects related to:

- chatter
- history
- sharing
- the Apex debug log
- approval requests
- communities

Once you select your object, you'll need to identify your directory and select a filename. If the .csv file you identify does not already exist, a new file will be created. In Figure 15-2, I have selected the Case object to be exported.

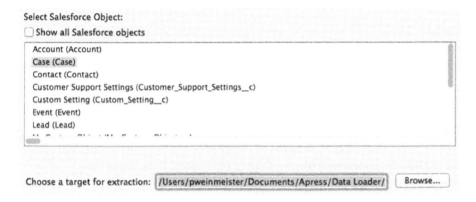

Figure 15-2. *Selecting an object is the first step for all functions within Data Loader[1]*

When you click the "Next" button, you will be presented with an interface that allows you to configure two critical elements:

- the subset of records to be extracted
- the fields to be included in the output file

You can declaratively build a SOQL query to identify which records you want to include. You may not realize that every time you configure a workflow rule using criteria or build a list view, you are actually writing a SOQL query. SOQL is Salesforce.com's own language that can be used to manipulate data. You are not provided a lookup dialog, so you'll have to provide the record ID if you're using a relationship field in your query. Here's an example of a SOQL query that displays five fields and contains two conditions:

```
Select Id, CaseNumber, ContactId, AccountId, Status FROM Case WHERE CreatedDate>
2015-01-01T01:01:01Z AND Status != 'Escalated'
```

---

[1] All Salesforce.com screenshots in this chapter © copyright Salesforce.com, Inc. Used with permission.

You can get as precise as you want with your query to potentially limit your records to the exact set you desire. However, I'd encourage you to balance precision with invested time at this stage. I would definitely encourage you to reduce your record set by including a few heavy-hitting conditions. For example, if you're limiting your set to one record type, a particular date, or a specific field value, it is simple enough to add the corresponding condition. However, if you find yourself adding more than three conditions, do keep in mind that you can further manipulate the data outside of Salesforce.com with relative ease. I would recommend a similar approach when considering your fields. If you only need a few fields, you should take a few minutes to select them to avoid receiving a huge dump of data in your output file. However, if you need the majority of fields, it might not be worth your time to individually select each field. For extracts with large field sets, I would suggest selecting all fields and worrying about column deletion outside of Data Loader.

Once you've set which fields and records you want to include, you'll notice that the corresponding SOQL query is visible. If you feel comfortable, you can directly edit the query to make further modifications. After you confirm that you do want to proceed with the export, you'll get a confirmation of the number of successful and unsuccessful records. With exported data, you shouldn't see a positive number in the error column. Records are either exported or not and those that are exported are considered successful.

Inserting Data

With Data Loader, you can insert large volumes of data to create new records in Salesforce.com with relative ease. Like with exporting (and all other functions), you'll need to identify the target object. Additionally, you'll need to have a properly formatted .csv file containing the records to be created within your org. When preparing your file, keep in mind the following factors:

- Relevant **validation rules, workflow rules**, and **triggers** will apply. If you do not want them to be considered, you will have to update the rules, triggers, and/or data being loaded accordingly. For example, you could update rule criteria to exclude records with certain data present and then update your data to match that exclusion scenario.

- **Object permissions** and **field-level security settings** will apply. For example, if you do not have write access to a particular field, you will not be able to include that column in the insertion.

- **Page layout requirements** and restrictions will not apply. So, if a field is required on the one active page layout for an object, it has no bearing on the data being imported via Data Loader.

Figure 15-3 shows how permissions, rules, and triggers might impact a data insert when using Data Loader.

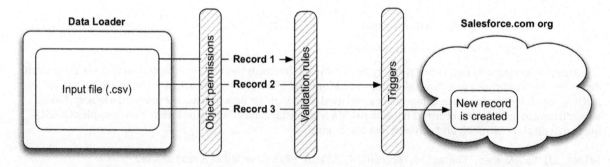

Figure 15-3. *Object permissions, validation rules, and triggers can all restrict the ability to manage specific data. In this example, three records are in the Insert file but only one ends up getting created*

Once you have selected the file to be inserted and proceed, Salesforce will validate your file. You will be alerted of any empty columns and issues with the file that would guarantee a failure. However, it's critical to understand that a successful validation does not mean that your records will be inserted. The validation does not take any internal org rules into consideration.

▪ **Note**   To avoid spending unnecessary time verifying the format of your file, consider exporting at least one record from the same object first. You can then use that export file as your template for importing. This will not only ensure that your columns are named properly but also that the field values are formatted correctly.

Once your validation has completed, you will map the column names within your .csv file to the object's "writable" fields. Read-only and system fields, for example, will not be available for mapping selection. If no existing maps exist, you will need to click "Create or Edit a Map" to define the field-mapping rules. As shown in Figure 15-4, the field-mapping interface includes two sections: the Salesforce.com fields and the file column headers. You can manually drag a Salesforce field down to match a file column header or you can "automatch" Salesforce.com fields to columns. I use this feature frequently, but I would provide a word of caution here: Only use the auto-match feature under the following conditions:

- You have appropriately named the file column headers (as previously mentioned, you may want to export a file via Data Loader and use that as your import template).

- You are familiar with the fields on the target object.

- You are attentive to detail.

Match the Salesforce fields to your columns.

Clear Mapping	Auto-Match Fields to Columns

Name	Label	Type
AccountId	Account ID	reference
AssistantName	Assistant's Name	string
AssistantPhone	Asst. Phone	phone
Birthdate	Birthdate	date
Department	Department	string
Description	Contact Description	textarea
Email	Email	email

Drag the Salesforce fields down to the column mapping.

File Column Header	Name
FIRSTNAME	
ID	
LASTNAME	
MAILINGCITY	
MAILINGCOUNTRY	

Figure 15-4. *Field-mapping interface with object fields at the top and file column headers at the bottom. You can automatch the fields or manually drag the object fields down to map them to file column headers.*

Once you've mapped your fields, you will want to carefully review them before proceeding. In Figure 15-5, you can see how your file's headers (on the left) match up with applicable fields (on the right).

File Column Header	Name
Fax	Fax
FirstName	FirstName
ID	
LastName	LastName
MailingCity	MailingCity

Figure 15-5. *A view of file column headers post-mapping*

Once you've gone over the information, you have the option of saving that mapping for future use. This is especially helpful for deployments. Since you may have to hand off data creation responsibilities, it's much more reliable to provide a mapping file that can simply be loaded than to assume someone else will set the proper mappings.

You'll proceed to insert the records from your file. As with the export process, you will receive a confirmation of successes and errors. Make sure to carefully review your errors to determine if they were expected or not based on your org's configuration.

Updating Data

Updating data via Data Loader overlaps significantly with the process of inserting data, with a few key differences. The main difference with updating is that you must include the record ID of the record you are updating. To do this, you export the data you need and make sure to include the ID in the selected fields list. With that exported file, you can simply update your field values in other columns and submit the modified file for update. The key is to make sure that you do not modify the ID column, as it is the only place to identify existing records using Update. Figure 15-6 shows a scenario in which data is exported using Data Loader, edited, and then updated (once again, using Data Loader).

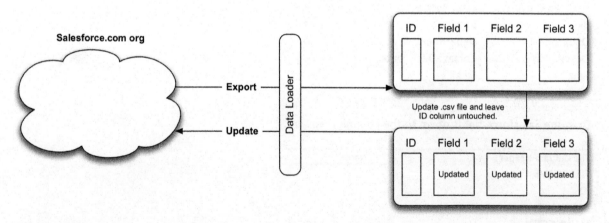

Figure 15-6. *In this example, a three-step process includes extraction ("Export"), transformation (manual editing via a spreadsheet application), and load ("Update"). The ID field will need to be left untouched for a successful update.*

■ **Note** Make sure that your spreadsheet application does not automatically change your file format from .csv to something else. Only .csv files will work with Data Loader.

Upserting Data

If you've ever used an ETL (Extract, Transform, and Load) tool in the past, you won't find too many surprises with the "Insert" or "Update" functions within Data Loader. The "Upsert" function, however, is a different beast altogether. "Upsert" allows to you submit a data set that includes existing and/or new records; Salesforce.com will make the proper determination and either insert a new record or update an existing one. This activity centers around the External ID field shown in Figure 15-7. Unless you include a column containing the Salesforce record ID, you must have a field designated as an External ID on your target object to perform an upsert. You should be aware of the following factors when considering external IDs:

- The Email, Geolocation, Number, Phone, Picklist, Text (not Text Area), and URL fields can be set as external IDs.

- You may identify more than one field per object as an external ID (up to seven).

- The External ID field that is selected to identify the records via an upsert cannot be blank.

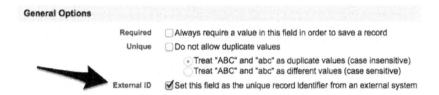

Figure 15-7. *Checking off the "External ID" checkbox when editing a field to identify it as an external ID*

When you are upserting within Data Loader, you will be given the option to select either the Standard ID field or a different field that has been designated as an External ID. Figure 15.8 shows a custom Case field, External Ticket ID, that can be selected during the Data Loader upsert process as an External ID field.

To match on Case, use either the Id field or an external ID field.

Select the field for matching on Case:

```
External_Ticket_ID__c
Id
```

Figure 15-8. *You can select the Salesforce.com record ID or an external ID to be used as the primary identifier in an upsert. In this example, the record ID and the field External_Ticket_ID__c (an external ID) are both available for selection.*

Next, you will identify the field to use for related objects. This field would be used if the records you're upserting have a relationship to another object via a Relationship field and you are referencing an External ID field value instead of a Salesforce.com record ID.

Once the upsert is complete, you will receive notification of the result. You'll notice that the results column will show one of two different values for successfully submitted records: "Item Updated" or "Item Created." If no existing record matches an external ID in the submitted file, a new record will be created. Figure 15-9 gives an overview of a hypothetical scenario involving an upsert.

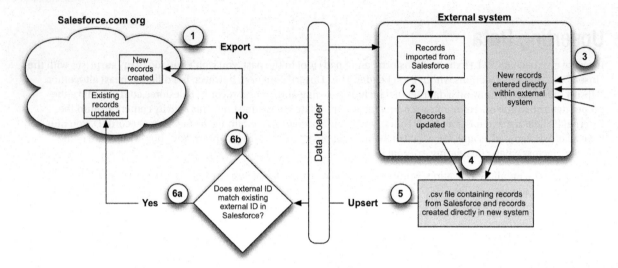

Figure 15-9. *A potential step-by-step process for an "Upsert" use case*

Deleting Data

In addition to exporting, inserting, and updating data, you can delete records as well. You have two options for doing so: "Delete" or "Delete All." The only difference between the two is that "Delete" performs a "soft" deletion, placing the records in the organization's recycle bin, and "Delete All" performs a "hard" deletion, from which records cannot be recovered. To delete data, you only need the record IDs. Upload your file containing the IDs of the records to be deleted, and that's all there is to it. Obviously, be careful to double-check your data before you perform a deletion.

Other Considerations

There are, of course, numerous options and alternatives for the approaches discussed in this chapter. You should consider the following:

- **Exporting via reports**: If you want to quickly export data outside of Salesforce.com to be used in a future update, consider using the Salesforce.com report builder; just make sure to include the record ID in your selected fields. You can export the data directly as a `.csv` file.

- **Import wizards**: Salesforce.com offers a number of built-in import wizards to guide you through importing data. You should review these, as there may be an advantage to using the wizards in some scenarios.

- **Date formats**: Dates will need to be formatted as follows: for date fields, use YYYY-MM-DD and for date/time fields use one of the following formats: YYYY-MM-DDThh:mm:ss+hh:mm, YYYY-MM-DDThh:mm:ss-hh:mm, or YYYY-MM-DDThh:mm:ssZ.

- **Settings**: Carefully review the Data Loader settings. In particular, pay attention to the "**Bulk API**" settings. These can be advantageous when handling later amounts of data.

- **History/Backup**: Make sure back up your Salesforce.com data often. Take a look at the "**Data Export**" option and consider scheduling an export of your org's data.

- **Command Line**: Data Loader can be programmed at the command line to schedule activities to manage your data.

Recap

In this chapter, I discussed the need to manage your data, specifically focusing on how to use the Data Loader tool for your approach. Any solution you build will affect data and, if you're the one responsible for managing that data, you'll be thankful to have a powerful solution such as Data Loader to facilitate that activity. You learned about seven Data Loader functions, paying special attention to "Export," "Insert," "Update," and "Upsert." If you get familiar with Data Loader, you'll have no problem quickly managing large amounts of data within your org.

■ ■ ■

CHAPTER 16

Managing Your Environments and Deploying Your Solutions

In the scramble to produce valuable and impactful functionality for your organization or clients, it can become all too easy to overlook the need to have a solid plan in place to manage your development/testing environments (called "sandboxes" within Salesforce.com) and deploy your work. However, I would implore you to prioritize this highly in your overall Salesforce.com development life cycle process. A thoughtfully configured sandbox model combined with a well-planned deployment approach will significantly increase your chances for long-term success as you build and deliver solutions. In this chapter, I will delve into the world of sandboxes and deployment within Salesforce.com and provide guidance on the way to approach them and key considerations that should be made.

The Salesforce.com Sandbox

The term *sandbox* refers to a development or testing environment within Salesforce.com. A sandbox is created as a copy of the current production org and is provisioned with all of the configuration, code, and setup data (i.e., metadata) from that org; record data may be included, depending on the type of sandbox. While the sandbox is initially a replica of production, it is not automatically synched with production in any way. It is important to understand that changes in production will not automatically be reflected in a sandbox.

Types of Sandboxes

Salesforce.com has a few different types of sandboxes that can be created. It is useful to be familiar with each to understand the pros and cons of provisioning a new sandbox of a particular type. Figure 16-1 provides an overview of sandbox types.

Figure 16-1. *You can create four different types of sandboxes. All of them include a mirror of production metadata; Partial Data and Full sandboxes include data in addition.*

Full Sandbox

A Full sandbox includes all of the metadata *and* data from your production org. All object records, custom setting records, and the like will be available in your Full sandbox. This would, for example, include all of the Case records created in your production environment as part of your customer support department. Likewise, all Opportunities created by your Sales team would be copied to the sandbox. A few additional options are also made available:

- **Field history:** You have the option of copying a configurable amount of field history data from production.

- **Chatter data:** You can include the Chatter posts and activity from production if desired.

There are two primary considerations you'll want to make when setting up these options: First, do you have concerns about file storage limits in your sandbox? If so, consider avoiding inclusion of Chatter data. Field History data does not count against your data storage limits. Second, are you looking to provision the sandbox as quickly as possible? If so, avoid copying any field history or Chatter data. Overlooking these items will expedite the provisioning time of a Full sandbox.

As a standard, production orgs are provided with one Full sandbox available for use. As a result, the application of a Full sandbox must be thoughtful and strategic. If you look at the three main activities that occur within a sandbox—development, testing, and training—it becomes clear that a Full sandbox would be much more useful for testing or training than for development, since data volume is more often a dependency for test execution and training than it is for development.

Partial Data Sandbox

Partial Data sandboxes are very similar to Full sandboxes except that they only allow a subset of data to be copied to the sandbox from production. Salesforce.com offers a "sandbox copy engine" that assists with the selection of data to be copied. Up to ten thousand records of each selected object will be included in the copy. Additionally, file and data storage limits of five gigabytes apply (although this could increase at a later date).

■ **Note**   Each sandbox type has a different limit for file and data storage. Object records count against data storage; content, files, and Chatter feeds count against file storage.

Developer and Developer Pro Sandboxes

Developer and Developer Pro sandboxes include no data from production; they only consist of metadata. This is often sufficient for testing needs. If additional data is needed, you can manually create it via the UI (as a production user would) or load in a set of data via Data Loader. If you needed a smaller set of data, there's really no need to provision a Full or Partial Data sandbox. For example, let's say you need a sample of Accounts, Contacts, Opportunities, Cases, and Leads; you can create files of 10–100 records for each quickly with relative ease.

The only differences between Developer and Developer Pro sandboxes are the limits for file and data storage. A Developer sandbox can hold up to 200 megabytes of each, while a Developer Pro sandbox can hold up to 1 gigabyte of each.

Refreshing a Sandbox

When you create a sandbox, you can be confident that its metadata precisely aligns with the metadata in production. However, the two environments will inevitably diverge, and your sandbox will, to some degree, fall out of synch with your production org. In order to make them consistent again, Salesforce.com provides the ability to refresh a sandbox after a specific period of time has passed since the last refresh or the creation date if it hasn't yet been refreshed. The process is illustrated in Figure 16-2. In reality, a refresh is essentially the same as replacing your existing sandbox with a new sandbox of the same name. All of the metadata from production is copied to your sandbox, overriding the existing configuration, code, and setup data. Additionally, the existing data in the sandbox is wiped out.

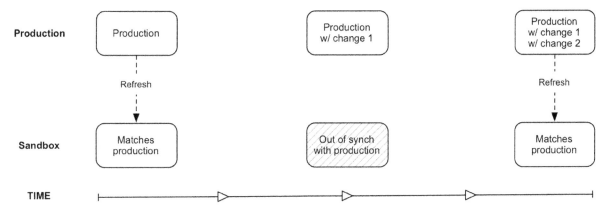

Figure 16-2. *Over time, your sandbox will diverge further and further from the production org. However, you can refresh your sandbox to synch it up with production again. Depending on the sandbox type, the current data in production will be copied to your sandbox during a refresh.*

It is a good idea to refresh your sandbox at the following intervals:

- **Full:** Every 29 days
- **Partial Data:** Every 5 days
- **Developer Pro:** Everyday
- **Developer:** Everyday

The refresh feature can extremely beneficial when developing solutions. New functionality may be based on metadata or records that exist only in production. A refresh can mirror records in production in your sandbox for you. You may find that your sandbox is in need of a refresh while you are working on something. However, before you do a refresh, be extremely careful that there is nothing in progress that is stored only in your sandbox, as there is the possibility of it getting overwritten. To avoid this happening, you have three primary options:

- Complete your work and deploy it to the parent environment.

- Save your work outside Salesforce.com in a way that will allow a quick recreation of the solution if need be.

- Deploy your work to a "sibling" environment (another sandbox connected to the same production org) and then deploy back to your sandbox after the refresh has completed.

Each option is unique and will depend on your particular situation. The main takeaway is to ensure that you do not lose any work in progress.

Designing Your Sandbox Model

Once you have familiarized yourself with the different types of sandboxes, you'll need to set up a model for your sandbox environment. It goes without saying that the right model for you will differ from the right model for others. Although there is no one-size-fits-all setup that will meet the needs of all organizations, what follows are some common considerations that will set you up for potential success.

Determining Your Needs

Before you start creating sandboxes on a whim, think about how you'll use them. Here are some possible activities that may be required:

- development

- unit testing

- system/integration testing

- performance/load testing

- user acceptance testing (UAT)

- training

- demonstrations

By thinking through how your environments will be utilized, you'll have a better idea of how many sandboxes you'll need and which types. For example, if you have only one or a few developers building solutions to be implemented in production, you likely won't need a large number of development sandboxes (Developer or Developer Pro). On the other hand, if you have large organizational departments that require detailed training and demonstrations, you'll benefit from a Staging/UAT sandbox (ideally, the type would be "full").

Assessing Availability and Cost

When your production org is initially set up, you'll have a certain number of each type of sandbox available for use. The number can differ significantly based on your agreement with Salesforce.com. Typically, you'll have one Full sandbox and multiple Developer sandboxes. Extra sandboxes are usually not cheap, so have a solid justification prepared if you feel that you need to purchase one. Figure 16-3 shows the sandbox availability and use within an example production org. To get to this screen, navigate to **Setup ➤ Sandboxes or Setup ➤ Data Management ➤ Sandboxes** depending on your user interface settings.

Sandboxes

Sandboxes are special organizations that are used to test changes or new apps without risking damage to your production data or configuration. Sandbox Templates are used to create new Sandboxes containing specific data sets.

Available Sandbox Licenses			
Developer	**Developer Pro**	**Partial Data**	**Full**
18 Available (3 in use)	0 Available (1 in use)	0 Available (0 in use)	0 Available (1 in use)

Figure 16-3. *By viewing your sandboxes from your production org, you can confirm how many of each sandbox are available or in use. This screenshot is just an example; each org is different.*[1]

Designing and Building the Sandbox Environments

After determining your sandbox needs and availability, you can create a logical model for your sandbox environment. As I previously mentioned, there is not a cookie-cutter approach that will work for everyone; however, I will propose one possible model that could be used as a baseline. Your exact situation may warrant additional sandboxes or a smaller footprint.

Development

The lowest tier of your sandbox model will represent those environments that see the greatest frequency of change, which would be your development environments. Additionally, there may multiple developers or development teams working simultaneously; it is recommended that each development group have a separate sandbox to prevent conflicts. These would likely be Developer or Developer Pro sandboxes.

System/Integration Testing

When you have multiple development environments, you should consolidate the disparate development activities into one environment. To achieve this goal, you will need to create a system/integration testing environment that all of the development environments feed into. Broader testing can be performed in this type of environment since it includes all development activity. It would likely be a Developer or Developer Pro sandbox. Figure 16-4 shows a possible configuration of development and system/integration sandboxes.

Figure 16-4. *Multiple development sandboxes and a parent integration sandbox will allow you to consolidate all development work in one org. All of these would likely be Developer or Full sandboxes in Developer.*

---

[1]All Salesforce.com screenshots in this chapter © copyright Salesforce.com, Inc. Used with permission.

User Acceptance Testing/Staging

Although your system/integration testing sandbox should contain all of your changes, you may want to have an additional sandbox for the purpose of user acceptance testing and/or staging. This environment will be a mirror of production the majority of the time; the exception would be when new functionality is pushed to the environment to be user acceptance tested or staged for a short period of time. This serves two purposes: it allows a stable, controlled environment to be used for UAT or staging, and it provides an org that can be used for a production deployment "dry run." You can run through your full deployment and it should be completely successful. If not, you have another opportunity to correct your deployment process and steps before anything reaches production. This environment would typically be a Full sandbox.

Performance/Load Testing

Depending on your needs, you may choose to have a separate environment for performance/load testing. If you'll be performing a significant number of automated activities in an org or measuring the speed of particular actions, you may want to consider obtaining a second Full sandbox. The content in this sandbox would not go directly to production but would instead be an endpoint for deployment. In other words, the latest changes would be deployed both to this sandbox as well as to the UAT/staging sandbox; in the final release you would move the UAT/staging sandbox to production.

■ **Note**   Contact Salesforce.com directly if you need additional sandboxes. Keep in mind that they must be purchased.

An Example Sandbox Environment

Figure 16-5 shows an overall sandbox environment based on the hypothetical sandboxes mentioned earlier.

Figure 16-5. *An example sandbox model that could be used to manage new functionality*

Deployment

Once you have designed and created your sandbox model, you will need to establish a plan to deploy your changes from your original environment to the next sandbox "tier." Outside a few exceptional situations, it is highly recommended that you create a clear deployment plan and adhere to it. Although a "quick fix" in production may seem to be a harmless time-saver in the moment, the true cost may end up being many hours of lost time as a result of miscommunication and/or a conflict at some point in the future.

To deploy your Salesforce.com functionality, you'll need to use an appropriate tool to move the corresponding changes. A number of tools are available to you, including:

- Change sets
- Force.com Migration Tool
- Eclipse: Force.com Integrated Development Environment (IDE)
- MavensMate: Force.com IDE
- Workbench

To follow the path of development without code, I will only focus on the primary declarative option, change sets, in this chapter. Personally, I do use Eclipse in addition to change sets and would recommend reviewing it and some of the other tools available, especially if you are familiar with code migration tools outside of Salesforce.com.

Change Sets

Change sets are groupings of components that can be deployed from one org (the source org) to another org (the target or destination org). Both the destination and the target org can be either a sandbox or a production org. The factor that makes change sets truly unique is their declarative nature—the entire process can be done within the Salesforce.com user interface with only clicks of the mouse (in addition to naming some text and describing the set).

Deployment Settings

The first step in using change sets is to configure your deployment connections, or authorization directions. Deployment connections define which orgs (sandboxes or production) are allowed to serve as a destination org for a specific target org. To set up your deployment connections, you will need to log in to the destination org and check off which orgs may push change sets to it. To do this, navigate to **Setup ➤ Deploy ➤ Deployment Settings** and click the name of the applicable target org. Figure 16-6 shows the edit screen for this setting.

Figure 16-6. *In the "Upload Authorization Direction" section, you can enable deployment connections by checking off "Allow Inbound Changes" and "Allow Outbound Changes" so that the changes will be received from the target org*

Figure 16-7 depicts the sandbox model, now with direction to show the allowable path of change set deployment.

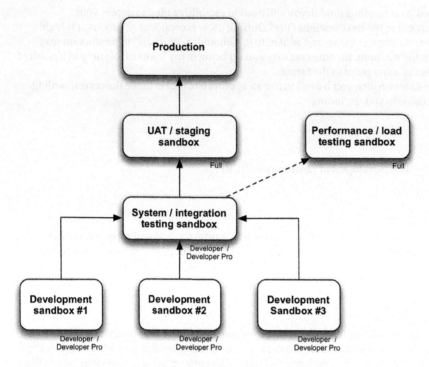

Figure 16-7. *This diagram adds direction to the sandbox model represented in Figure 16-5*

Change Set Content

To add content to your change set, navigate to **Setup ➤ Deploy ➤ Outbound Change Sets ➤ New**. Once your set has been created, you can add a large variety of Salesforce.com development components to it. Among many other components, you can include the following types:

- custom objects

- custom fields

- page layouts

- workflow rules, field updates, and email alerts

- validation rules

- custom report types

- record types

- sharing rules

To add a component, select the component type, click the specific component you want to add, and click the "Add to Change Set" button, as shown in Figure 16-8.

Figure 16-8. You can select a component and click "Add to Change Set" to include it in your change set

Additionally, you can include profiles to be a part of your change set. This will carry over certain profile-specific attributes in the deployment. For example, let's say you have a new custom field with field-level security configured differently for various profiles. If you do not include profiles in the deployment, no profiles will have access to your new field; however, by including the applicable profiles, your field-level security settings will carry over.

You should also take advantage of the "View/Add Dependencies" button that is available within your change set before proceeding. This button will identify any potentially dependent components that should also be considered for deployment. After clicking the button, carefully review the components to determine whether they should be included. Page layouts can be used to illustrate an example. Assume that your set includes an updated page layout that exposes a brand-new custom field; the "View/Add Dependencies" functionality will reveal the new custom field to you and allow you to add it to the set.

Deployment Process

Once you have finalized your change set, you are ready to deploy it to the desired target org. To do so, click the "Upload" button from within your change set and select an available org as your target org, as shown in Figure 16-9. Click the "Upload" button to submit your set.

Upload Details   Upload   Cancel

Target Organization   ▌ = Required Information

	Name	Description	Type	Platform Version
⦿	Production	Production organization	Production	31.0

Figure 16-9. To deploy your change set, select the appropriate org and click "Upload"

You'll need some patience here; it can take a while (10–15 minutes) before your set is available within the target org. You will be notified by e-mail of a successfully submitted change set, but it may take another 5 minutes before the set can be accessed.

At this point, you'll have two options: You can simply validate the deployment of the change set or go ahead and deploy it. A validation of the deployment will simulate a deployment and inform you of whether the process will be successful if actually deployed; no components in the set will actually be introduced to the target org. This can be a huge time-saver in the deployment process. Let's say you have a deployment planned for Friday at 10 p.m. If you attempt your deployment for the first time on Friday at 10 p.m., you may be disappointed to find out that an error was encountered. This means creating a new change set and redeploying it, which can take up your valuable time. By validating the deployment earlier in the day on Friday, you can identify potential errors and get your set ready for a punctual deployment free of any errors.

When you are ready to make changes to the target org, click "Deploy." Like with the validation process, this will validate your deployment and, if applicable, run all Apex tests. If successful, everything in your change set will now be a part of the target org.

Deployment Approach

In an ideal situation, you would package up everything related to a specific release and deploy it via one change set. This should be attempted whenever possible. If successful, you'll be done with deployment relatively quickly. The reality, however, is that an all-at-once approach can be extremely time consuming if deployment issues are encountered. If you have more than a few errors, peeling back the layers can require numerous iterations and analysis and potentially waste your time. As an alternative, consider grouping related components and deploying them separately. For example, you might place all new objects and fields in one change set, and follow that with another set containing workflow rules and validation rules. There is no perfect solution for all users. Consider your situation and choose an approach that makes the most sense for you.

Other Considerations

Keep in mind the following considerations when deploying change sets:

- **Deploying "down:"** You can deploy down (e.g., from production to a sandbox) in addition to deploying up. There may be times when a change is made in a higher-level environment and you need to synch it up without making all changes manually. In these cases, consider a deployment connection that is bidirectional.

- **Manual changes:** Some changes must be done manually. For example, "Case" and "Email-to-Case" settings cannot be deployed from one sandbox to another. Make sure you plan your deployment accordingly.

Recap

No matter how amazing your work is, it won't provide much value if it never sees the light of day (i.e., if it fails to get deployed to production). To successfully manage your solutions within Salesforce.com, you will need to create the appropriate sandboxes to meet your needs and establish a thorough, sensible plan for deployment. Your deployment can be done via change sets or a variety of other tools. Make sure to assess your options carefully. With an effective sandbox model and an effective deployment strategy, you'll be able to deliver functionality where you want and when you want with relative ease.

■ ■ ■

CHAPTER 17

Next Steps in Your Path to Development Excellence

So, what's next? Besides taking the obvious step of applying what you've learned in your everyday job and building up your experience in the different areas, there are additional opportunities for continuing your path of learning within the world of Salesforce.com development.

Success and Developer Communities

Salesforce.com has done an amazing job of building collaborative sites where you can get involved and interact with peers in the ecosystem. The following two communities are particularly valuable:

- **Salesforce Success Community for users:** (`https://success.salesforce.com`) This community is designed for administrators, power users, consultants, and basic-to-intermediate developers.

- **Salesforce Developers:** (`https://developer.salesforce.com`) This community provides an outlet for developers, including those at advanced skill and experience levels.

In both communities, you can find useful articles, ask questions, get answers, submit ideas, and more. They are both valuable resources for anyone who likes to learn more or help others to do the same. Set up a profile and start collaborating!

Social Media

If you're reading this book, it's probably a safe assumption that you're at least minimally active in the realm of social media. If so, I would highly recommend using your Twitter account to follow some users and entities that regularly share valuable, unique information related to Salesforce.com. Here are some Twitter accounts you may want to follow:

- **@PhilWeinmeister:** Hear from me with useful updates! I share my blog posts and other insights here.

- **@Salesforce:** This is the main Twitter account for Salesforce.com. It allows you to stay up to date on news, announcements, and overall innovation.

- **@SalesforceDevs:** This account sends out tweets about a variety of development topics. It is a great resource for staying on top of the latest within the world of Salesforce.com development. A good portion of the content involves coding, but it's also valuable for declarative solutions.

- **@SalesforceU:** Here, you can get the latest news, updates, tips, and tricks to help you get the most out of Salesforce.com training and certification.

- **@AppExchange:** The Salesforce1 AppExchange (`https://appexchange.salesforce.com`) sends out tweets about thousands of different apps.

- **@ForceDotComLabs:** Force.com Labs publishes apps written by Salesforce.com employees. and sends out its updates here.

- **Salesforce.com & Force.com MVPs:** This group includes some of the best and brightest, who bring insight and new content to the Salesforce.com ecosystem, sharing a ton of helpful tips and feedback for the larger community. (Go to `www.salesforce.com/mvp/mvplist.jsp` for a list of specific individuals to follow.)

Dreamforce

Dreamforce is Salesforce.com's bigger-than-life annual megaconference held in San Francisco each summer or fall. If you pay attention to advertised offers and start looking early, you can snag a discounted pass that will give you full access to the event. This conference offers a plethora of resources. I would specifically recommend the following two areas of the conference:

- **Sessions:** Salesforce.com offers hundreds of sessions in which you can hear from employees, users, and other developers about best practices, real-world lessons learned, and helpful tips. These sessions can serve as minitraining for you to take your skills up a notch.

- **Developer Zone:** At Dreamforce, you'll find extensive resources for developers of all skill levels. Visit the zone and get involved. You may even score some swag while you're learning the latest-and-greatest development features.

In addition to Dreamforce itself, a number of city-specific events are held around the world. For example, Salesforce.com hosts smaller, Dreamforce-like events as part of the Salesforce World Tour. Look for an event coming to your town in the near future.

Certification

If you're not already familiar with Salesforce.com's certification program, you should be! Salesforce.com provides a thorough, well-organized offering of meaningful certifications that allow you to convey your knowledge in a particular area. As of 2015, at least seven different certifications exist, with more likely to come. This book's content relates most directly to the Salesforce.com "**Certified Force.com Developer**" exam. However, it is not an official certification guide and some components of the exam may not be covered in depth. To learn more about the developer exam or to obtain a free study guide, navigate to `http://certification.salesforce.com/developers`.

Additionally, some of what you've learned in this book will help you prepare for the two administrator-focused exams: "**Salesforce.com Certified Administrator**" and "**Salesforce.com Certified Advanced Administrator**." Some of the content in these exams is more introductory or focused on nondevelopment items (e.g., setting up new users), but there is some content that is covered in this book. To learn more about the administrator exams, navigate to `http://certification.salesforce.com/administrators`. Good luck getting certified!

Help, Webinars, and User Groups

Salesforce.com has spent many thousands of hours compiling extremely useful help documentation. Some very intelligent, eloquent employees have devoted detailed attention to providing information on each piece of the platform, allowing you to take full advantage of the entire system. You can find the main help page at `https://help.salesforce.com/apex/HTHome`. As part of the overall help documentation, Salesforce.com produces a number of guides to using specific features in PDF format. A full list is available at `https://help.salesforce.com/HTViewHelpDoc?id=quicktour_tips.htm`.

You can also get live help from Salesforce.com's periodical webinars. These are free Web sessions that offer information on particular features and functionality. You can find upcoming events at `www.salesforce.com/events/webinars`.

Another resource is other developers in your local area that you can get involved with. Whether through Salesforce.com or not, you can find groups that regularly meet and share the experiences, tips, and tricks they've gained through their own development. You can find Salesforce.com's list at `https://success.salesforce.com/userGroups`.

A Final Word

The world of Salesforce.com is vast and dynamic, with opportunities to build solutions on the platform continuing to expand. A unique facet that sets it apart is the fact that you can develop powerful, meaningful applications without producing a line of code, and it's not a secret that Salesforce.com places a strong emphasis on that ability to build solutions declaratively. An array of new features and functions are released triannually, allowing you to take what you produce to the next level. It's an exciting time to be a part of what's happening and I wish you the best in all of your future Salesforce.com development endeavors!

Index

Get the eBook for only $10!

Now you can take the weightless companion with you anywhere, anytime. Your purchase of this book entitles you to 3 electronic versions for only $10.

This Apress title will prove so indispensible that you'll want to carry it with you everywhere, which is why we are offering the eBook in 3 formats for only $10 if you have already purchased the print book.

Convenient and fully searchable, the PDF version enables you to easily find and copy code—or perform examples by quickly toggling between instructions and applications. The MOBI format is ideal for your Kindle, while the ePUB can be utilized on a variety of mobile devices.

Go to www.apress.com/promo/tendollars to purchase your companion eBook.

Apress®
THE EXPERT'S VOICE™

CPSIA information can be obtained at www.ICGtesting.com
Printed in the USA
LVOW02s2007080715

445461LV00008B/167/P